WAYWARD FEELING

Audio-Visual Culture and Aesthetic Activism in Post-Rainbow South Africa

HELENE STRAUSS

Wayward Feeling

Audio-Visual Culture and Aesthetic Activism in Post-Rainbow South Africa

UNIVERSITY OF TORONTO PRESS
Toronto Buffalo London

Toronto Buffalo London
utorontopress.com

ISBN 978-1-4875-4058-6 (cloth) ISBN 978-1-4875-4060-9 (EPUB)
ISBN 978-1-4875-4059-3 (PDF)

African and Diasporic Cultural Studies

Library and Archives Canada Cataloguing in Publication

Title: Wayward feeling : audio-visual culture and aesthetic activism in post-rainbow South Africa / Helene Strauss.
Names: Strauss, Helene, author.
Series: African and diasporic cultural studies.
Description: Series statement: African and diasporic cultural studies | Includes bibliographical references and index.
Identifiers: Canadiana (print) 20220130345 | Canadiana (ebook) 2022013054X | ISBN 9781487540586 (cloth) | ISBN 9781487540609 (EPUB) | ISBN 9781487540593 (PDF)
Subjects: LCSH: Art and social action – South Africa. | LCSH: Art and society – South Africa. | LCSH: Sound art – South Africa. | LCSH: Video art – South Africa. | LCSH: Aesthetics – Social aspects.
Classification: LCC N72.S6 S77 2022 | DDC 701/.030968 – dc23

We wish to acknowledge the land on which the University of Toronto Press operates. This land is the traditional territory of the Wendat, the Anishnaabeg, the Haudenosaunee, the Métis, and the Mississaugas of the Credit First Nation.

This book has been published with the help of a grant from the Federation for the Humanities and Social Sciences, through the Awards to Scholarly Publications Program, using funds provided by the Social Sciences and Humanities Research Council of Canada.

University of Toronto Press acknowledges the financial support of the Government of Canada, the Canada Council for the Arts, and the Ontario Arts Council, an agency of the Government of Ontario, for its publishing activities.

Canada Council for the Arts Conseil des Arts du Canada

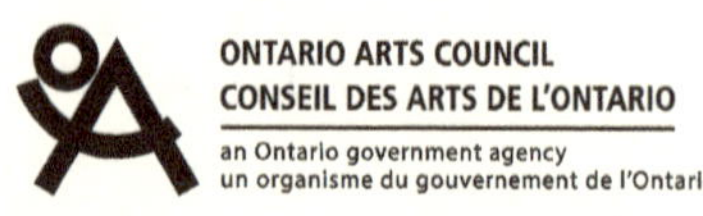

Funded by the Government of Canada Financé par le gouvernement du Canada

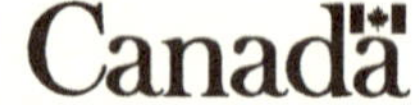

To Tulsi Banana,
our wayward, hyperaesthetic stray.

Contents

Preface

On 24 October 2020, I woke to the news that the South African anti-mining and environmental activist Fikile Ntshangase had been murdered. At around 6:30 pm on Thursday, 22 October, four men entered her home in Ophondweni, KwaZulu-Natal province, and shot her to death in front of a thirteen-year-old child. Ntshangase was a leading member of the Mfolozi Community Environmental Justice Organisation (MCEJO), which has been involved in a protracted legal dispute with Tendele Coal over its planned extension of the Somkhele opencast coalmine, located a stone's throw from the Hluhluwe-iMfolozi nature reserve in KwaZulu Natal (Greenfield; Kockott and Hattingh). The organization opposed the expansion of Tendele's mining operations in the area because of what many in the local community viewed as a truncated consultation process – one that led to the granting in 2016 of additional mining rights to Tendele for an area covering over 222 square kilometres – and because of the company's failure to comply with environmental laws (Kockott and Hattingh). The latter is tied to widespread concerns about the environmental impacts of opencast mining. These include the contamination of groundwater sources and the degradation of air quality, to which a host of respiratory and other human health problems have been ascribed (Borralho).

Ntshangase's assassination was the latest atrocity brought on in a year that delivered more than its fair share of grief. The struggles of Ntshangase and others opposed to extractive capitalism's ongoing disregard for human and environmental health are at the coalface, literally, of growing global awareness of a rapidly intensifying planetary climate crisis. The latter was thrown into sharp relief in 2020 by the COVID-19 pandemic, which radically transformed social and economic relations around the globe in a matter of weeks. A corollary of consumer capitalism's harmful relationship with non-human life and non-life alike, COVID-19 offers a prelude to the devastating threats to human survival that climate change is predicted to deliver if the destruction of wildlife habitat and biodiversity for the sake of mining, industrialized agriculture, and human housing continues apace (Vidal; Volz). The virus struck a heavy blow to the comforting fictions that wealth and technological innovation – what Naomi Klein refers to as "magical thinking" (189) – might insulate some from the inescapable interdependence of human and non-human ecologies. These are fictions to which communities such as those Ntshangase advocated for have never had easy access. As Kathryn Yusoff explains, recent expressions of concern about "the exposures of environmental harm to white liberal communities" conceal a much longer planetary legacy that saw these harms "knowingly exported to black and brown communities under the rubric of civilization, progress, modernization, and capitalism" (14).

Wayward Feeling is located in the wake of some of these histories of harm as they unfold affectively in the post-apartheid South African present. The manuscript for this book was submitted just as the planet suddenly retreated into the quarantined physical space of the home, even as it opened, for some, to new digital realms. Though much has changed in the interim, the relevance of *Wayward Feeling* to an understanding of contemporary public culture and its affective expression has simultaneously been heightened, as rage, anxiety, and despair in the face of historical dispossession, as well uncertainty about the post-pandemic future, catalysed new forms of global protest action. I draw attention, in these prefatory reflections, to Ntshangase's murder in part because it connects with a host of concerns that coalesce in the chapters of this book, in turn amplified by the evolving pandemic.

The mineral revolution that started to reshape South Africa from the mid-nineteenth century onwards has arguably been the leading historical driver of contemporary social, racial, economic, gender, and environmental injustice in the country. Though the book does not explicitly place the South African afterlives of resource extraction at its centre, they reverberate through its pages, from the extractive histories of rubber referenced in chapter 1; to the devastating massacre of the miners at Lonmin Platinum, Marikana, in 2012 (chapter 3); to the 2015 #RhodesMustFall protests highlighting the links between the legacy of one of the founders of the De Beers mining company and the forms of economic, emotional, and epistemic injustice shaping contemporary higher education (chapter 4); to the connections that I draw between breathing as an autonomic respiratory mechanism central to the body's capacity to regenerate and regulate stress and a larger respiratory crisis that confronts a planet increasingly choking on the mining industry's toxic waste (chapter 5 and the conclusion).

As I drafted the conclusion at the start of South Africa's 2020 lockdown, I was struck by the pertinence of the book's overarching concern with waywardness – what Saidiya Hartman calls "an improvisation with the terms of social existence ... when there is little room to breathe" (228) – to the threats posed by the novel coronavirus to human respiratory health. In the months since these lockdown restrictions were first imposed, the breath and breathing took on renewed significance, not least in the aftermath of the death of African-American citizen George Floyd in May 2020. Though the phrase "I can't breathe" has long been a rallying cry among decolonial and racial justice activists in the United States and South Africa alike, as I point out in chapter 4, Floyd's merciless asphyxiation by white Minneapolis police officer Derek Chauvin during an interminable nine minutes and twenty-nine seconds – while he repeatedly cried "I can't breathe" – drew attention anew to the suffocating nature of racial injustice in the United States and elsewhere (Apata). At the time, Floyd's death was the latest in a long history of similarly brutal police killings of Black US citizens, yet what made his murder unique was the fact that it was captured on video, quickly going viral online, and unleashing an unprecedented wave of antiracist protests around the globe.

These events struck a powerful chord with my third-year students and me as we tried to navigate the digital divide – suddenly amplified by South Africa's pandemic lockdown – while working through the readings assigned for our seminar course on the literary, cultural, and aesthetic politics of mining in South Africa. With the images of George Floyd's killing that flooded our social media feeds still seared into our mind's eye, we could not fail to notice the prevalence of the breath in our mining curriculum, from the miner who had contracted "the sickness of the lungs" that "ate a man's body away" (107) in Peter Abrahams's classic 1946 novel *Mine Boy*, to struggles for breath in the poetry of Alfred Temba Qabula, Ingrid de Kok, and Benedict Wallet Vilakazi, to the hidden health legacies of South African gold and platinum mining exposed in documentary films directed respectively by Rehad Desai, Aliki Saragas, and Richard Pakleppa and Catherine Meyburgh (the latter's 2018 film *Dying for Gold* appositely produced by their independent film production company, Breathe Films). Yet our course texts, like the many forms of audio-visual and aesthetic mediation at the centre of this book, do not simply bear witness to these scenes of suffocation; they harness the embodied sensorium very deliberately to chart a wayward path beyond histories of loss, trauma, and injustice.

The racial justice protests that the death of George Floyd sparked in the United States coincided with a time of intensified securitization in South Africa, as the African National Congress (ANC) government tried to enforce its quarantine measures. Activist efforts by the Black Lives Matter movement in the United States to defund the police brought South African histories of police brutality targeting Black communities again into painful focus, exposing structural racism's latest incarnation in the country. The South African Police Service in fact kills a staggering three times as many people per capita as do the police in the United States (Stuurman). Since the government imposed its first strict national curfew, so-called pandemic policing has resulted in the deaths of at least ten South African citizens as well as the criminalization of thousands, for mostly minor infractions (Trippe). Collins Khosa, for instance, was strangled and killed by members of the South African National Defence Force (SANDF) in the privacy of his own home after being suspected of having alcohol in his front yard (the initial lockdown included the prohibition of alcohol and cigarette sales). Sibusio Amos, likewise, was followed to his home and shot to death by police after being found drinking at an informal bar (lockdown-related police brutality is subject to an ongoing inquiry by the government's Independent Police Investigative Directorate, though Amos's death remains uninvestigated).

Inspired in part by worldwide Black Lives Matter protests, thousands of South Africans gathered on 9 June 2020 in protest against lockdown-related police brutality. Recent months also engendered renewed protests against the ongoing scourge of gender-based violence (addressed in chapter 5 of this book), exacerbated by a lockdown that saw countless women and gender nonconforming people confined at home with their abusers. During the first five days of the initial lockdown, the police's gender-based violence hotline received approximately 2,300 calls, nearly three times the pre-lockdown rate (Harrisberg). The gruesome murders of women such as Tshegofatso Pule, Naledi Phangindawo, and Sanele Mfaba fuelled the latest social media campaign to address the country's deplorable rates of domestic abuse and femicide, a reality subsequently declared South Africa's second pandemic by President Cyril Ramaphosa.

As social justice activists the world over breathed a collective sigh of relief, at least temporarily, in response to the outcome of the 2020 presidential election in the United States – not least for the implications for a climate crisis reaching its tipping point – it bears noting that the recent revitalization of anti-racist, feminist, anti-imperialist, and economic justice movements in the wake of Floyd's death, and in light of social inequalities heightened by the pandemic, was in many ways prefigured in the Global South (see for instance Makhulu, "Trump"). In South Africa, in particular, increasingly inventive methods of insurrectionary citizenship have been giving shape, since at least the mid-2000s, to feelings of despair, disappointment, and rage at the many forms of injustice that colonialism and apartheid continue to trail in their wake, messianic promises on the part of the post-apartheid state notwithstanding. By way of an extended conversation with multiple genres of aesthetic activism and audio-visual culture in South Africa, *Wayward Feeling* offers some insight into this difficult, painful, and, at times, regenerative affective archive. What follows explicitly foregrounds the South African context, but readers interested in some of the disruptive aesthetic and audio-visual strategies propelling publics towards a more affectively discriminating engagement with extractive and racial capitalism's ever-unfolding global forms will find multiple points of connection.

Acknowledgments

Wayward Feeling drew life from countless networks of support and inspiration. Key among these are the filmmakers, artists, audio-visual activists, and critical cultural theorists whose gift of time, labour, creativity, and courage enabled the conversation that follows. This gift nourished not only the insights that shaped this book, it also nurtures the soil from which the most urgently needed alternatives to contemporary racial and extractive capitalisms are starting to germinate in South Africa and beyond. We live in a time of considerable emotional upheaval resulting from the many forms of historical injustice converging in the current planetary climate crisis, in turn intensified by increasingly intrusive technologies of digital mediation. Though the path-breaking work done by feminist, decolonial, and queer cultural and creative workers who have long parsed the affective grammars of injustice is not always credited in more recent studies associated with the so-called affective turn, there can be no doubt that they have offered – and continue to offer – some of the most innovative, historically grounded vocabularies for making sense of our turbulent global present. If *Wayward Feeling* will achieve anything, I hope it is to amplify some of these debts.

The writing of this book benefited immeasurably from the inspiration offered by friends and colleagues across at least three continents. Some of its most bountiful ideas took root while I was working at McMaster University in Canada, where colleagues and friends modelled forms of ethical intellectual engagement of which I will be forever in awe. *Wayward Feeling* owes its greatest debt to Susan Spearey, without whose discerning intelligence and unstinting generosity it would never have come to fruition. Sue selflessly set aside her own deadlines every time I completed a chunk of this work to offer insight and reassurance. The arguments presented here would have been much impoverished without this dedication of intellectual and emotional labour. The joyous friendship and enthusiasm of Jesse Arseneault and Susie O'Brien likewise served as a cornerstone to this work. Their example in the classroom, on the page and in life, continues to remind me why I do this work in the first place. Mary O'Connor has been a much-loved mentor whose brilliance and grace in navigating the hazards of the corporate university I am always striving to emulate. Phanuel Antwi, Sarah Brophy, and Y-Dang Troeung count among the book's earliest and most vital interlocutors; I deeply cherish the privilege of having been able to learn from and collaborate with them. Nadine Attewell, Jessie Forsyth, Asha Jeffers, Allison Mackey, Dana Mount, Malissa Phung, Heather Snell, and Gena Zuroski have shared their time, work, care, and much more. I owe a special thanks to the late Don Goellnicht, who was the first to invite my partner Wayne and me over for supper after I took up my post at McMaster. I miss his friendship and his unsurpassed talent for sniffing out a secret. Warmest thanks are due also to Diana Brydon, whose invaluable mentorship early on opened many doors. I am especially grateful to the following friends, neighbours, and former colleagues in Canada for guidance, laughter, and inspiration: Nandi Bhatia, Chandrima Chakraborty, Subho Chakravarty, Daniel Coleman, Sarah D'Adamo, Cathy Grisé, Cindy Hindle-Stranak, Derek Jenkins, Jennifer Jones, Saikat Majumdar, Peter Mountford, Sarah Olutola, Tunji Osinubi, Christina Pangilinan, Prabhjot Parmar, Wendy Pearson, Anne Savage, Jessica Schagerl, Claire Senior, Antoinette Somo, Peter Walmsley, Kerri Withers, Tim Versteeg, and Lorraine York. Thanks especially to Lorraine for much-needed advice in the final stages of this project.

Friends and colleagues in South Africa have broadened my horizons and enriched my life in ways I will never be able to repay. Since moving back home, I have benefited from countless acts of kindness without which I would not have mustered the sanity and sustained focus that writing in a world of endemic institutional distraction requires. Of the people instrumental in my hiring at the University of the Free State, I am particularly grateful to Jonathan Jansen for the lively culture of curiosity and critical deliberation that he fostered during his time as rector and vice chancellor, and for clearing the space within which the best kind of teaching, learning, and research in my department could be pursued. My colleagues in the department of English have carried the weight of frequently inhumane work- and marking-loads with remarkable equanimity and good humour. During my tenure as department chair, Susan Brokensha, Mariza Brooks, Thinus Conradie, Iri Manase, and the late Margaret Raftery all on occasion helped me to make time for working on this project. I am deeply thankful to them for this generosity, as well as to the following colleagues for maintaining the climate of collegiality and mutual support within which my own ideas could mature and our students could thrive: Philip Aghoghovwia, Rick de Villiers, Nonhlanhla Dlamini, Colleen du Plessis, Carla Els, Carlo Germeshuys, Hanta Henning, Stacey-Lee Khojane, Manuela Lovisa, Ntsutle Mafisa, Rodwell Makombe, Sipho Maqubu, Faith Mkwesha, Kudzayi Ngara, Oliver Nyambi, and Carrie Timlin. I owe Kudzayi Ngara a special word of thanks for his fortitude and wit during the years we spent together in the trenches while he served as Qwaqwa subject head. A thousand thank yous are owed to the wonderful Patsy Fourie, whose warmth and unfaltering professionalism eased my transition back home, and made it possible to find the time to write while navigating administrative chaos. Candice Reynolds likewise provided a beacon of no-nonsense intelligence and strength that made coming to work a joy. For her kindness and creativity, I also thank Karen McGuire, who went well beyond the call of collegiality and consideration during the time it took me to complete this book.

I have been lucky to learn from several brilliant under- and postgraduate students over the years. For illuminating my thinking in the classroom and beyond, I thank in particular Glow Chang, Tanaka Chidora, Alexandro Daniels, Tamia Dicks, Sherredine Dunn, Suné du Plessis, Charlene du Plooy, Tammy Fray, Sinoxolo Gcilitshana, Dominique le Breton, Tracy Keegan, Rene Lombard, Nontsikelelo Lukhele, Lorette Marais, Refiloe Matsoso, Nhlanhla Mghobozi, Nthabiseng Mokoena, Yanda Mbopa, Zander Olivier, and Doreen Tivenga. The always-inspiring Dian Weys has been a long-standing source of support. I am especially thankful to the students in my "Archives of Feminist Rage and Love in (South) African Literature and Culture" postgraduate course, from whom the insights in chapter 5 benefited in particular. Our community of feminist killjoys has brought me incomparable joy over the past few years.

At the UFS, several other friends have buoyed me through various stages of this project by sharing their work, wisdom, and care. Jackie du Toit and Neil Roos are a wellspring of sage advice, and created invaluable opportunities for writing and sustained intellectual engagement. I drew much inspiration from the generative conversations and collaborations enabled by Andre Keet and Pumla Gobodo-Madikizela during their time at the UFS. For nourishing company I am especially thankful to Makhosazana and Philip Aghoghovwia, Janine Allen-Spies, Mariza Brooks, Megan Doney, Dennis Francis, Rob and Rindi Gordon, Mpho Jama, Mariana Kriel, Nadine Lake, Lis Lange, Joy Owen, Millie Rivera, Rachel Stewart, Lihlumelo Toyana, Dionne van Reënen, and Rosa Williams. For the gift of our annual "Women's Night" and more,

I thank Suzanne Human, Johanet Kriel, and Annie van den Oever. I am indebted to the brilliant Candice Thikeson for letting me pick her brain on several occasions. The incomparable Zubeida Jaffer graciously allowed me to vent during a difficult stage of this process and offered great writing advice. Kristina Riedel in particular has been a port in a storm; she has been remarkably generous with her friendship.

The book further benefited from the brilliant writing and, on occasion, advice of Ingrid de Kok, Vanessa Farr, Adam Haupt, Gugu Hlongwane, Danai Mupotsa, Sally-Ann Murray, Grace Musila, Martin Rossouw, Meg Samuelson, Kirk Sides, Kylie Thomas, Ross Truscott, Shaun Viljoen, Timothy Wright, and Sandy Young. Of the many recent theorists in South Africa and elsewhere who have blazed the wayward feminist trails followed by this work, the following have carved the deepest grooves into my head and heart: Sara Ahmed, Gabeba Baderoon, Rita Barnard, Lauren Berlant, Ann Cvetkovich, Saidiya Hartman, Neville Hoad, Desiree Lewis, Zethu Matabeni, Leigh-Ann Naidoo, and Sarah Nuttall. Pumla Dineo Gqola deserves every accolade she gets and a million more. Her pioneering body of work has been at the vanguard of South African feminist theorizing for some time now, and never ceases to raise the bar for me and my students. *Wayward Feeling* would be a lesser book without the gift of her mesmerizing example, her boundless generosity, and indefatigable spirit.

Occasions to present this material to audiences in South Africa, Canada, the United States, Germany, and elsewhere have been indispensable to me in gathering my thoughts into their present form. Notable among these are the many events organized by the Association for Cultural Studies (ACS) in which I have had the privilege to participate in recent years, either as part of the biennial Crossroads in Cultural Studies conferences or of the smaller ACS Institutes. This community has been remarkably welcoming and intellectually wayward in all the best ways, and for this I thank the following people in particular: Gil Rodman, Janneke Adema, Margie Borschke, Stephen Chan, Catherine Driscoll, Udo Göttlich, Matt Jordan, Ana Mendes, Aljosa Puzar, Matthias Wieser, Rainer Winter, Handel Kashope Wright, and Fan Yang. I am grateful for an invitation from Ronit Frenkel, Pamila Gupta, and Peter Vale to share work at the Johannesburg Institute for Advanced Studies; this experience informs some of my thinking in chapter 4 in particular. Derek Hook and Margareta Palacios have been valuable interlocutors, and I am enormously thankful for the opportunity I was given to present some of this work at Birkbeck, University of London, and Duquesne University, Pittsburgh, as part of the "Affective Archives" research collective. Derek has generously offered incisive feedback on much of my work. I owe a singular debt of gratitude to the brilliant Kerry Bystrom for her kindness in hosting me as a research associate at Bard College, Berlin, during the final months of writing this book. Thanks so much for granting me the time – and such an unforgettable space – to get to the finish line.

My heartfelt thanks go to Handel Kashope Wright, Boulou Ebanda de B'béri, and Keyan Tomaselli, the co-editors of the African Cultural Studies Book Series at the University of Toronto Press, for their enthusiastic endorsement of the project. Special thanks to Handel for his patience and encouragement from the outset, and for his kind invitation to present an early incarnation of this work as part of a Spotlight Session at the Tampere ACS Crossroads. I am grateful also to Mark Thompson, Barbara Porter, and Anne Laughlin, my editors at the University of Toronto Press, for so expertly shepherding my words from manuscript to book.

The research has benefited from funding tied to two consecutive ratings from the National Research Foundation (NRF) of South Africa (Grant Numbers 119020 and 85999), as well as from associated funding awarded by the University of the Free State. I acknowledge that opinions, findings, and conclusions or recommendations expressed in any publication generated by NRF-supported research are my own, and that the NRF accepts no liability whatsoever in this regard. I would not have been able to finish the manuscript were it not for a research leave granted in 2019, and for this I thank Corli Witthuhn, Heidi Hudson, and Chitja Twala in particular. I also thank Lee Goliath, Largo Mogopodi, and Aubrey Madiba at the UFS library for exemplary and speedy assistance with all my research-related requests.

I am grateful to the anonymous readers of this manuscript engaged by the University of Toronto Press for their astute feedback and for compelling me to add the preface. The book is the better for it. A much shorter and earlier version of chapter 1 was published in "Spectacles of Promise and Disappointment: Emotional Publics and Quotidian Aesthetics in Video Installations by Berni Searle and Zanele Muholi," *Safundi: The Journal of South African and American Studies*, vol. 15, no. 4, October 2014, pp. 471–95; reprinted by permission of the publisher (Taylor & Francis Ltd., http://www.tandfonline.com). A portion of chapter 3 appeared in "Managing Public Feeling: Temporality, Mourning and the Marikana Massacre in Rehad Desai's *Miners Shot Down*," *Critical Arts: South-North Cultural and Media Studies*, vol. 30, no. 4, August 2016, pp. 58–73; copyright © Critical Arts Projects & Unisa Press, reprinted by permission of Informa UK Limited, trading as Taylor & Francis Group, www.tandfonline.com on behalf of Critical Arts Projects & Unisa Press.

For the daily gift of clarity and wonder I thank my beautiful global community of yoga teachers and friends, especially Rowena Johnson, Anja Kuehnel, Satya Katiza, Kevin Sahaj, Zani Ludick, Johannes de Villiers, Trudie Strauss, and my first teacher, Katie McClelland. Deepest thanks to Dulcie Marais, for always being my girl, and to Anita Bothma, for picking up all the balls that I drop on the mom and school front. Ntombizodwa Vivian Japhta and Daniel Lemoen: I am eternally grateful for the patience and harmony you bring to my life. Margie Kemp: thanks for the kind gift of childcare and company during a crucial research trip. Cora Teske and the wonderful Teske family: I treasure your enduring friendship and appreciate your hospitality while I was on research leave in Germany.

Tulsi Banana, Mia, Hazel, Josephine, Stoffie, Chloë, Ivy, and Tipsy – my feline and canine kin: I cannot imagine a life without the daily delights of your antics and attention. Johan and Erna Myburgh, Vanessa, Naomi, Lia, Ghali, Luke, Emile, Celdri, Ash, Belinda, and Heinie: I am so lucky to call you my "fabulous family." Erna's boundless love and prophetic wisdom continue to radiate through each of us, compelling us to try harder every day to live up to our best selves. Louise, Steph, Herman, Trudie, Edrich, and Lehan: your love and laughter are the foundation upon which all of this is built. My parents, Danie and Tharina Strauss: there are not thanks enough for the lifelong gifts of your wise counsel, financial and emotional support, and unfaltering love.

Finally, my deepest gratitude goes to Wayne and Disa, who have sustained me through every syllable of this book. You soften my sharp edges and inspire me to engage the world from a place of trust and kindness first and foremost. I cannot believe my good fortune in having come into your orbit.

I dedicate this book to Tulsi Banana, our wayward, hyperaesthetic stray. Thank you for being my first guide into the complex reciprocity of body, sense, and world.

WAYWARD FEELING

Introduction

It is no accident that the student protests that started to spread through South Africa in March 2015 were sparked by a statue – at the time prominently on display at the University of Cape Town (UCT) – of Cecil John Rhodes (1853–1902), mining magnate, politician, and one of the most dedicated disciples of the British imperial project. The fact that the statue of Rhodes could still occupy such a prominent place at one of South Africa's foremost universities in the year 2015 speaks powerfully to some of the failures of the reconciliation projects put in place in the immediate aftermath of white minority rule. That his statue would inspire such depths of anger and resentment more than twenty years after legislative apartheid ended and more than a hundred years since Rhodes's death further reveals the deep historical roots of contemporary South African political disaffection. That these protests did not, in fact, erupt sooner attests to the anaesthetizing effects of post-apartheid nation-building initiatives and attendant projects of affective management. It is safe to say that the anaesthetic has now worn off.

This book navigates this steadily expanding terrain of unvarnished feeling. If the South African national government under Nelson Mandela and Thabo Mbeki tried to defuse racial tensions by promoting affective attachments to the ideals of interconnection, nonracialism, and national unity as the country's dominant organizing principles, more recently a growing segment of the South African citizenry have found themselves adrift from the certainties promised by these ideals. As Sisonke Msimang phrases it in a 2016 opinion piece in the *New York Times*, many South Africans have started to "reclaim their power over a sentimental mythology about forgiveness and racial harmony that has been, for at least a decade, inauthentic and out of step with the realities of most people's lives" ("Making"). Indeed, as some of the failures of nation-building, political accountability, land reform, infrastructural capacity-building, educational advancement, and attendant forms of economic, gender, and racial injustice are becoming increasingly difficult to conceal, widespread disaffection has started to power creative new forms of insurgent citizenship.[1]

Of the many examples of organized dissent one could list here, the so-called hashtag student uprisings associated with the #RhodesMustFall and #FeesMustFall movements have perhaps been most vocal about the ways in which the reconciliation projects of the early post-apartheid years have stifled meaningful discussion of colonialism and apartheid's material and affective legacies, and of the need to finally look their causes squarely in the face. As feminist and decolonial activist Simamkele Dlakavu explains in an opinion piece on the role of white allies in Black student resistance, "the so called 'rainbow nation' and 'post-racial' youth of South Africa are starting to reject the labels imposed on them. They feel that those terms have derailed meaningful justice and reconciliation in these 21 years of our democracy" ("Is There Space"). In their mission statement, the Rhodes Must Fall activists – a collective made up of students and staff members at the University of Cape Town – clearly articulate their struggle as motivated by the ongoing experience of racism and attendant forms of structural injustice on the part of Black people in post-1994 South Africa, and explicitly place "black pain" (6) at the forefront of their struggle.[2]

These perspectives highlight at least two concerns that are central to the argument developed throughout this book. First, the emphasis on the part of the Rhodes Must Fall collective and allied Fallist movements on Black pain is symptomatic of a long lineage of feminist, queer, and decolonial approaches to the embodied mind that has recently come to revitalize the popular vernacular of dissent. In their resistance to forms of alienation at once material, curricular, and emotional, student activists in effect compelled a renewed centring of the sensorial body and its experiential distance from forms of happiness associated with a good life promised – but never fully delivered – by the post-apartheid state. Second, by revealing a legacy of psychic division deeply rooted in the unequal distribution of racialized suffering at the heart of South Africa's colonial history, these activists telegraph some of the themes that run through much recent scholarship on affect: that the personal and the political, the social and the psychic, are intimately entangled, and, by extension, that our emotional lives reflect not simply our direct experiential biographies but in fact constitute archives of larger historical and political forces that are more often than not inaccessible to our conscious selves.

Wayward Feeling marshals some of the critical, creative, and activist vocabularies to emerge in South Africa in recent years to consider the complex affective claims that the past continues to make on present-day political and everyday life nearly three decades since the end of apartheid. The book asks what contemporary South African audio-visual culture and aesthetic activisms might tell us about the forms of power that circulate through embodied feeling in a "post-rainbow" South Africa, an era which I periodize, for reasons that I elaborate on in the next chapter, as the years roughly since 2006, when the rape trial of former president Jacob Gedleyihlekisa Zuma took place. How do racism, sexism, and other forms of structural disenfranchisement continue to assert themselves in affective terms, and how have these terms been recast in spaces both public and intimate in recent years? How have terms such as disappointment, rage, and melancholia – read here as political emotions that surge unpredictably across the social – come to energize contemporary cultural forms and aesthetic activisms? What are some of the affective resources that people in contemporary South Africa draw on to make difficult lives bearable?

I argue that the tension between aspiration and achievability in post-rainbow South Africa has yielded modes of feeling that increasingly disrupt the thrall of the post-apartheid promise of a better future for all, even as widespread attachment to the utopian ideals of the anti-apartheid struggle continues to shape dissenting political organizing and cultural production. In short, the book maps *wayward feelings* – defined broadly as those affective shifts that are difficult to control or predict, that fail to conform to publicly prescribed or sanctioned feeling, that reach beyond confinement and capture – across scenes of intimate encounter and aesthetic articulation by way of analyses, for instance, of the relationship between emotion and politics in contemporary South African protest and consumer cultures, of the expectant dimensions of mood in visual youth autobiography, of the management of public feeling both prior and subsequent to the Marikana massacre, of aesthetic activisms associated with the #RhodesMustFall and #FeesMustFall student protests, and of the multigenerational, multisensory resonances that echo through South African archives of women's cultural production and activism.[3]

In the course of this introduction, I map some of the temporal currents surging through South Africa in the aftermath of apartheid before considering how an aesthetic lens might help to animate the intersections of history, politics, and the embodied sensorium in the South African present. I also explain in greater detail what I mean by *wayward feeling*, and what a reading of audio-visual culture and aesthetic activisms through this framework might bring to making sense of post-rainbow times.[4] *Wayward Feeling* is particularly interested in the potentially transformative capacities of audio-visual culture's affective sway, even as it remains cautious not to assume that the autonomic energies prompting the transmission of affect will necessarily yield progressive political outcomes. Much of the labour of variously amplifying, recomposing, nuancing, and mobilizing the "affective surplus" (Gill and Tyler 79) produced by disaffected South African publics has been done by (audio)visual activists, filmmakers, and performance artists, and it is this work that is the main focus of my book. By way of analyses of works by filmmakers and (audio)visual activists such as Berni Searle, Zanele Muholi, Sarah Chu, Evelyn Maruping, Rehad Desai, Chumani Maxwele, Sethembile Msezane, and Gabrielle Goliath, I develop a set of key terms and rubrics for working through the relationship between post-rainbow structures of feeling and the material, experiential, and affective body. These include the terms "sensual and emotional pedagogies" and "quotidian aesthetics" (chapter 1), "expectant mood" and "wayward agency" (chapter 2), "counter-affective lingering" (chapter 3), "wayward aesthetics of commemoration" (chapter 4), and "resonant feminist listening" (chapter 5).

Bewildering Times

As South Africa continues to grapple with the realities of continuing, if not worsening, inequality post-apartheid, a growing chorus of cultural theorists and public commentators have started to ponder the relationship between social and psychic time. A range of conceptual frameworks has been offered for making sense of what Anna-Maria Makhulu calls a country that is not simply "out of sorts but out of time" ("Reckoning" 260). Derek Hook describes the temporal order of the post-apartheid era as bidirectional, tugging between competing notions of achievable post-apartheid progress and the many "instances where adequate structural change has either not come to pass or stalled, threatening even in some cases to regress, to reverse into an intractably backward trajectory" (*(Post)apartheid* 6). In the aftermath of the 2012 Marikana massacre in particular – the most deadly attack by the security forces of the state on its own citizenry since the end of apartheid – the critical emphasis seems increasingly to land on the backward temporal slide identified by Hook. A proliferating vocabulary for diagnosing this temporal order includes "precarious time" (Lincoln 99), "the new old" (Nuttall, "Afterword" 280), "the now-time" or "present imperfect" (van der Vlies, *Present* 6, 21), "post-revolutionary time" (Wright 199), the "almost-times" (Msimang, "Zuma's"), "historical dissonance" (Naidoo 2), and "autumnal" time (Barnard, "Introduction" 9).

Timothy Wright, for instance, identifies in South Africa's post-2012 historical consciousness a melancholic attachment to the ghosts of revolutionary futures past. Inspired by anthropologist David Scott's argument in *Omens of Adversity* (2014) that the failed Grenada Revolution (1979–83) following the Reagan administration's 1983 invasion brought about "the beginning of the end of a whole *era* of revolutionary expectation – indeed, of revolutionary socialist possibility" (4), Wright points to a post-apartheid South African temporality that is likewise "marked by a sense of afterness" (199). Yet unlike the impression of "ruined" time that characterizes post-revolutionary Grenadan consciousness and that brought an end to a global sense of socialist and decolonizing possibility initially sparked by the 1955 Bandung conference, post-apartheid temporality hovers somewhere between fulfilment and failure, or, as I phrase it in the next chapter, promise and disappointment.

In the South African context, Wright suggests, revolutionary time has been dampened but not entirely extinguished, as "the allegory of emancipationist redemption ... continues to exert force on the South African imagination" (199). Post-revolutionary time, then, "possesses a dynamic turbulence in which the hegemony of neo-liberal time is always under threat from the return of a reborn revolutionary time" (199). Indeed, as I demonstrate in chapter 1, reborn revolutionary time continues to draw its affective charge from the post-apartheid promise-in-revision, as the promise of nonracial harmony has come to be supplanted by the promise of radical economic reform, most insistently articulated by the Economic Freedom Fighters (EFF).[5]

In her recent overview of the post-apartheid literary imagination, Rita Barnard likewise draws on Scott's argument to position local South African temporal specificities alongside global ones. Though there are many examples of South Africa being historically out of sync with the rest of the world – not least of which the anachronism that was apartheid state racism – there are, as Barnard points out, a number of congruities between the local and global experience of time. These include "the paranoia characteristic of the Cold War era and, in recent years, a pervasive feeling of disappointment and diminished expectations, a sense of entrapment in the distracted present of social media and consumption, and an intensification of rage and impatience: all of which, however various, are identifiably transnational predicaments" ("Introduction" 4). Barnard's is a post-apartheid temporality that swivels between the sense of stasis that attends inhabiting the global political economy of neoliberalism and moments of acceleration delivered by various forms of contemporary protest, hinting at "imagined futures in the very ruin of Mandela and Tutu's rainbow nation dreams" (7).

Yet for Barnard there is also more to the story than this tension between neoliberal suspension and post-rainbow activist acceleration. In the global afterlives of extractive capitalism, another temporal framework emerges as the "vernal metaphors" (8) associated with myths of progress so prevalent during the early South African transitional years are gradually superseded by "autumnal" ones. Here Barnard draws on Anna Tsing's reading, in *The Mushroom at the End of the World: On the Possibility of Life in Capitalist Ruins* (2015), of the possibilities for improvising multiple futures that stem from relinquishing our attachment to liberalism's linear teleologies of progress in the face of an unfolding planetary climate catastrophe. The need for these forms of improvisation became particularly pronounced in 2020, as the uncertainties introduced by the COVID-19 pandemic required the navigation of multiple, overlapping temporal logics (Jordheim et al.). Barnard locates the "autumnal affect" that structures these imagined global futures also locally, "in the blighted urban areas, the dusty townships, and the drought-stricken rural areas of South Africa where lives continue to be creatively patched together on the improvisatory edges of global modernity" ("Introduction" 9).

Promise and disappointment, fulfilment and failure, suspension and acceleration, vernal and autumnal. Each of these dichotomies to some extent signals what I elsewhere refer to as the "bewildering affective timelines" ("Affective Return" 225) of thwarted expectation in the aftermath of apartheid. They convey something of the "yo-yo effect" that Ronit Frenkel and Pamila Gupta identify in a South Africa "that tends to swing between fear and optimism, pessimism and hope, on a regular basis" (2). It is fair to assert then, as Leigh-Ann Naidoo does in her 2016 Ruth First Lecture, that the meaning of our times still evades capture:

> We are, to some degree, *post*-apartheid, but in many ways not at all. We are living in a democracy that is at the same time violently, pathologically unequal. Protest action against the government – huge amounts of it, what in most other places would signal the beginning of radical change – often flips into a clamour for favour from that very government. Our vacillations, contradictions and anachronisms are indication that what time it is, is open to interpretation. (2; emphasis in original)

From these bewildering temporalities, Naidoo saw briefly arise, in the revolutionary aspirations of student activists, a form of time-travelling: an experiment with "hallucinating a new time" by "forcing an awareness of a time when things are not this way" (2), a time beyond the structural violence of South Africa's apartheid past and its obstinate hold on the present. In practice, the protests were a clear example of post-rainbow activist acceleration, of Wright's "reborn revolutionary time" (199), the window to which has since in many ways closed. Yet alongside Barnard, I find in the students' collective hallucination – emergent also in countless other forms of insurgent organizing and aspirational life-making against the odds in contemporary South Africa – hints of the kinds of improvisational possibility that Tsing so compellingly identifies in the matsutake mushroom's "willingness to emerge in blasted landscapes" (3), and in the "precarious livelihoods" (4) that have been formed around global practices of mushroom collecting – what she terms "collaborative survival in precarious times" (2).

Taking my cue from Naidoo, I conceive of *Wayward Feeling* as a book-length hallucination of sorts, invested in tracing some of the many imaginative means by which South Africans have refused to relinquish their dreams of a better future. As the Marxist philosopher Ernst Bloch once memorably phrased it, "we never tire of wanting things to improve" (*Principle* 77).[6] Yet as modes of wayward feeling, aspirational hallucinations are also far from predictable in form, substance, and outcome, propelled as they are by affective energies that pulse erratically beyond the purview of our clear-cut analytical frames. Even as we scramble to gain some conceptual purchase on the chronopolitics of South Africa post-rainbow, the psychic experience of time continues to test our expectations, as the analyses of audio-visual culture and aesthetic activism that I offer in the chapters to follow reveal.

(An)aesthetics

Conceived of in the cauldron of South African higher education in these turbulent times, *Wayward Feeling* finds particular resonance in the local voices of those who refuse to sever the aesthetic from the political, the aesthetic experience from the aesthetic object, the cognitive from the emotional. In short, the book considers how political and social shifts in contemporary South Africa unfold aesthetically, a term taken here to refer to the messy socio-cultural and material worlds of sensate perception and embodied feeling, and to the many forms and genres of cultural mediation and everyday life through which these sensations travel.

In what follows, audio-visual and performative modes of cultural production in particular take preference as sites of aesthetic mediation and transmission. Alongside the many feminist, queer, decolonial, and affect theorists referenced throughout the book, I advocate for a return to older understandings of the term aesthetics, as concerned less with the realm of taste, beauty, and artistic merit than with the domain of sensation, perception, or feeling. The former understanding of the term gained prominence in Europe subsequent to the publication of Alexander Baumgarten's *Aesthetica* (1750), in which the study of art and beauty first came to be linked to notions of good and bad "taste." Baumgarten's reappraisal of the term consolidated its narrow use as a conduit for reinforcing existing class and moral distinctions, an early manifestation of what theorists such as Thorstein Veblen and Pierre Bourdieu would later identify as forms of socio-cultural differentiation central to the distribution of power in consumer capitalism.[7] Aesthetics in this modern usage thus became a significant evaluative force in the study of both art and the experiences associated with it.[8] Ben Highmore helpfully traces the shift from classical understandings of aesthetics towards more recent approaches in order to delineate his own preferences for a return to the former:

> Once upon a time the word "aesthetics" ... gestured thought toward the great left-over: the bodily creature; the paths of often unruly emotions; the whole sensual world in all its baseness and brilliance. Emerging as a named area of inquiry only in the mid-eighteenth century, the history of aesthetics can be seen to follow a wayward path of increased intellectual specialisation, increasingly limiting itself to only certain kinds of experience and feeling, and becoming more and more dedicated to finely wrought objects. Once taken out of their lively solution, such discrete objects (artworks, powerful feelings of awe in the face of nature) were left beached on the shores of disciplinary knowledge. Marooned by an attention designed to praise and appraise them, art objects were often shorn of the very thing that aesthetics originally sought to engage with – the sensual, material entanglement with the socio-natural world. (*Ordinary* x)

In popular usage, as Highmore points out, the older meanings no longer widely associated with aesthetics can still be located in the terms anaesthetics or anaesthesia (as well as synaesthesia or hyperaesthesia). From the Greek root *anaisthetos*, the term anaesthetics refers to a dulling of the senses, an inability to experience both distressing and pleasurable feeling.[9] In her appraisal of the generational fault lines that separate the time-travelling student activists from their elders, Naidoo in fact invokes this sense of the term when she writes that "many in the anti-apartheid generation have become anesthetized to the possibility of another kind of future" (5). South African arts writer Lwandile Fikeni likewise calls for a return to forms of aesthetics located "in the lived social experience – in the senses, the feelings, the emotions" (5). He reads recent student activisms in particular as enabling such a return, as protestors engaged in "the aesthetics of rage" as they channelled public feeling beyond the gallery into the streets.[10]

As the inverse of anaesthetics, then, aesthetics calls forth an enlivening of the senses that makes us responsive to the social and material worlds we inhabit, a responsiveness positioned throughout this book within the shifting dynamics of political and social coexistence. Unsurprisingly, it is the classical sense of the term that has captured the attention of those whose work aligns with the recent turn to affect in social and cultural theory. This turn to aesthetics in its earlier, broader sense has proved particularly generative for considering the sociality of intimate, subjective life and for mapping the feelings and forms, moods and modes, by which history, politics, and culture have come to pulse through the body. If within the discourse of aesthetics we find a historical tension between elitist forms of cultural and political withdrawal, on the one hand, and a path towards understanding the historicity and collective embeddedness of individualized feeling, on the other, *Wayward Feeling* is interested in aesthetics to the extent that it might guide us towards the latter.[11]

Wayward Feeling

This turn towards the embodied sensorium has animated this project from the outset, and draws momentum in part from growing interest in the relationship between the psychic and the social on the part of a range of South African cultural and social theorists in the aftermath of apartheid. Though no monograph has as of yet examined how audio-visual culture and aesthetic activisms mediate the "post-rainbow" structural circulation of power through embodied feeling, *Wayward Feeling* shares common ground with work by a number of theorists concerned with the intersections of private feeling and public culture in post-1994 South Africa. Some of this work was generated by the widely discussed South African Truth and Reconciliation Commission (TRC) that concluded in 1998, but significant contributions have also been made more recently by those theorizing the psychosocial – if not always explicitly affective – dimensions of apartheid's afterlives.[12]

In the shadow of an intensification of protest action on the part of disaffected publics in recent years, political emotion and public feelings have slowly started to emerge as objects of study among scholars in the fields of South African literary, art, and (visual) cultural studies in particular. Examples include Marietta Kesting's *Affective Images: Post-apartheid Documentary Perspectives* (2017), which examines the visual mediation and circulation of affect in a range apartheid-era and post-apartheid photographs and films, and Andrew van der Vlies's *Present Imperfect: Contemporary South African Writing* (2017), a study of some of the affective, formal, and temporal dimensions of specifically literary engagements with post-apartheid disappointment. Additional touchstones include Pumla Dineo Gqola's *Rape: A South African Nightmare* (2015), *Reflecting Rogue: Inside the Mind of a Feminist* (2017), and *Female Fear Factory* (2021); Kerry Bystrom's *Democracy at Home in South Africa* (2016); Danai Mupotsa's work on public feelings across a range of contemporary (South) African visual and celebrity cultural sites; Neville Hoad's *African Intimacies: Race, Homosexuality and Globalization* (2007); Brenna Munro's *South Africa and the Dream of Love to Come: Queer Sexuality and the Struggle for Freedom* (2012); Deborah Posel's readings of the affective dynamics of the post-apartheid public sphere; and Jay Pather and Catherine Boulle's edited volume *Acts of Transgression: Contemporary Live Art in South Africa* (2019).

The affective excesses generated by the slow pace of post-apartheid redress are increasingly acknowledged by these interlocutors and others as central to any understanding of our times. Jay Pather and Catherine Boulle, for instance, find in examples of recent embodied aesthetic activism an increased inability to "articulate the distension of the time" (1) via conventional communicative means, as feelings carefully managed during the country's transitional period – what I elsewhere term "rainbow anaesthetics" ("Wayward" 4) – can no longer be contained. Their edited volume of often deeply personal reflections on the transgressive forms and feelings emerging through contemporary live art is framed deliberately as a response to a post-apartheid political economy producing "an overflow of emotion that is in excess of language" (14). In the same volume, cultural critic Sarah Nuttall likewise embraces "histories of feeling, epistemologies of emotion" as a heuristic lens for the "intense psychic energies … at work in periods of upsurge and turbulence" ("Upsurge" 43). As she phrases it, "tracing the meaning of a time through communities of affect enables the emergence of unconventional figures of the political. Put differently, emotions are an integral – and visceral – dimension of the grammar of the political itself" (43).

This book considers specifically those "wayward" feelings endemic to post-rainbow times. I conceive of waywardness in three intersecting ways:

(1) as a form of defiant survival in contexts of extreme daily hardship;
(2) as an aesthetic strategy that aims to awaken viewers and listeners to the sensorial realm of embodied feeling; and

(3) as an epistemic and methodological commitment to undoing what Ramón Grosfoguel has termed the "epistemic racism/ sexism" foundational to the Cartesian "knowledge structures of the Westernized University" (73).

In the first instance, my understanding of waywardness derives from a number of sources concerned with what Homi Bhabha once referred to as the "affective experience of social marginality" (172) in postcolonial contexts. Most recently, Saidiya Hartman's deeply moving and generative *Wayward Lives, Beautiful Experiments: Histories of Social Upheaval* (2019) conceives of waywardness as the many improvisatory everyday struggles to evade regulation, surveillance, and violence on the part of Black women living in Harlem and Philadelphia in the United States at the turn of the twentieth century. To be wayward, she writes, is "to be deeply aware of the gulf between where you stayed and how you might live" (227). Waywardness, she goes on, is "the avid longing for a world not ruled by master, man or the police … the social poesis that sustains the dispossessed … Waywardness articulates the paradox of cramped creation, the entanglement of escape and confinement, flight and captivity" (227).[13] Waywardness, as the "everyday struggle to live free … when there is little room to breathe" (227, 228), can be identified in affective terms throughout this book, for instance, in the playful aesthetics of Berni Searle and Zanele Muholi as they chart avenues of escape for those whose sensory, experiential realities irritate dominant modes of feeling, and in the creative strategies of defiant endurance that Sarah Chu, Evelyn Maruping, and the women represented in their films craft as moody daily experiments in "how-to-live" (Hartman 228).

Readers familiar with the work of feminist and queer theorist Sara Ahmed will recognize in these wayward feelings traces also of the figures of the "affect alien" or "willful subject" that she pursues, for instance, in *The Promise of Happiness* (2010) and *Willful Subjects* (2014).[14] Whereas affective alienation takes shape in contexts where dominant expectations regarding what a person should feel are experienced as suffocating, the wilful subject is one who strays "from the paths they are supposed to follow" (Ahmed, *Willful* 21) because these paths simply do not accommodate them. Alongside Ahmed, I have an interest in disappointment as a political feeling with deep historical reach; my own interest lies, in the book's initial chapters, less in disappointment itself than in that to which it gives rise. Wayward feeling is located in this beyond.

As the book proceeds through scenes of contemporary labour, decolonial, and feminist activism in the later chapters, wayward feelings emerge increasingly as aesthetic strategies by means of which viewers and listeners are summoned into greater responsiveness to forms of bodily and psychic suffering that, to varying degrees, differ from their own experiential positioning. My interest in these forms of aesthetic engagement stems in no small part from an abiding awareness of my own location as a beneficiary of the systemic privileges conferred on me by South Africa's apartheid and colonial history, and, by extension, from the ongoing search for ethical ways of responding to historical and contemporary violence and trauma. This search is echoed in a concern articulated by Athena Athanasiou and Judith Butler in their conversation on the term "dispossession," which they read as a marker of the crucial ethical challenge posed to the unified, sovereign subject by its constitutive others, on the one hand, and of the various forms of social abjection – symptomatic, for instance, of colonial occupation, forced migration, unemployment, and poverty – whereby precarity comes to be unevenly distributed, on the other:

> Both of us found ourselves returning to the question, "What makes political responsiveness possible?" The predicament of being moved by what one sees, feels, and comes to know is always one in which one finds oneself transported elsewhere, into another scene, or into a social world in which one is not the center. And this form of dispossession is constituted as a form of responsiveness that gives rise to action and resistance, to appearing together with others in an effort to demand the end of injustice. (3–4)

If contemporary political disenchantment is the affective culmination of the country's legacy of colonial and apartheid dispossession, how does one cultivate political responsiveness to the experiences of those for whom these histories of loss live on and continue to take on new forms? What might works of audio-visual aesthetic mediation reveal about the psychic energies that at once fuel and elude larger structures of feeling, and about the viewer's and listener's own positioning within this affective landscape? What are some of the aesthetic forms by which political disillusionment has come to be channelled to produce better ways of listening to those excluded from political, social, and psychic membership in contemporary South Africa? My analysis, in chapter 3, of the "counter-affective labour" conducted by a filmmaker such as Rehad Desai to galvanize and sustain public outrage in relation to the Marikana massacre constitutes one possible response to Athanasiou and Butler's question. My reading, in chapter 4, of the wayward aesthetics of commemoration whereby artist Sethembile Msezane for instance enlivens histories of dispossession through the enfleshed sensorial body likewise charts possibilities of ethical spectatorial responsiveness, as does my call in chapter 5, via Gabrielle Goliath's powerful sonic installations, for approaching the afterlives of sexual and gender-based violence through a method of resonant feminist listening.

The audio-visual texts and performances considered in each of these chapters are noteworthy for their stubborn refusal to conceive of deliberation as detached from passion, which brings me to my third approach to waywardness as a non-Cartesian epistemic and methodological investment. The book is propelled throughout by my wayward feminist leanings, which invariably steered me towards feminist, anti-racist, and queer theory responsive to the non-ideational dimensions of embodied experience that cannot simply be reduced to rationality's other, but stand in complex, conjoined relation to it. This orientation also accounts, as I explain below, for my choice of the word "feelings" in the title as a term that I take throughout as a blanket category that encompasses related terms such as emotion, affect, sentiment, and mood.

In brief, as Jan Slaby and Christian von Scheve point out in their editorial introduction to a recent "Key Concepts" guide to *Affective Societies*, "the long-standing assumption in social theory of a dichotomous opposition between affectivity and rationality turns out to be grossly inadequate" (3). Indeed, work in neuroscience has increasingly been confirming that the different parts of the brain responsible for functions including heartbeat, respiration, attention, emotion, language, and abstract thought are vitally interdependent. As Maia Szalavitz and Bruce Perry explain, the four regions of the brain "work in concert, so it is impossible to separate 'rational thought' from emotion. Even the most sophisticated decisions and analyses require positive and negative emotion; otherwise, it is impossible to determine which choice or idea is 'better' and which isn't. Valuing anything – even an idea – as 'good' or 'bad' requires feeling" (18). Or as James Jasper phrases it in his study of the role of emotion in politics and social movements, "feeling and thinking are parallel, interacting processes of evaluating and interacting with our worlds, composed of similar neurological building blocks" ("Emotions" 286).[15]

In their volume on affect, emotion, and rhetorical persuasion in mass communication – conceived in part in response to the election of Donald Trump as president of the United States and the triumph of the "Leave" campaign in the UK Brexit vote in 2016 – editors Lei Zhang and Carlton Clark likewise demonstrate that "facts and reason alone are not the answer to our problems" (5). Referencing, for instance, the oft-cited work of Hugo Mercier and Dan Sperber on what has come to be known as "confirmation bias" – namely the tendency of people to gravitate towards information that confirms their beliefs and to discard information that challenges them – Zhang and Clark posit the concept of "heartfelt reasoning" (8) as a return to the Aristotelian rhetorical notion of the enthymeme. The authors conceive of enthymeme not simply as an incomplete form of informal logic, as is commonly the case; they highlight its affective dimensions as central to argumentation and to understanding how rhetorical persuasion works in what has been popularly labelled the "post-truth" age of the present.[16]

The insights that these theorists draw on and develop have in fact been a mainstay of much feminist and queer theorizing on emotion and feelings for some time (central also to the well-known feminist refrain that the "personal is political"), and it is this long theoretical legacy to which *Wayward Feeling* is particularly indebted. As international and African feminist theorists alike have demonstrated at length, the fiction of objective knowledge as detached from embodied location has been historically complicit in a range of gendered, racial, and other exclusions, as I explain in greater detail in chapters 4 and 5.[17] Anticolonial philosopher Ramón Grosfoguel further explicitly links Cartesian philosophy to what he calls the four genocides/epistemicides of the long sixteenth century, namely "against Jewish and Muslim origin population in the conquest of Al-Andalus, against Indigenous people in the conquest of the Americas, against Africans kidnapped and enslaved in the Americas and against women burned alive, accused of being witches in Europe" (73). With these histories in mind, he identifies a missing link in Enrique Dussel's argument that Descartes's famous maxim "I think therefore I am" in the seventeenth century was enabled by the preceding 150 years of "I conquer therefore I am": "What links the 'I conquer, therefore I am' (*ego conquiro*) with the idolatric, God like 'I think, therefore I am' (*ego cogito*) is the epistemic racism/sexism produced from the 'I exterminate, therefore I am' (*ego extermino*) … as the new foundation of knowledge in the modern/colonial world" (77).

My interest in this book in the affective legacies of these histories of suffering that attended the globalization of European capitalist modernity, as well as their epistemological and material aftermath, is shared, then, by decolonial, anti-racist, queer, and feminist critical theorists working in both the Global North and South, and, as many of these theorists have pointed out, is hardly a new scholarly agenda if we take into consideration the intellectual inheritance of work on the embodied effects of colonialism as well as of homophobic, misogynist, racist, and other forms of violence.[18] These legacies are not always acknowledged by those anthologized in recent volumes on affect, but they do point to important junctures of past, present, and future conversation about cultural theory from the South to which *Wayward Feeling* hopes to contribute.[19]

It bears stating that much of the research generated by so-called affect theorists working in the North owes significant intellectual debts to the theoretical and experiential legacies of the Global South. I am not interested here in tracing intellectual origins – "theory is for use," as James Ferguson puts it ("Theory" 3). But it is worth noting both the striking relevance to South African contexts of work on political emotion produced in the Global North, and the fact that much of this work in fact germinates from anti-colonial and other social justice concerns at the heart of much cultural theorizing in South Africa and elsewhere in the Global South. Many of those working at institutions in the North who theorize the relationship between emotional and social justice in fact bear "scholarly signatures that are simultaneously north and south" (Comaroff and Comaroff, "Theory"). Much of the work coming out of the "Feel Tank Chicago" and the "Public Feelings" projects in the United States, likewise, shares a concern with "the affective legacy of racialized histories of genocide, slavery, colonization and migration" (Cvetkovich, "Public" 464) that also animates this book.

My preference for "feelings" as an umbrella term that signals intersubjective and trans-material energies registered, for instance, across sensory, cognitive, psychic, autonomic, visceral, respiratory, and atmospheric terrains of embodied sociality stems in part from my longstanding engagement with this body of work. Unlike those committed to reserving the term "affect" for pre-personal, nonintentional, noncognitive processes (what Melissa Gregg and Gregory Seigworth call "visceral forces beneath, alongside, or generally *other than* conscious knowing, vital forces insisting beyond emotion" [1]), and "emotion" for socially and culturally mediated conceptualizations and appraisals of felt experience, I heed Sara Ahmed's warning that, in certain contexts, "the affect/emotion distinction can operate as a gendered distinction" ("Afterword" 207).[20] I am drawn to the term "feelings" in part for its capaciousness, for how it signals the physicality of the experiential, and for the historical preference given to it in feminist and queer scholarship, even as I enlist a range of related terms through the course of this book to do similar work. (I provide a brief genealogy of the term "mood," for instance, in chapter 2 in an effort to get a better grip on post-rainbow modes of youth feeling.)[21] Feelings are messy and unpredictable, and have histories that stretch well beyond the immediacies of social encounter.

By prompting a conversation between contemporary South African audio-visual culture and national and international scholarship on affect, emotion, and feeling, then, my aim is in part to expand the terms within which historical injustice and structural inequality have been considered in a South African context, and to broaden the theoretical orbit of those studying affect from Northern vantage points. Yet in the spirit of waywardness, the book also refuses to yield to the demands of prestige-driven academic cultures that insist on the exhaustive citation of a ready-made roster of Continental philosophers or academic superstars located in the generously funded institutions of the Global North. Even as I engage with the work of some of these theorists, *Wayward Feeling* favours a critical methodology aimed at amplifying local aesthetic practice and theorizing, and is fundamentally motivated by the long-standing refusal, on the part of African queer and feminist theorists, to privilege academic forms of knowledge production over the creative, imaginative, and everyday aesthetics and cultural work emanating from local South African contexts. The latter are approached throughout this book as generative modes of critical cultural theorizing in and of themselves, and inform some of the shifts in register towards the end of this book as I explicitly claim the personal as political by drawing on some of my own experiences in higher education. These aims may also, in hindsight, account in part for the gender imbalance of the book, as it clearly privileges the work of women and genderqueer artists, filmmakers, and (audio)visual activists, including lesser-discussed creative work not yet considered in other studies of South African audio-visual culture.

~

Each of the chapters to follow stages an encounter with one or more of the aesthetic genres within which power has been held to account over the past fifteen or so years. These include video installations, conceptual artwork, visual youth autobiography, documentary film, live art, and multimodal performative and sonic installations. These are read, at least in part, for their formal, generic characteristics, and for how they mediate the failures of both dominant and resistant structures of feeling to fully account for the social sensorium of everyday experience under conditions of material dispossession, bodily suffering, trauma, and psychic alienation. My methods for selecting these particular films, performances, and installations were inevitably somewhat wayward – as befitting a study of this nature – in that they were informed by my own fluctuating feelings in relation to South African public culture during this time. The aesthetics that made it into this study demanded my attentions specifically for how compellingly they mediated some of the most widely discussed moments of public upheaval and state repression during these years, and how captivatingly they articulated some of the affective complexities that attend the post-rainbow encounter between the public and the intimate.

My discussion of these works follows a more or less chronological order, from the earliest work by Muholi and Searle, released respectively in 2008 and 2009–11 (chapter 1), to the most recent of the audio-visual installations by Goliath, namely *This song is for…*, first staged in 2019 (chapter 5). This order is reflected also in the chronology of scenes of protest and spectacular violence that inform the later chapters in particular, from the 2012 Marikana massacre, to the hashtag student protests, to feminist organizing against the ongoing surge in gender-based violence that again took on staggering new forms in 2019 and 2020. Whereas the first four chapters foreground visual modes of aesthetic mediation – with only intermittent attention paid to the aural – in the fifth chapter I challenge my own ocularcentrism as I explicitly privilege sound as the dominant site of analysis (chapter 4, in fact, briefly considers the olfactory sense as well). Each of these chapters follows the post-rainbow contours of waywardness variously as a site of creativity, improvisation, and play, as a strategy of defiant survival – even thriving, as a mode of aesthetic articulation and transmission, and as a challenge to those who would deny the interdependence of cognition and affect, rationality and feeling.

Chapter 1, "Troubling the Rainbow Promise," suggests that the spectacles of promise and disappointment that have marked the transitional and post-rainbow periods are key indicators of some of the political emotions that might be mobilized as potential political resources in contemporary South Africa. Recasting disappointment as a mode of wayward feeling and politics, I read the video installations "Black Smoke Rising" (2009–11), by Berni Searle, and "what don't you see when you look at me?" (2008), by Zanele Muholi, as instructive examples of an expansive everyday aesthetics that engages viewers in a "sensual pedagogy" (Highmore, *Ordinary* 53–4). Situated firmly within a larger emotional culture of post-rainbow feeling, these artworks enlarge the social sensorium by drawing attention repeatedly to forms of everyday experience that tend to escape dominant frames of perception. There is a real urgency in bringing an affective lens to contemporary South African public, protest, and audio-visual cultures, particularly given how emotional publics in this context have responded to state violence and various other forms of injustice in the past fifteen or so years. The chapter's conceptualization of disappointment's "thick present" (Haraway 1) explicitly opens up contemporary South African public and consumer cultures and aesthetic activisms to analyses of their affective wiring, an approach that is vital to understanding the full complexity of everyday struggles for greater personal and political freedom and social justice.

Chapter 2, "Moody, Expectant Teens," reads the films *Made in China*, produced by and starring Sarah Chu, and *Where Is the Love?*, co-directed by and starring Evelyn Maruping, as examples of (tele) visual auto-biography as a self-styling genre that reveals the at once expectant and foreclosed dimensions of youth feeling in contemporary South Africa. The chapter suggests that the tension between desire and achievability for young people trying to negotiate structural inequality constitutes the very temporality of the expectant affects that suffuse the methods and moods of youth visualization in these films. If other chapters include examples from contemporary South African (audio) visual culture engaged in relatively explicit forms of aesthetic activism, the acts of political dissent that these films engage in are perhaps more deliberately personalized and therefore less overtly visible and calculated. Yet the strategies of visual self-styling adopted in these films have much to tell us about the cultural and affective politics of the post-rainbow public sphere, and about the uncertain temporalities that both inform and give rise to forms of wayward agency in constrained surroundings.

Sarah Chu and Evelyn Maruping (in collaboration with the rest of the group involved with the making of their films) both engage in forms of mood work as they try to counter the affective toll of despair-inducing conditions that stem from extreme poverty, xenophobia, racism, and patriarchy's relationship to early reproduction. Yet their films are not equally successful at manufacturing horizons of possibility that feel achievable both within and beyond their diegetic worlds. Whereas *Made in China* follows the fairly typical script of resolution, overcoming, and (national) incorporation that tends to afflict particularly the coming-of-age genre and the genres of intimate mediation peculiar to late consumer capitalism and its therapeutic industries, *Where Is the Love?* fails conspicuously to move beyond the sadness expressed by its tearful youth subjects, a failure due in part to the fact that the experience of social *im*mobility conveyed by the film's young mothers so demonstrably eclipses dreams of a different life. Yet the wayward feelings that swirl through these films also push against any attempt at generic containment, in turn revealing disappointment to yield unpredictable experiments in life-making.

In chapter 3, "Managing Public Feeling," I read some of the political decisions made and sentiments expressed in relation to the 2012 Marikana massacre for what they reveal about the post-rainbow temporalities of securitization, and about the forms of affective engineering they set in motion. I suggest that the affective and temporal dimensions of attempts at containing perceived threats to financial and political stability on the part of South Africa's business and political elites are central to understanding increasingly violent and repressive securitization and crisis management strategies deployed in response, for instance, to recent labour unrest, student protests, and the coronavirus pandemic. Though I identify these strategies specifically in relation to the Marikana massacre, the analytical and temporal scope of the chapter extends also to scenes of affective containment that characterized public culture in the immediate aftermath of apartheid. I identify in Rehad Desai's award-winning documentary film *Miners Shot Down* (2014) an example of how the mismatch between national structures of feeling and the lived, embodied sensorium might be aesthetically mediated to enable better conditions for the work of mourning the deceased miners. The chapter is particularly concerned with the extent to which the film is able to move beyond the truncated timelines of the journalism of sensationalism, spectacle, and distraction as it searches for ethical ways in which to mediate extreme violence and bodily pain. The chapter suggests, in short, that we conceptualize postcolonial melancholia as a strategy of counter-affective, wayward aesthetic lingering that might open the violence and temporalities of spectacle to the otherwise obscured pasts, futures, and presents of slow violence.

Chapter 4, "Feeling the Fall," positions aesthetic activisms associated with the 2015–17 student protests within the epistemic terrain historically liable for the widespread normalization of the mind-body, reason-emotion dichotomy in South African public discourse. In this context, the charge of unreasonableness – and by implication, of being blinded by emotion or rage – so frequently levelled at student activists reveals, in hindsight, a tendency to underestimate the complexities of intellectual-affective engagement on the part of many of these protesters, and the critical anti-colonial and feminist legacies that have informed – in both implicit and deliberate ways – their embrace of the affective, experiential body in the struggle for better student access to South Africa's tertiary institutions. The chapter proceeds via a reading of two events that unfolded in relation to the toppling of the statue of Cecil John Rhodes at the University of Cape Town in April 2015. The first is the act that initiated the Rhodes Must Fall campaign, namely activist Chumani Maxwele's throwing of human excrement onto the statue on

9 March 2015. The second is a performance piece titled "Chapungu – the Day That Rhodes Fell," staged by artist Sethembile Msezane on the day when the statue was finally removed from its plinth overlooking the UCT rugby fields. I conceive of these performances as archives of feeling that work aesthetically to distil affect's historicity and sociality into embodied commemorative form. I argue that these wayward commemorative activisms bring histories erased from the colonial record into animate, corporeal focus by offering an aesthetic portal into a past that resists museumification.

In chapter 5, "Feminist Resonance," I build on my reading of the cultural politics of Black and feminist rage in chapter 4 to theorize "resonant feminist listening" as a method of engaging feminism's multisensory affective archives. I argue, first, that to listen resonantly requires attending to the repeated historical censoring, disciplining, and erasure of feminist feeling in South Africa, and to bring these feelings into the present to feminist ends. I draw on two examples here to make my point: (1) the apartheid-era editorial interference in Miriam Tlali's *Muriel at Metropolitan* (1975), the first English-language novel to be published by a Black woman in South Africa, and (2) the feminist afterlives, in digital times, of the rape trial of former president Zuma. I then suggest that Gabrielle Goliath's performative installations *Personal Accounts* (2014), *Elegy* (2015–present), and *This song is for…* (2019–present) draw her audiences into an immersive experience of resonant listening, as she compels them to engage South Africa's scourge of gendered-based violence in ethically implicated, somatosensory ways. Goliath shatters the safety of detached observation, instead drawing audiences viscerally into the experience of mourning and traumatic recall by harnessing the affective charge of rhythm, sonics, and breath, and thus calling upon them to account for their own relation to the suffering of others. Goliath's wayward performative aesthetics reach pointedly beyond the ocularcentric power-knowledge regimes foundational to European capitalist modernity and patriarchy, and to their exclusion of certain bodies from certain spaces, academic and otherwise.

I conclude the book by briefly considering the wayward embodied politics of the "shut down," which I read variously as a strategy used by dissenting publics to get the attentions of those in power, as a form of trauma-induced emotional withdrawal (discussed at various points in the book), as a response to a global pandemic, and as a mode of slowing down and repair following times of upsurge. I draw here in part on my own experiences of inhabiting the corporate university in South Africa during the years it took to write this book, as I revisit *Wayward*

Feeling's most pressing theoretical and political claims, and imagine some of the futures to which this work might lead.

In her study of the productive and disruptive dimensions of "black rage" in the context of the contemporary United States, and of the challenge that the Black Lives Matter movement poses to "liberal democratic demands that anger be ejected from political, public, and popular deliberations over racial inequality and social justice", Debra Thompson points to the "contrast between Western liberal ideas of universalism, such as the principle of equality before the law, and the pragmatic experience of democracy, which is constituted through the ways these universal principles and democratic institutions (e.g. the police) produce and reproduce racial hierarchies" (460, 462). Almost thirty years after the end of minority rule in South Africa, *Wayward Feeling* still finds comparable contrasts between the aspirational goals enshrined in the 1996 Constitution, and the lived, affective experience of racial, gendered, class, and other forms of inequality. The following chapters present only some of the many sites one could have chosen for better understanding these contrasts, and in no way claims comprehensiveness, but it does reveal the work of aesthetic mediation and activism to pose an important challenge to forms of affective exclusion endemic to post-rainbow times.

1

Troubling the Rainbow Promise

The cover image chosen for this book is that of a burning tire. It is a spectacular, arresting image that features prominently in the visual iconography of global mass protest. As a sign, variously, of modernity and mobility, of waste economies and waste management, of extractive capitalism and environmental destruction, as well as of poverty and resistance in varied formats, the tire carries a heavy symbolic freight. The burning tire is an image that resonates powerfully in South African visual culture, as it evokes painful histories of social upheaval and racialized struggle conveyed during the apartheid years, for instance, in the terrifying phenomenon of necklacing. More recently, it has come to figure also in the spectacles of promise and disappointment that have marked post-rainbow times.[1]

It is unsurprising therefore that the tire has made its way into the video installations of two of South Africa's most celebrated visual and conceptual artists, Berni Searle and Zanele Muholi. The book's cover image is taken from the initial part of a video trilogy by Searle entitled "Black Smoke Rising." The installation includes three consecutive single-screen projections respectively titled "Lull," "Gateway," and "Moonlight." The image is included in the first part of this trilogy, namely "Lull," a long-take sequence shot that offers this portrait of the burning tire as a counterpoint to earlier scenes of natural tranquillity, as the artist, positioned in an idyllic nature scene, calmly rocks back and forth on a swing made of recycled tire. The screenshot used to open this chapter is taken from Muholi's installation "what don't you see when you look at me?"[2] It features the artist, partly covered in feathers and visible only from the waist down, playfully jumping in and out of a black tire positioned at the centre of a white room. Here the tire figures counterintuitively as a site of play, as a safe haven or place of belonging,

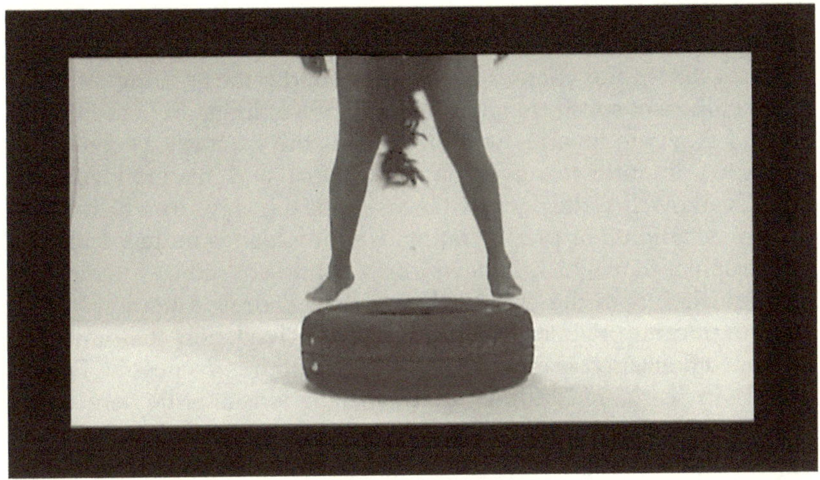

Figure 1.1 Still frame from Zanele Muholi, "what don't you see when you look at me?," 2008. The video installation from which the image is taken can be viewed online at https://www.youtube.com/watch?v=wlbM8Ic7w-Q. © Zanele Muholi. Courtesy of Stevenson, Cape Town/Johannesburg and Yancey Richardson, New York.

even as it evokes connotations of corporeal disciplining, violence, and gendered spectacle.

Taken together, these art projects are highly suggestive for thinking through some of the tensions that have troubled the South African public sphere in the past fifteen or so years, when the post-apartheid promise of a better life for all started to lose its lustre. In what follows, I read these audio-visual texts as conveyors of some of the emotional cultures produced in the aftermath of apartheid, and consider the unique contribution that they make to current debates on political and aesthetic activism.[3] I suggest that these texts offer a particularly useful point of entry into an analysis of the shifting post-apartheid "culture of spectacle"– to stretch Njabulo Ndebele's apartheid-era phrase (*Rediscovery* 43) – that informs the resistant aesthetics considered throughout *Wayward Feeling*. Through a set of complex affective-aesthetic gestures, "Black Smoke Rising" and "what don't you see when you look at me?" highlight the troubling domestication of spectacular scenes of violence in contemporary South Africa, yet they also chart possible "escape routes"

(Papadopoulus et al. xv) from the messy intermingling of promise and disappointment in the post-rainbow present.

As my aim in this chapter is in part to ponder the ongoing influence of the culture of spectacle on ordinary habits of living in post-rainbow times, I gravitate towards work that reads the spectacle as complexly entangled in intimate, everyday emotional and material cultures. Ann Cvetkovich writes, for instance, about the ways in which "what counts as national or public trauma is that which is more visible and catastrophic, that which is newsworthy and sensational," which she distinguishes from the "small dramas that … draw attention to how structural forms of violence are so frequently lived, how their invisibility or normalization is another part of their oppressiveness" ("Public" 464). Both Searle and Muholi, in the installations at issue here and in their larger body of work, have come to be known for their unique ability, through the use of their own physical bodies as well as numerous everyday objects of gendered and queer intimacy, to open the sensational and spectacular to the kinds of "small dramas" of which Cvetkovich writes.[4] By way of making sense of these artistic interventions and the emotional cultures from which they emanate, I briefly examine spectacles of promise and disappointment as sites of cultural and temporal contestation in contemporary South Africa. I do so in an effort to understand the shift from what is frequently referred to as "liberation euphoria" – and the at times euphoric fantasies of a future South Africa that marked dominant public discourse and nation-building initiatives in the period immediately following the political transition – towards an emotional culture marked increasingly by expressions of disappointment.[5]

I then consider how the art installations by Searle and Muholi might contribute to a larger project – in queer and feminist theory in particular – invested in mobilizing negative affect as "a possible resource for political action" (Cvetkovich, "Public" 460). As Andrew van der Vlies phrases it in his study of the value of a turn to affect for understanding contemporary South African literary forms, "bad feelings … index a potential to reinvigorate the political" (*Present* ix). Inspired by a number of theorists invested in disappointment's directionality – its power to illuminate and provide insight, to adapt Audre Lorde's reading of the "uses of anger" (124) – I turn to iconographies of struggle and difficult emotions in an effort to "[depathologize] the emotions of protest and [to illuminate] otherwise obscured aspects of contentious politics" (Gould 19). I suggest that acts of aesthetic mediation such as those by Muholi and Searle help to enact disappointment less as a sustained state of affective dysphoria than as a wayward structure of feeling that is ultimately propelled by what Saidiya Hartman calls "occult visions of other worlds and dreams of a different kind of life" (228). Having said this, the chapter resists what Cvetkovich calls "pastoralizing or redemptive accounts of negative feeling," even as it "embraces categories such as utopia and hope" (*Depression* 6) in the wake of the emancipatory post-struggle promise.[6]

Spectacles of Promise and Disappointment

In a September 2019 opinion piece Zaheera Jinnah comments on the links between yet another wave of gender-based violence and femicide, the ongoing scourge of xenophobic violence that again flared up towards the end of 2019, and multiple recent forms of protest action:

> Over the past few days South Africa's major cities have burst into flames. This is not new. Co-ordinated and sporadic acts of violence linked to service delivery protests, xenophobic sentiments and public outrage are part of the DNA of post-apartheid South African politics.

Public disaffection over the country's staggering unemployment rate, skyrocketing poverty, and the state's abiding inability to deliver infrastructure and services to all of its citizenry has, indeed, taken on spectacular and unpredictable new forms in recent years.[7] Yet as a mode of political engagement and exaggerated signification, the spectacle in fact reaches deep into South African history. In his now canonical essays on the "spectacle of social absurdity" (*Rediscovery* 33) that preoccupied the anti-apartheid literary imagination, Njabulo Ndebele identifies the "spectacular" as a category central to the apartheid social order and its representational counterpart, recognizable across the spectrum of apartheid political and everyday life:

> … the monstrous war machine developed over the years; the random massive pass raids; mass shootings and killings; mass economic exploitation the ultimate symbol of which is the mining industry; the mass removals of people; the spate of draconian laws passed with the spectacle of parliamentary promulgations; the luxurious life-styles of whites: servants, all encompassing privilege, swimming pools, and high commodity consumption; the sprawling monotony of architecture in African locations, which are the very picture of poverty and oppression. The symbols are all over: the quintessence of obscene social exhibitionism. (31–2)

Ndebele's point about the spectacular here pertains specifically to anti-apartheid literature, which he suggests finds itself in the grip of a "society of posturing and sloganeering; one that frowns upon subtlety of thought and feeling, and never permits the sobering power of contemplation, of close analysis, and the mature acceptance of failure, weakness, and limitations" (42). Yet as feminist theorist Pumla Dineo Gqola suggests, Ndebele's "critique of literary predictability is theoretically applicable to spaces beyond the literary impulse that was his primary concern in the body of work cited" ("Difficult" 61). Responding to the spectacle of the 2006 Jacob Zuma rape trial, Gqola extends Ndebele's theorization of the spectacle to make sense of the gendered public sphere in the post-trial political landscape. She reads the spectacular as "a trope that has characterised South African public culture for centuries before … from the primacy of the body under colonialism/slavery, through the contestations Ndebele critiques in 'protest literature,' to the violent masculinities which silence dissent in post-apartheid South Africa" (63).

While 1994 consigned many of the spectacular excesses of colonialism and apartheid to history, those inhabiting contemporary South Africa will also recognize the disturbing longevity of many of the examples of "social exhibitionism" included in Ndebele's list. Indeed, renewed sensitivity to precisely this longevity is at the root of the reborn revolutionary time that I reference in the introduction, marked, in turn, by what Timothy Wright identifies as a melancholic attachment to the promises of emancipation delivered in the immediate aftermath of apartheid. These melancholic attachments are arguably enduring in part because of the spectacular forms that the emancipatory promise assumed in the early transitional years – though not in the strictly negative sense of which Ndebele and Gqola write. The various nation-building initiatives launched during these years in fact evoked a somewhat different meaning of the spectacle, namely the staging of a series of events, projects, or symbols before the public gaze as objects of "marvel or admiration" (OED).[8] The many symbolic transformation projects initiated at the time – including the now exhausted Rainbow Nation trope, the rhetoric of reconciliation spawned by the Truth and Reconciliation Commission, as well as ex-president Thabo Mbeki's African Renaissance project – predictably exerted a powerful force on a citizenry until then conscripted to the *longue durée* of frustrated expectation under colonialism and apartheid. While not all national subjects occupied the same ideological, experiential, or material position in relation to the promises of a more socially just South Africa contained in these initiatives, there can be no denying the force with which myths about national reconciliation and upward mobility came to fuel public sentiment during these years.

Though it has been a while since the early transitional incarnation of the *spectacle of the promise* started to lose its grip on the South African imagination, I draw attention to it here for what it reveals about the futures to which it tethered South African publics, and for how an attachment to those futures have inflected post-rainbow structures of feeling. The following words, delivered by Nelson Mandela on the occasion of his inauguration as president of South Africa on 10 May 1994, are instructive:

> Out of the experience of an extraordinary human disaster that lasted too long must be born a society of which all humanity will be proud ... We enter into a covenant that we shall build the society in which all South Africans, both black and white, will be able to walk tall, without any fear in their hearts, assured of their inalienable right to human dignity – a rainbow nation at peace with itself and the world ... We are both humbled and elevated by the honour and privilege that you, the people of South Africa, have bestowed on us, as the first President of a united, democratic, non-racial and non-sexist government ... Never, never, and never again shall it be that this beautiful land will again experience the oppression of one by another. (540–1)

Elevating the promise into a covenant, Mandela's address here serves to "make the future into an object, into something that can be declared in advance of its arrival" (Ahmed, *Promise* 29). As a performative utterance, a promise is in fact structurally proleptic, as Judith Butler's early work on gender performativity taught us (*Gender* 171–80). Finally released from the "extraordinary disaster that lasted too long," as Mandela phrases it, South African public feeling came to be readily cathected to this aspirational future. In fact, the end of minority rule constituted such a long-awaited realization of the promise of the ANC's anti-apartheid struggle that the lines between the present and the futurity of Mandela's emancipatory covenant came to be easily blurred – a slippage further enabled by the "politics of enchantment" that characterized the Mandela presidency (Posel, "Madiba Magic" 72).[9]

This blurring accounts in part for the many other spectacular promises to which the end of apartheid made the South African public imagination susceptible, including the promise of nonracial national belonging, the promise of work, the promise of consumer access, the promise of gender and gender-queer justice, and, with renewed emphasis in the post-rainbow years, the promise of economic freedom and land redistribution. The country's forceful re-entry into a hyper-consumerist world order post-1994, for instance, conscripted South Africans to a cultural condition akin to what Guy Debord had in mind when he described the commodification of everyday life in postwar France. According to Debord, the images produced by the mass media in a consumer society inherently shape social relations and penetrate the most intimate recesses of our daily lives, a condition exacerbated in recent years by the increasing ubiquity of mobile screens as accelerants of the "colonisation of social life" (29).[10] Though hardly a new phenomenon in South Africa, particularly among the beneficiaries of apartheid, conspicuous consumption has taken on spectacular new forms in the post-apartheid context, where systemic social inequality is frequently camouflaged under a surface of conspicuous consumer display. These patterns of consumption do more than simply mask the structural inheritance of racial capitalism, however; as an aspirational mode of self-expression, conspicuous consumption has historically come to shape the very narratives through which freedom and liberation are expressed for many of the racialized subjects of colonial and apartheid biopolitics.

Deborah Posel points out, for instance, that the aspiration for liberation has frequently been articulated by post-apartheid publics through the discourse of consumer promise, disapproval expressed by a range of critics vis-à-vis the spectacular exhibition of wasteful affluence notwithstanding.[11] Posel traces the historically constitutive relationship between the making of race and the regulation of consumption in South Africa, and suggests that, "if blackness was produced as in part a restricted regime of consumption, the politics of enrichment could readily adopt the discourse and symbolism of emancipation" ("Races" 173). In other words, in light of this history of the biopolitical regulation of Black consumer aspiration and spending, post-apartheid articulations of political liberation in terms of the right to acquire and display consumer goods are unsurprising. Yet to yoke liberation goals to the promises offered by consumption is necessarily to court disappointment, given that access to the means required for conspicuous consumer spending continues to be circumscribed for most, and that debt has in fact subjected many South Africans to new forms of disenfranchisement, as Deborah James argues at length in *Money from Nothing: Indebtedness and Aspiration in South Africa*.

The redemptive consumer promises listed here are tied also to the promise of work that Franco Barchiesi critiques in *Precarious Liberation: Workers, the State and Contested Social Citizenship in Postapartheid South Africa*. Barchiesi points out that in post-apartheid South Africa, the promise of social inclusion, citizenship, and a dignified life contained in the government's valorization of waged employment has, in reality, become the site of extreme disappointment for the majority of the country's citizens, not least because of the overwhelmingly precarious and exploitative nature of wage-earning work in an era of transnational and financial capital. Barchiesi defines "workers' melancholia" (*Precarious* 247) as the result of an attachment to imagined forms of normative capitalist employment that in fact have never provided the foundations of a decent life, yet are still promised by those on both the right and the left of the political spectrum in spite of mounting global evidence that such a life is out of reach for most. Disappointments associated with both unemployment and the precarious nature of many forms of employment gave rise most notably to the culture of masculinist spectacle that attended Zuma's 2006 rape trial and his subsequent political ascent, as well as the many forms of organized dissent that plagued his presidency. As Barchiesi phrases it, the melancholic workers' imaginary of the Zuma era tended to be a conservative one that linked "images of decent work, what is left of past promises of redemption [through] wage labour … with ideas of family respectability, strict gendered division of household tasks, masculine power and national purity, where 'disrespectful,' crime-prone youth are kept out of the streets and under control, women are confined to domesticity, reproduction and care, and immigrants don't 'steal' national jobs" ("Melancholic Object" 54).

Alongside Barchiesi, I read the events preceding and following the 2007 Polokwane conference – which definitively set in motion Zuma's rise to the presidency – as an important turning-point for South Africans then still firmly yoked to the post-apartheid spectacle of the promise.[12] I find Barchiesi's assessment of the melancholic workers' imaginary as assuming particularly masculinist and xenophobic forms at the time especially helpful for clarifying my own decision to delineate post-rainbow times as the years roughly following the Zuma rape trial. Terms including "transitional," "post-TRC," "post-transitional," "post-Polokwane," and "post post-apartheid" reflect increasingly convoluted attempts at periodizing the shifting state of post-apartheid public feeling.[13] The term post-rainbow incorporates all of these classifications to the extent that it signals some of the affective complexities that attend efforts to overcome the injustices of the country's apartheid and colonial past, or, more precisely, the injustices that remain in the wake of Mandela's rainbow promise. In a sense, then, the "post-rainbow" is less of a temporal than an affective marker. Nevertheless, I demarcate the mid-2000s as a temporal threshold here for two reasons. First, the Jacob Zuma rape trial, which took place in 2006, served to heighten the tension between South Africa's progressive 1996 Constitution and the legal, political, and social tenacity of gender injustice in particular in the country. Second, the years since roughly the mid-2000s also witnessed a remarkable rise in public articulations of disaffection with the failure of the state to deliver on its early transitional liberation promises, earning the country its unenviable reputation as the "the protest capital of the world."[14]

To pause briefly on the first of these reasons, for South African feminists in particular, the Zuma rape trial delivered a disheartening reminder that the "non-sexist government" promised in Mandela's inaugural address was still far from realized. I am not alone in having experienced the Zuma rape trial as a watershed moment. In her 2007 book on this trial, feminist theorist and activist Mmatshilo Motsei explains, for instance, that for her, the "trial was both a form of victimization and a moment of reawakening ... I know from talking to other people that the South African political landscape will never be the same again" (18). Pumla Dineo Gqola likewise reads the rape trial as a defining moment in the shift from post-1994 optimism about the possibility of gender justice. In her work on the culture of masculinist spectacle heightened by the trial, cited earlier, she explains for instance that she was much more optimistic about the struggle against rape and other forms of gender-based violence prior to the Zuma rape trial, even as she knew that the statistics did not support her optimism. "After the trial," she writes, "having witnessed ... how far people were willing to go to terrorise a woman in defence of a powerful man, it is clear to me that something drastic needs to change before this culture consumes us whole" (*Rape* 10). As I elaborate in chapter 5, the implications of the Zuma rape trial were far-reaching, and continue to shape the terms within both violent misogyny and the long-term fight for substantive gendered citizenship have unfolded in the more than fifteen years since.

Though the rainbow trope is often taken to refer primarily to the ANC government's efforts to build a *nonracial* democracy post-1994,[15] the right to be protected against discrimination on various grounds, including gender and sexuality, were in fact key to Mandela's rainbow covenant, though not often publicly and popularly embraced as such (rights explicitly safeguarded, in fact, by the 1996 Constitution). By identifying the trial as roughly inaugurating "post-rainbow" times, I stubbornly insist on the centrality of gender and sexuality to the larger project of decolonial redress reclaimed, for instance, by student activists involved in the 2015–17 Fallist protests. Yet my aim here is less to impose a teleology than to trouble dominant periodizations that have overlooked the trial's constitutive reshaping of the (gendered) landscape of post-apartheid disillusionment. No feminist account of the South African political landscape will miss the trial's role in disturbing post-apartheid psychic time, even as one has to acknowledge this moment as one among many subsequent *spectacles of disappointment* that have gradually served to awaken South African publics from rainbow anaesthesia's at once euphoric and numbing effects.

Disappointment here figures as the refusal to conceal or convert the bad feelings disavowed by the spectacle of the promise, a refusal that might serve hopeful political ends but that frequently also ends up contributing to what Barchiesi calls "an authoritarian, chauvinist social order presiding over the continuous brutality of the market" ("Melancholic" 54). Aside from events surrounding the Zuma rape trial, examples of the post-rainbow spectacle of disappointment arguably include the widely publicized outbreaks of xenophobic violence in 2008, 2015, and 2019 (and less-publicized incidents in between); the ongoing community protests against, for instance, poor service delivery, failures of land reform, inadequate sanitation and electricity infrastructures, a crumbling education system, corruption, and a lack of political accountability, particularly during the years of the Zuma kleptocracy, but in many instances continuing apace under president Ramaphosa; wide-ranging labour unrests and strikes; student protests, as well as ongoing feminist activism (considered in greater detail in chapters 4 and 5 respectively).[16] I group these disparate examples of public affect together with an awareness that each of these is informed by a unique set of political aims, ideological investments, and modes of organization (the intersectional forms of justice advocated by feminist and many student activists since March 2015 differ markedly, for instance, from forms of misogynist rage expressed in defence of Zuma outside his trial courtroom, or the public anger displayed in attacks on foreign black Africans that continue to recur with alarming regularity). I am also cognizant of the fact that disappointment as an individualized feeling has been registered in many complex ways and at different moments since the end of apartheid (in fact, for many of the beneficiaries of apartheid, the end of apartheid no doubt registered as a feeling of disappointment that the apartheid project failed). Yet I am not simply tracing the expression of private feelings here, but am reading these events as part of a larger emotional culture of disappointment that has found political expression in myriad unpredictable – and not always progressive – ways.

My interest in these events as spectacles of disappointment stems further from their shared attachment to the redemptive rainbow promise. In this regard, one may well ask how xenophobic violence, for instance, fits into this list when anger is directed not first and foremost at the failures of the post-apartheid state, but instead at those considered foreign.[17] Many reasons have been given to account for recent articulations of "exceptionalist chauvinism" (Msimang, "Belonging") on the part of xenophobic South African publics, not least of which are the divisive tactics of apartheid and colonial forms of statecraft through which the production of difference came to settle into the country's social psychology.[18] Yet nearly three decades since apartheid's legislative demise, there can be no denying that decisions made by the post-apartheid state to curtail transnational mobility from other African countries have exacerbated the problem. The architects of rainbow nationalism unfortunately missed a crucial opportunity to re-embed post-apartheid South African collective imaginaries within a larger pan-African landscape, former president Thabo Mbeki's efforts at positioning the country as part of a continental African Renaissance notwithstanding (Comaroff and Comaroff, "Nature" 645). As a result, the experience of having endured and overcome apartheid – on the part of both white and Black South Africans – has emerged as an unspoken prerequisite to partaking of the benefits of post-apartheid citizenship, which for many, as much of this book indicates, unfortunately continues to remain largely aspirational. More to the point, one of the key forces at the root of contemporary xenophobic violence can be identified in the willingness of many of those in the thrall of the post-apartheid promise to turn to violence to defend that promise, what Loren Landau appositely calls "the demon of violence living within a society prepared to turn on itself to exorcise those it sees as denying the promise of post-Apartheid power and prosperity" ("Loving" 216). An attachment to patriotic, parochial futures emerged in this regard as a particularly pathological symptom of the messianic liberation promise. Indeed, as Achille Mbembe phrases it in his 2019 Ruth First lecture on the need to rethink Africa's colonial borders, "So much having been so carelessly lost in a relatively short time – things priceless, to which no quantifiable value can be attached – anger and rage have become endemic. Speech itself is at risk of being silenced, so great is the disappointment" ("Ruth").

State responses to collective articulations of disappointment have also assumed increasingly repressive forms, exemplified most lethally in the 2012 Marikana massacre, as I discuss in chapter 3. These include the spectacularly violent deaths of the Marikana miners, many of whom were shot in the back, as well as of protestors such as Andries Tatane, whose April 2011 death at the hands of the police has been referred to as a "watershed moment in public perceptions of state violence after apartheid" (Jacobs and Wasserman), of unarmed student protesters such as Shaeera Khalla, who in October 2016 was shot thirteen times in the back with rubber bullets at close range by public order police, and of Collins Khosa, who died, as I noted earlier, on 22 April 2020 at the hands of the SANDF. These scenes of violence, which reflect a post-apartheid political climate marked by the continued "global vulnerability of the black body" (Ndebele, "'Iph'indlela" 137), also point to a larger state "necropolitics" violently enforced by a police force trying to quell rising levels of discontent on the part of increasingly vocal emotional publics.[19]

In this context, disappointment – a term that refers literally to a feeling of dissatisfaction that results from the failure of having one's expectations met, but that I also read as signalling broader experiences of discontent and disquiet – until fairly recently still functioned at the level of individualized post-apartheid feeling, or, in Raymond Williams's terms, as a premonitory affective state not yet fully available to large-scale definition and expression.[20] Yet in the increasingly frequent eruption of spectacles of disappointment across the country, one also sees the translation of these individualized feelings into something more socially tangible and forceful. In her analysis of consciousness-raising work done by feminist groups in the 1960s and 1970s in the United States, Deborah Gould explains that social movements have the capacity to recast inchoate, individualized feeling into a force for social change. She demonstrates how, in this context, "individualized understandings of what many women were experiencing as an inchoate sense of things simply not being right – what many called depression" were challenged by pointing "to the social origins of that feeling state, renaming it anger. That interpretive emotion work encouraged women to understand themselves and their situations in new ways and indeed to *feel* differently, to feel angry rather than depressed and self-questioning" (34).

In South Africa, similar emotional pedagogies are at work in the labour of social protest movements, yet as my reading of post-apartheid xenophobic violence for instance attests, not all forms of collective disappointment articulate into non-violent futures. This fact has been borne out repeatedly on an international scale in recent years, as countries ranging from the United States, the United Kingdom, Brazil, India, and Turkey found themselves in the grip of xenophobic nationalist sentiment stoked by fear-based authoritarian populist leadership. To assume, in fact, that post-rainbow disappointment will necessarily deliver greater social justice is to remain in the thrall of the utopian promise and its beguiling teleologies of linear progress and safe futures. To think of promises and disappointments in strictly dichotomous terms is to continue to overlook the many ways in which past failures and disappointments can inspire new promises, in turn delivering both gains and remains. It helps here to situate the rainbow promise along the longer historical continuum that Jennifer Wenzel addresses in her reading of the afterlives of the famous anti-colonial prophecy that led to the Xhosa Cattle Killing of 1856–7, and of the many promises and failures shaping public sentiment since. Inspired by Walter Benjamin and Ernst Bloch's respective readings of the affective surplus left by past revolutionary aspirations, Wenzel's analysis of the cattle-killing's failure serves in part to trouble linear readings of the historical trajectory of the anti-apartheid struggle. As she considers the links between this history of promise and disappointment, and the state of post-1994 revolutionary desire, Wenzel suggests instead that "reading the afterlives of anticolonialism retrospectively, while holding a sense of inevitability in abeyance – either inevitable devastation or inevitable liberation – might recover modes of dreaming difference that would transform remembered prophesies of acolonial restoration into prophetic memories of postcolonial justice" (28). Andrew van der Vlies makes a similar point in his assessment of literary engagements with post-apartheid disappointment, eschewing, via Bloch, sequential approaches to the narrative of postcolonial overcoming in favour of a method attentive to "multiple simultaneous imperfect *presents*" (*Present* 21; emphasis in original).

If, as Hannah Arendt suggests, "promises are the uniquely human way of ordering the future, making it predictable and reliable to the extent that this is humanly possible" (92), what might be gained from developing a different relationship with the present of futures past, as some South Africans have indeed started to do post-rainbow? Alongside Anna Tsing's point, cited in the introduction, about the possibilities for improvising multiple futures that come into view when we relinquish our attachment to linear narratives of progress, Donna Haraway's approach to times of (climate) turbulence is particularly helpful for troubling the prolepsis of the promise:

> In urgent times, many of us are tempted to address trouble in terms of making an imagined future safe, of stopping something from happening that looms in the future, of clearing away the present and the past in order to make futures for coming generations. Staying with the trouble does not require such a relationship to times called the future. In fact, staying with the trouble requires learning to be truly present, not as a vanishing pivot between awful or edenic pasts and apocalyptic or salvific futures, but as mortal critters entwined in myriad configurations of places, times, matters, meanings. (1)

In their sensorially rich engagements with precisely this "thick present" (Haraway 1) of post-apartheid disappointment, Searle and Muholi in fact model some of the "subtlety of thought and feeling" that Ndebele calls for in his critique of the spectacle, as they redirect some of the revolutionary energies trailing broken rainbow promises to aesthetically wayward ends.

Quotidian Aesthetics and Emotional Publics

The artworks of Searle and Muholi are approached here as examples of what the everyday life theorist Ben Highmore refers to as "quotidian aesthetics" (*Ordinary* 53). Specifically, through their use of the objects of everyday life in their video installations, and their playful engagement with the routines and rhythms of daily living in spaces of precariousness, Searle's and Muholi's work reveals an approach to aesthetics attentive to the quotidian world of sensation, what Highmore calls "our lively sensitivity to stimulus from without and within; our sensate connectivity to a world of things and other people; our responsiveness to a world of feelings" (x–xi). As I explained in the introduction, such an approach departs from inherited understandings of aesthetics as concerned primarily with regulating the boundaries of beauty and artistic merit; instead, the world of quotidian aesthetics in Highmore's usage is a world entangled in the dense socio-cultural thicket of affective and sensate perception and feeling, an ordinary life-world that "engages us in a sensual pedagogy (a shaping of perceptions, of sentiments, of discernment) that is constitutive of our sociality" (53–4).

By way of explanation, let me start by returning to the tire in Searle's and Muholi's respective installations as the symbolic fulcrum for the emotional publics that spectacles of promise and disappointment respectively sustain. Both Searle and Muholi defamiliarize the tire by using the device of *détournement*, a means whereby an everyday object or signifier from a capitalist system is refigured and placed within a new context to serve the potential disruption or undoing of the spectacle.[21] As an object of consumer-capitalist excess and its colonial roots in rubber extraction, the tire is *detourned* in their work to gesture to possibilities of subversion, protest, play, care, creativity, conservation, and recovery even as it critically signals scenes of consumer spectacle and histories of resistant violence.[22] Their *detourned* usage of the tire as a symbol also neatly draws together memories of violent social upheaval that centrally define emotional cultures in the aftermath of apartheid, on the one hand, and the affective force of a symbol of "a growing and pervasive 'air of discontent'" (Searle, "Black Smoke Rising") in present-day South Africa, on the other.

In the work of Searle in particular, where the burning tire is used deliberately as a symbol of political protest that exerts a powerful affective force on any viewer familiar with South African history, aesthetic form is given to structures of wayward feeling, the complexity of which, as Couze Venn remarks in a different context, is "difficult, if not impossible, to convey through other registers[;] they incite a level of participation in the events and experiences represented that encourage emotional-cognitive engagement" (6) on the part of the viewer.[23] In these installations, produced and released prior to the notable proliferation and intensification of public protest action including and following the Marikana massacre in particular, we see an example of what Raymond Williams means when he suggests that structures of feeling frequently find semantic articulation in art and literature before they do so anywhere else: "not by derivation from other social forms and pre-forms, but as social formation of a specific kind which may in turn be seen as the articulation (often the only fully available articulation) of structures of feeling which as living processes are much more widely experienced" (133).

The title of the first part of Searle's trilogy, namely "Lull," is particularly allusive as an accompaniment to the successive single-shot projections of the swinging and then burning tire that gradually obscures the natural landscape behind the thick black smoke that it generates. Aside from the obvious reference to how the culture or society of the spectacle lulls its members to structural inequality and environmental degradation as lived, everyday experience, the title also carries more sinister, threatening undertones as a sign of temporary tranquillity that precedes a storm. The term "lull" thus evokes an anticipatory, future-orientated temporality that augurs a yet-to-be-determined disruption on the horizon. Yet unlike the anticipatory safety offered by the promise, the futurity of the lull is firmly anchored in a combustive, troubled present from which it anticipates an as yet unknown affective and political disturbance.

Read alongside the title of the trilogy as a whole, namely "Black Smoke Rising," the term "lull" signals the tense, unnatural calm that precedes a collective uprising in the face of continued experiences of social, political, and civic exclusion. References to these forms of exclusion are at the heart of the trilogy in the sense that each of the three parts explicitly signals spectacles of disappointment in post-rainbow South African contexts: whereas both "Lull" and "Moonlight," through their generative usage of the burning tire as a symbol, allude to the kinds of social protest that have marked South African public culture for at least the last fifteen years, "Gateway" references the controversial N2 Gateway Housing Project of the South African government, which was opposed especially by local residents who were evicted from their homes along the N2 corridor to make way for the project.[24]

Yet the installation's title also gestures to a slightly different set of associations. In one of its online versions, the accompanying text includes the song "Rock-a-Bye Baby," a lullaby that disturbingly ends in a rocking cradle falling from a tree, baby and all. On one level, the lullaby here signals that possibilities for violence are inherent in even the most intimate, everyday rituals of care and kinship. On another level, Searle's juxtaposition of scenes of domesticity and parental tenderness with the spectacular scenes of violence gestured at by the burning tire encourages viewers to think the spectacular and the quotidian as messily entangled, and as woven through the continuous present of everyday experience. That the scenes of parental care evoked by the lullaby and the rocking swing have historically been gendered female is significant in terms of the larger politics of gendered spectacle central to contemporary South African public life. As Desiree Lewis points out in her analysis of spectacles as sites where meanings over gendered embodiment, nationhood, and power are publicly contested, these spectacles provide important "sources for the fictions, symbols, memories and narratives that are central to individuals' ... sense of gender and personhood" ("Gendered" 127). As she puts it, the epistemic and physical disciplining of particularly Black women's bodies that are frequently enacted in the form of public spectacle "has been central to the construction of masculinist citizenship and nationhood [in post-apartheid SA since ...] authoritarian cultures draw on, and are rationalised by, gendered behaviour and language, by somatic symbols and meanings through which notions such as citizenship, order and the healthy social body are imagined" (128).

The quotidian aesthetics of Searle's work are also revealed in the numerous allusions to waste that the trilogy evokes, allusions which clearly convey the kind of autumnal affect that Anna Tsing and Rita Barnard identify in extractive capitalism's ruins (*Mushroom*; "Introduction"). In each of the three parts, objects that have come to be associated with superfluity – of things, people, and the spaces they inhabit – are foregrounded. Specifically, in "Lull" and "Moonlight" the burning tire is used to stage the domestication of spectacular scenes of violence in everyday South African life, whereas in "Gateway" a small house that is gradually engulfed by flames only to be exposed as nothing more than a copy of the original, easily reduced to what looks like corrugated paper and then ashes, represents itinerant living in informal settlements where people are continually at the mercy of forces beyond their control. These representations, tied together through the recurring trope of fire – which powerfully signals violence and bodies in pain, on the one hand, and cleansing, renewal, and a stripping of illusion and fakery, on the other – allude to what Zygmunt Bauman calls a "culture of waste," characterized both by "*an acute crisis of the human waste disposal industry*" and the increasingly widespread vulnerability of "human beings bereaved of their heretofore adequate ways and means of survival in both the biological and the social/cultural sense of that notion" (*Wasted* 6–7; emphasis in original). These disposable objects and symbols of precariousness – placed as they are in relation to scenes of intimate emotional sociality such as parental tenderness and play ("Lull"), failed efforts at homemaking ("Gateway"), and the emotional hardships encapsulated in the searching of a garbage dump as a means of survival ("Moonlight") – convey violence as profoundly systemic, namely as what Slavoj Žižek calls the "often catastrophic consequences of the smooth functioning of our economic and political systems," the kind of "violence inherent in a system: not only direct physical violence but also the more subtle forms of coercion that sustain relations of domination and exploitation, including the threat of violence" (2, 9). They also prefigure some of the forms of "excremental insurgence" that erupted in Cape Town in response to the abysmal state of sanitation across the region – subsequently deployed also with explosive emotional force by #RhodesMustFall activist Chumani Maxwele, as I discuss in chapter 4.

That these signifiers are frequently assembled against the backdrop of scenes of natural or pastoral tranquillity (as in the representation of a seemingly idyllic natural landscape in "Lull" or of the liquid moonlight that steadily engulfs Table Mountain in "Moonlight") is significant further as a way of complicating tired binary distinctions between the human and so-called natural environment. Such distinctions make it possible to detach our concern for human and non-human life respectively from one another; it also reinforces the faulty assumption that the natural world is utterly separate and removed from the human world. By drawing the attention of viewers to the complex intersections of these environments, Searle in effect enlarges the scope of environmental concern without capitulating to neoliberal approaches to environmental activism and conservationism, where the latter mobilize concern for the environment to the detriment of interest in other equally important political issues.[25]

These references are crystallized especially in the third part of the trilogy, namely "Moonlight." In this segment, a distant view of Table Mountain is foregrounded by a wasteland of scorched earth and ecological destruction where people walk around in search of scraps of reusable waste. Against this backdrop, a burning tire is dragged back and forth along the ground until the entire frame is covered in flames and smoke, casting Table Mountain in the distorting shadows of the flowing black smoke and blue moonlight, in which it seems to dissolve into liquid. The installation is accompanied by a faltering rendition of Beethoven's Moonlight Sonata (from which it derives its title), a fitting soundtrack in light of the controversy that surrounds the naming of the composer's famous work. Derived from a review by poet Heinrich Rellstab published five years after Beethoven's death, in which Rellstab suggested that the first movement reminded him of the play of the moonlight on Lake Lucerne, the title has subsequently been criticized as "a misleading approach to a movement with almost the character of a funeral march" (Kennedy 598). This pairing – of the play of the moonlight and the allusions to death evoked by the faltering funeral march – provides a suitable emotional register for the trilogy's closing engagement with the "'problems of (human) waste and (human) waste disposal' [that] weigh ever more heavily on the liquid modern, consumerist culture of individualization" (Bauman, *Wasted* 7).

Alongside the other jarring symbols of social precariousness that populate the trilogy, the final instalment has the capacity to arouse troubled feelings: unease, anxiety, fear, apprehension, discontent, and disappointment. In registering these emotions, viewers are not simply engaged in private acts of feeling, they become part of an affective sociality – what Lauren Berlant calls "intimate publics," namely "strangers formed into communities by affective ties; and the assumptions of shared emotions and worldviews that precede, create, and then often render anxious and ambivalent, such publics" (Berlant in Prosser, "Life Writing" 180). Such affective prompting, the effect of which will necessarily be determined at least in part by the viewer's experiential and socio-cultural background, arguably has the capacity to move viewers, however awkwardly and momentarily, beyond the fraudulently individualizing emotional cultures of neoliberal consumer capitalism. As Daniel Coleman suggests in his defence of reading – which I take here to refer to the reading of a variety of works of the creative imagination, including audio-visual aesthetic texts – the privacy of reading "allows a person to engage ideas, scenes, or possibilities that she or he may not have the wherewithal to countenance in public or before peers. We talk about reading as escape. Maybe it's an escape from loneliness, but it's not an escape from the world. The privacy of reading is not solipsism. It's connection to a wider range of experience" ("Why does") and, one might add, of feeling.

The trilogy's references to burning commodities and waste – in both its material and figurative senses – offer an associative link that provides strange insights into some of the ways in which the spectacle of the consumer promise has been incorporated into the quotidian in contemporary South Africa. In particular, Searle's images call to mind what Megan Jones, in an analysis of township youth culture, has referred to as "conspicuous destruction" (209). Jones's argument unfolds in the context of her discussion of a particularly striking incarnation of the consumer promise that took hold among young people in post-apartheid South African townships, where "forms of commodity display … are less about wealth attained than wealth and belonging aspired to" (210). Specifically, her discussion centres on the practice of *i'khothane,* whereby expensive consumer goods such as designer clothes, shoes, and other objects of material distinction are "set alight in a display that asserts wealth through indifference to the commodity" (209). Here consumer goods are destroyed arguably as a way of both affirming and contesting the spectacle of the consumer promise. On the one hand, the spectacular visibility of these wayward performances of wastefulness can be read as a mode of assertiveness that defies the marginalization of township youth. On the other hand, *i'khothane* exposes the promise of the commodity to be both empty – in the sense that the use value of the commodity is reduced to its capacity for aspirational signification – and extremely seductive. In Searle's usage, the burning tire as a social text thus gestures to forms of disruptive consumption tied complexly to the messy daily strategies of living in the context of consumer capitalism and its wasteful excesses.

Read collectively, Searle's video installations weave together colonial, apartheid, and post-apartheid signifiers as a way of drawing viewers affectively into the emotional cultures generated by the intersection of civic protest, consumer capitalism, and the dense present of everyday life. Zanele Muholi's work similarly inhabits these intersecting symbolic and affective sites, yet does so from a slightly different vantage point. "what don't you see when you look at me?" features the artist's naked body in a variety of poses with three highly suggestive everyday objects: a tire, a sausage, and feathers. The visual images are accompanied by a number of sounds, including the voice of the artist reciting, at varying tempos, the poem "I ache for you," by Yvonne Onakeme Etaghene. The artist's body and these objects are then deliberately placed against a white backdrop, a gesture that Muholi describes as follows:

> *What don't you see when you look at me* is a video installation that examines the act of Western looking/gazing, of seeing, of perception, and ultimately of mapping. It asks what registers and is imagined in a viewer's mind when glancing at a black female body "against" a white background ... My performance is a way of returning the gaze, as I am looking out from the "white" space my body inhabits, and by which it is surrounded. I look away from it, but the viewer will always see my subjectivity: a black, naked, female body "against" and in opposition to "whiteness." Due to centuries of European exploitation and oppression, black women were never allowed, taught, or socialized to capture their own (positive) images or explore their own sexual and erotic freedom, and to look back, stare back. (Muholi, "what don't you see ...")

The political intervention that this installation makes clearly unfolds on multiple terrains simultaneously, but for the purposes of this analysis, I start by focusing on the tire as a site of symbolic contestation before briefly considering some of the representational and affective work done by the installation as a whole. If, following Searle, we are to read the tire as a symbol of political protest and as a referent for post-rainbow spectacles of disappointment, Muholi's artwork both affirms and refigures these connotations. As in Searle's "Black Smoke Rising," the tire in Muholi's installation powerfully draws out the sense memories of viewers conversant with South Africa's history of resistance to state violence, yet to the artist, a black tire also paradoxically represents "a safe haven/womb or a place of belonging" ("what don't you see ..."). As an object that saturates the everyday lives of those who inhabit the margins of global consumer capitalism, where burnt tires are not only the source of highly carcinogenic respiratory toxins but also of wire sold as scrap metal that provides alternative means of economic subsistence, Muholi's reading of the tire as a site of prenatal safety gestures ambivalently to the recuperative power of acts of creative mediation. Muholi's spirited engagement with the tire, the sausage, and feathers as sexually charged metaphors goes beyond simply challenging conventional hetero- and cisnormative codings of embodiment, desire, and maternity; it also asks of viewers to consider the significance of play as a site of wayward epistemic and aesthetic activity.

If aesthetic activity is read as having the capacity to enliven us to the world of sensate perception, as Highmore suggests, the playfulness at issue here might be said to contribute to altering the horizons of the sense-able, the audible and the visible, a political project central to Muholi's creative oeuvre.[26] As a self-proclaimed visual activist, Muholi has long walked that fine line between attuning available structures of recognition to the experiential complexities of queer intimacy, on the one hand, and refusing, on the other hand, to let such a politics of recognition, however expansive, contribute paradoxically to a narrowing of the terrain within which sexual life might be imagined. (This is a paradox that Judith Butler explores in their work on kinship, where they elaborate on the importance of having one's demands for political recognition met even as one remains vigilant to the risks of further exclusion and violation that follow from such an extension of normative structures of intelligibility).[27] Critics such as Kylie Thomas, Gqola, and van der Vlies have commented on this dimension of Muholi's work, showing their photographic installations to not only resist "endeavours to name, tame and classify" but also to offer "a new archive of affect and affiliation … concerned to reclaim alternative, subordinated – if not subaltern – identities that do not conform to the narrative endorsed by the self-appointed spokespeople of any given (majority dominated) polity" (Gqola, "Through" 622).[28]

Muholi's long-standing concern with altering available frames of legibility to reflect the experiential complexities of specifically Black lesbians and gender-nonconforming people in South Africa, for whom both the threat and the lived reality of extremely violent forms of bodily and epistemic disciplining has long been the norm, emerges clearly in "what don't you see when you look at me?" Each of the symbols in this video installation is haunted in some way by the violence that has historically attended the experience of subjection on the grounds of, for instance, sexuality, sex, gender, race, and class. Yet through Muholi's creative, playful project of *détournement*, these everyday objects also yield possibilities for wayward re-signification. The tire, as already mentioned, is a signifier heavy with histories of resistant violence in South African contexts. In Muholi's conceptualization, however, the tire is also opened up to alternative semantic and experiential registers, signalling the entanglement of this everyday object in gendered economies of intimacy, love, comfort, care, and creativity (as their reading of the tire as "a safe haven/womb or a place of belonging" does [Muholi, "what"]).[29]

The sausage, in turn, immediately calls to mind the signifying force of the *phallus* in the context of violent patriarchy, where, specifically in South Africa, hate crimes such as "curative" or "corrective" rape are used to violently discipline Black lesbians and gender-fluid people. In other words, by drawing on this fraught symbol, Muholi highlights the difficulties of reading "black lesbian desire outside of the violence of both the present and the past," as Kylie Thomas phrases it ("Intimate Archive," 428). This reference to heteropatriarchal violence is reinforced in Muholi's own statement on the figurative meaning of the sausage, yet, as in their representation of the feathers, which they suggest signal both "a dark forest [and] pubic hair," there are also alternative connotations that emerge: "A sausage can be perceived as a *phallus* but at the same time represents what is inside the womb or intestines" ("what"). Here the cisnormative assumptions concealed by predictable readings of the sausage as *phallus* are exposed. By weaving together into a single signifier references to both male and female body parts in their conventional encodings, Muholi in effect draws the attention of viewers to epistemic and experiential complexities that are less than fixed in their gendered figurations. Muholi goes on to explain, perhaps with deliberate vagueness, that "what is inside the womb or intestines … can cause the confusion and struggle that comes with the agitation and emotions provoked by interference" ("what"). The words "confusion," "struggle," "agitation," "emotions," "provoked," and "interference" all reference the difficulties that attach to bringing the disciplinary force of state biopolitics and social censure to bear on LGBTQIA+ forms of intimacy and embodiment. That the "confusion" produced by such "interference" should be a site of "struggle" is significant, however, because it brings us back to the wayward feelings at the heart of both Muholi's and Searle's everyday aesthetics, a point to which I will return shortly.

Muholi's positioning of their own body against a white background similarly works to multiple ends. The whiteness of the space, as already indicated, becomes a sign of European colonial overdetermination. Yet the space is not inhabited acquiescently. Muholi places their naked body in numerous moving postures in relation to the objects they interact with, including poses that openly convey the experience of sexual pleasure; that signal anger, confidence, or assertiveness (especially where they stare straight into the camera, deliberately engaging the viewer's gaze); or that communicate a sense of playful silliness, as when they jump up and down on the sides of the tire. While the latter performance could be read as representative of the physical exercise techniques used, for instance, by the army to train soldiers, it could also signal Muholi's joyous participation in the child's game of hopscotch. Throughout these moments, parts of the artist's body spill beyond the frame of vision. Their movements and their body's placement in both the on- and off-screen space thus clearly allude to the inadequacy of heteropatriarchy and colonialism's frames of perception and articulate "an unwaveringly nuanced representation of Black lesbian identities that gestures to the impossibility of effective containment" (Gqola, "Through" 624). By placing the word "don't" in the installation's title, Muholi further draws attention to not only their own body's capacity for defiant signification; they also place the onus squarely on the viewer to consider the kinds of "sanctioned ignorance" (Spivak, *Death* 9) that sustain all affective attachments to privilege and discriminatory ways of seeing.[30]

Finally, the inclusion of Muholi's voice reading Ethagene's poem deepens the artwork's reflections on the tensions inherent in the desire to inhabit articulable, legible forms of intimacy, on the one hand, and the sensual and sensorial richness that lies beyond the normative, the rational, and the articulable, on the other. There is much to be said about this poem by way of analysis, but for the sake of this conclusion I highlight only one brief point. The threefold repetition of the line "I'm unable to articulate," which follows from the repeated line "I ache for you" at the start of the poem, not only serves as a statement of frustration, with an inability felt as a lack. As the emphasis heightens through repetition, the line turns from an expression of failure into a declaration of defiance, a deliberate refusal to capture linguistically and cognitively an embodied experience that pulses at the level of affective, aesthetic responsiveness. Muholi's defiance honours the potential contained in what Deborah Gould, in her discussion of the meaning of the term "affect," describes as a kind of "bodily, inarticulate, less-than-fully conscious, sensory experience" ("On Affect" 26), a reading reinforced by the poet's repeated but clearly inadequate attempts at fully verbalizing, through words such as "ache," "throbbing," "heartbeat," "deafening," "vibrate," and "kissed," the somatic sensation of being *affected* by another.

Read in context of the installation as a whole, Muholi's inclusion of Etaghene's poem registers intimate human communication to be shaped both by the expectation and experience of subjection and by the potentially transformative affective forces that pulse, at least in part, beyond the purview of prevailing regimes of social legitimation. The latter avenues of escape are referenced as part of a measured act of political defiance on the part of the artist to counter the condition of being looked at by actively looking, of being desired by desiring, of being theorized by theorizing, and of being cast as disappointing by enacting disappointment.

Wayward Politics

Both Searle's and Muholi's video installations grow out of a larger emotional culture of disappointment. Both these installations evoke the uncanny ubiquity of the spectacle in a country where the deplorable scale of misogynist violence continues to have a profound bearing on the post-rainbow gendered everyday. Yet they both also gesture to the possibility of inventing new forms of politics, fresh ways of seeing and listening, and novel ways of feeling in the face of overwhelming social inequality. Through their at once serious and playful aesthetic approach to contemporary South African struggles for equality, Searle and Muholi draw attention repeatedly to the density of everyday experience that tends to escape dominant frames of perception. Such work constitutes a form of wayward politics that operates beyond the conventional realm of statecraft or political protest. We might read this work as causing a disturbance in what Jacques Rancière calls the "distribution of the sensible" (*Dissensus* 54). The latter refers to the ways in which the apportioning of sense, space, and time structures what is visible, sayable, and audible within specific aesthetic and political regimes. This dynamic is shaped concurrently by activities of policing whereby the coordinates of social and political participation are drawn, on the one hand, and by the activities of dissensus and disruption by those whose speech previously registered only as noise or whose concerns have never been regarded as worthy of attention, on the other. For Rancière, "politics is aesthetic in that it makes visible what had been excluded from a perceptual field, and in that it makes audible what used to be inaudible" (*Philosopher* 226). The impact that these works of art can have cannot be calculated and measured in immediately tangible and material ways; these works operate both alongside and differently from more spectacular forms of street protest, some of which I address in subsequent chapters. But in a way this intangibility is where their power lies. I read these works as alternative, wayward forms of politics that are not necessarily tied to the immediate and the calculable, but to the slow work done by cultural workers, artists, and scholars in humanities disciplines who are engaged in enlarging the cognitive, discursive, and sensory terrains within which politics and social membership are currently confined. We need to pay attention to these forms of political intervention if the more immediately measurable forms of political engagement are to become possible.

The redistribution of the sensible enabled by these installations constitutes what Ben Highmore, following Rancière, calls a "moment of negativity": "in the rip all sorts of things are possible" (*Ordinary* 48). For Searle and Muholi, the latter moment of negativity is tied to the inability to look away from the many kinds of systemic violence that continue to shape daily life in South Africa in the wake of the rainbow promise. Yet in their work, disappointment also figures as a refusal to let go of an investment in the possibility of a better future. As such, disappointment as a negative affect is politically generative in ways that Sara Ahmed's work on happiness and the figure of the feminist killjoy can help to illuminate. In *The Promise of Happiness* and elsewhere, Ahmed considers how human desire is shaped by the attribution of happiness to certain objects or social ideals – such as heterosexual marriage or multicultural integration – "that circulate as social goods" ("Multiculturalism" 126). Framed in these terms, the question of happiness becomes a political question about what kinds of life choices people are directed towards by virtue of their supposed capacity to generate happiness. When someone fails to experience the pleasure that proximity to these ideals or social goods promises, that person becomes an "affect alien," namely someone who is "out of line with an affective community" (126). Feminists, for instance, frequently find themselves in this position when they fail "to find the objects that promise happiness to be quite so promising" (Ahmed, *Promise* 65). More than that, feminists tend to be held up as the cause of the unhappiness of others when they point to sexism or other experiences of discrimination. Put differently, feminists are often "read as being unhappy, such that situations of conflict, violence, and power are read as *about* the unhappiness of feminists, rather than being what feminists are unhappy *about*" (Ahmed, *Promise* 67; emphasis in original).

Ahmed warns that the imperative to be happy, to follow the promise of happiness, can become a powerful political obstacle to social justice activists who recognize precisely how much there is to be unhappy about (*Promise* 223). Following Audre Lorde, Ahmed articulates a political vision that calls for a heightened consciousness of the effects of violence and social inequality as a "struggle not so much to feel hurt but to notice what causes hurt, which means unlearning what we have learned not to notice" (216). In the aesthetic activisms of Searle and Muholi, disappointment functions similarly as a mode of wayward feeling that disrupts the fantasies upheld by the spectacle of the promise. As Ahmed puts it, "disappointment can be experienced as a gap between an ideal and an experience that demands action" (41). As such, disappointment continues to be aspirational, but in a way that is anchored less in the safety of utopian futures promised than in the messiness of presents lived. As feminist killjoys, Searle and Muholi both point to signs of injustice not simply to refuse to be happy but to mobilize disappointment as an affective driver of the difficult daily work of building a more inclusive, socially just present from the ruins of the promise. Their challenge may in fact be said to echo through each of the more headline-grabbing forms of political and aesthetic protest that I discuss in chapters 3 to 5. Yet in the next chapter I first consider some of the difficult and unpredictable ways in which young people in the country "survive disappointment" (Cvetkovich, *Depression* 6), as I deepen some of the insights regarding the entanglement of public culture and intimate feeling offered thus far through a study of expectant youth mood and its complex psychosocial temporalities. South Africans under the age of twenty make up at least a third of the country's collective population, and a reading of some of the daily strategies of affective self-styling to emerge from this demographic is therefore key to making sense of post-rainbow times.

2

Moody, Expectant Teens[1]

Braids: plastic, shiny, cheap synthetic strands of dreams-come-true make their way out from her underaged head.

Kopano Matlwa[2]

If moods are characterized by a tendency to linger, to be persistent and difficult to unsettle – contrasted, that is, to emotion and affect by virtue of having a longer duration (Felski and Fraiman, v; Rosfort and Stanghellini, 258) – how do we account for the moodiness of teens? Young people, to be sure, are often described as stubborn, wilful, or obstinate, as doggedly refusing to be moved from an opinion or course of action. The moods associated with youth obstinacy are assumed to be moods, then, that tend to hang around. Yet young people are also widely considered to be capricious, impulsive, or unpredictable, traits indicating sudden shifts in mood or behaviour. Writing about the centrality of gender and sexuality to the meanings historically assigned to mood, Clare Hemmings points out that "when mood attaches to women, it is likely to be characterized by its superficiality rather than its duration" ("In the Mood" 529). The point may well be extended to a reading of young people's assumed relationship to mood, and draws attention to the need to think of mood both in relation to the body and in terms of the body's relationship to representation. The assumed texture and duration of a mood then depend, it seems, in large part on the bodies to which it attaches and the meanings assigned to those bodies.

I turn to mood in this chapter on young women's visual autobiography for at least two reasons. First, as an affective state that comes to reside but does not entirely originate in an individual's body, mood by definition straddles the boundaries between the social and the psychic, the public and the private – in fact, mood precedes these very distinctions. As I am concerned in this chapter with visual autobiography as a self-creating genre through which private feeling enters public culture, I suggest that a consideration of mood can cast a heuristic light onto some of the affective textures of embodied youth self-representation in South Africa today. Second, I am interested in the nuances that a reading of mood as attunement – as a way of tuning in or being tuned in to social feeling – bring to understanding what seem to be the simultaneously expectant and foreclosed dimensions of youth feeling in post-rainbow South Africa.

My argument proceeds by way of an analysis of the films *Made in China* (Peerbhay) and *Where Is the Love?* (Ditshego), screened by the South African Broadcasting Corporation (SABC) in 2011 as part of the "I Am Mzansi: This Is My Story" documentary series. Made by a group of young South African filmmakers who were supervised by professional mentors, and sponsored jointly by the SABC, Born Free Media, and the loveLife initiative, the seven films in this series comprise a much-needed addition to a South African documentary filmmaking tradition that, as Jacqueline Maingard has shown, tended until relatively recently to be dominated by white male filmmakers (663). The films, which navigate through stories about, for instance, unplanned pregnancy, xenophobia, citizenship, body art, popular music, train surfing, poverty, sexual violence, and dancing, are each prefaced by the lines "Mzansi, up close and personal" and "I am Mzansi, and this is my story," which position these documentary accounts as part of an overarching narrative of post-apartheid youth experience, where anxious (auto)biographical revelation confronts the script of the idealized youth citizen.[3]

My curiosity about these films germinates from a concern that runs through this book, and that seems recently to have informed much of the research navigating the complex comingling of the public and the intimate, namely the tension that emerges when publicly prescribed or sanctioned feeling fails to coincide with the feelings called forth by our everyday lives. Building on my analysis, in the preceding chapter, of disappointment as a political affect that strikingly reveals the tension between how we are expected to feel and how we do feel – and the wayward feelings that emerge from this nexus – I suggest that the filmmakers of the "I Am Mzansi" series perform a number of complex rhetorical manoeuvres to balance the affective demands made by both generic convention and dominant emotional cultures, on the one hand, and the inability on the part of the storytellers to fully align their accounts of themselves with these demands, on the other. I read these films as positioned at the crossroads of "the happy fictions of success and inclusion that frequently characterize dominant accounts of multiculturalism, citizenship, neoliberal capitalism and (neo)colonial structures of governance, on the one hand, and the various interruptive texts and textures that emerge from the accumulated everyday experience of various forms of structural violence, on the other" (Antwi et al., "Postcolonial" 5). This tension seems to be particularly pronounced in post-rainbow South Africa, where democratization has brought the majority of young people "little prospect of employment, a vexing mix of rising expectations and declining prospects" (Posel, "ANC" 60), as my analysis in chapter 4 of the cultures of protest emerging among the so-called born-frees at universities also demonstrates.

What, I ask, can visual youth autobiographies as forms of "mediated intimacy" (Gill and Tyler 79) or "intimate exposure" (Bystrom 19) make known about the tension between prescribed and lived feeling in post-rainbow South Africa, and about technologies of intimate control that have to be navigated by contemporary audio-visual publics? How might a study of mood help to overcome the depoliticizing tendency central to the turn to the intimate self in the autobiography industry? What are the (audio)visual, affective, and generic strategies used by the filmmakers of *Made in China* and *Where Is the Love?* to imagine alternatives to psychic pain and the difficulties that young people confront in their everyday lives? In the section that follows, I first trace some of the historical shifts attendant to the public circulation of autobiographical feeling in South African visual culture. I then map some of the historical and more recent coordinates of scholarly conversation on mood, before considering how *Made in China* and *Where Is the Love?* attempt to align moody youth feeling with the affective and material expectations that accompany everyday life under contemporary racialized capitalism in South Africa.

Visual Youth Autobiography

In her work on the hidden, non-elite forms of representation and literacy through which ordinary African lives are conveyed, Karin Barber calls for a study of "tin-trunk texts," namely "letters, diaries, obituary notices, pamphlets, and other things that people across Africa often keep in boxes hidden under their beds" (ix). These texts, she writes, constitute an important archive for the study of the many and inventive forms of literacy that were emerging in people's ordinary lives in these contexts. They also evoke revealing new forms of social self-styling, of "personal publicity and collective privacy, modes of projection, distribution, multiplication and storage of lives and personalities for which we still need to develop a vocabulary" (12).

I suggest that the "I Am Mzansi" films might be approached as a comparable "tin-trunk" archive of texts, particularly to the extent that the films reveal new visual literacies that in turn make possible novel forms of self-projection in the context of contemporary visual culture. Admittedly, the films that I study here were broadcast on national television, and so form part of a body of audio-visual texts through which the mediation of certain personal stories has been officially sanctioned. One of the key aims of this chapter is therefore to consider how demands for a better future on the part of South Africa's young people tend to be channelled into conventional and dominant generic and affective formats. Yet the life-narratives conveyed in these films have a more complex relationship to mainstream visual culture and the elite literacies of which Barber writes. As films made by and about young South Africans whose wayward daily strategies of emotional and material survival tend to be crafted in response to social pressures that counteract these very efforts, the "I Am Mzanzi" documentary series in effect constitutes a rich archive of "tin-trunk" texts – conveyed, for instance, through oral testimony, photography, household items, commodities, and personal possessions, as well as sartorial and corporeal semiotics – that bring under-represented youth experience into broader circulation.

My interest in the "tin-trunk" dimensions of youth visual autobiography is enabled, in part, by a range of historical shifts related to the transmission and formal organization of the autobiographical voice in South Africa. The political transition of 1994 coincided not only with a lessening of anxieties surrounding the collective representativity of the individual autobiographical voice – a concern particularly prominent in the 1980s, when the autobiographical narration of personal trauma was more often than not tethered to – or made to serve – the larger, collective anti-apartheid struggle (Ellen Kuzwayo's *Call Me Woman* [1985] and Emma Mashinini's *Strikes Have Followed Me All My Life* [1989] constitute perhaps the two most prominent examples here).[4] The end of apartheid also opened up novel possibilities for self-narration facilitated by the global spread of new technologies of knowledge production and dissemination, and by the broadening of freedoms surrounding the representation and expression of bodily intimacy. Not only, in other words, did the post-apartheid era usher in a time of unprecedented openness surrounding previously criminalized, censored, and repressed articulations of interpersonal affect and hidden autobiographical detail, the range of platforms available for bringing subjective, "tin-trunk" interiority into public culture multiplied simultaneously.

This era saw an explosion of not only (auto)biographical writing by and about the post-apartheid political elite; non-elite or non-literary forms of autobiographical narration also gained greater visibility (a proliferation of literary autobiographies, memoirs, and other generic experiments with self-narration include texts by writers such as Sisonke Msimang, Malaika wa Azania, Antjie Krog, Zakes Mda, Chris van Wyk, Bonnie Henna, Damon Galgut, and J.M. Coetzee). The Truth and Reconciliation Commission, in particular, constituted a key site for the public mediation of non-elite inner lives (Bystrom and Nuttall 310–11). The South African Broadcasting Corporation's (SABC) coverage of the TRC hearings enabled South Africans to witness some of the most difficult moments of autobiographical revelation staged in the country's recent history, and marked the early stages of an era in which the particularly *(tele)visual* circulation of private experience and feeling became increasingly widespread. The TRC also "at least temporarily inaugurated a 'public-private sphere' where people previously defined as separate could imagine and feel their way into a shared public culture through empathetic engagement with people victimized by the apartheid regime" (310).

The post-apartheid public sphere has been a great deal more inclusive than that of the apartheid era, but has also exhibited many of the typical tendencies that have elsewhere accompanied mass-mediated communication under late capitalism, including "encouraging repertoires of self-disclosure and the authentication of opinion on the strength of personal experience; giving primacy to the visual image over the written word, and producing modes of conversation saturated with affect" (Posel, "Malema" 37).[5] The growing ubiquity of screens connecting people via an uninterrupted stream of images brought everyday lives and feelings into public circulation in unprecedented ways. What W.J.T. Mitchell in 1994 famously called the "pictorial turn" (20) has become even more differentiated and diversified in the intervening years, which have seen a surge in the range of and platforms available for visual cultural production. The latter in no small measure paved the way for what Kerry Bystrom and Sarah Nuttall, in their 2013 editorial introduction to a special issue of the journal *Cultural Studies* on the public South African lives of private selves, have identified as one of the key features of contemporary public culture in South Africa, namely an increasing preoccupation on the part of cultural workers with the public display of private feelings, experiences, and spaces, and with the body as a sign and a site of intimate encounter.

These trends are linked in part to the compression, within a global neoliberal paradigm, of political life into individualized and psychologized modes of public engagement, where the traffic in intimate affects via mass communication platforms such as reality television, social media, talk shows, and the tabloid and autobiography industries serves as a disciplinary technology of sorts.[6] Yet, as the films that I study in this chapter reveal, not all forms of intimate mediation necessarily work to reactionary ends as mechanisms for psychic makeover; the films under discussion here signal, instead, some of the difficulties faced by young people in South Africa as they try to manage the affective demands attendant upon the so-called crisis everyday of contemporary racialized capitalism, and of finding meaningful ways to respond to these demands. As Bystrom and Nuttall put it, "modes of intimate exposure suffuse diverse media forms and can speak in different keys to a variety of publics. They seem to be crucial in addressing both the challenges of the unfinished democratic transition and the aspirations and desires of the 'born free' generation" (311).

The accelerated transmission of autobiographical intimacy in contemporary visual culture, in other words, is bound to a tangle of dominant and negotiated modalities of thought and feeling. On the one hand, acts of visual self-narration might be seen to feed into the thrall of what Chris Hedges refers to as the "cult of distraction" enabled by the "commercial 'personalizing' of the world" (37). As Zygmunt Bauman puts it, "the task of holding society together … is being 'subsidiarized,' 'contracted out,' or simply falling to the realm of individual life politics. Increasingly it is being left to the enterprise of the 'networking' and 'networked' selves and to their connecting-disconnecting initiatives and operations" (*Does Ethics* 14–15). On the other hand, visual autobiography has become a medium for counter-cultural production and experimentation, for questioning precisely the individualizing tendencies attendant to the commodification of intimate lives, and "for reinvigorating public spheres … and fostering new forms of analysis and coalition" (Brophy and Hladki 5). In the South African context, artists and visual activists such as Sabelo Mlangeni, Usha Seejarim, Zanele Muholi, Sue Williamson, Mary Sibande, Nandipho Mntambo, and Berni Searle have long enlisted the (auto)biographical self in visual modes of social critique. These deliberate forms of aesthetic struggle serve, in this chapter, as an unspoken touchstone against which to read the corporeal and affective contestations and regimes of self-management that emerge in the autobiographical projects of young filmmakers under discussion in what follows.

Like Sarah Brophy and Janice Hladki in their collection on embodied politics in global visual autobiography, this chapter I approach "autobiography's relation to visual culture in terms of embodied political cultural practice" (7). Reading the visual public sphere as a forum premised neither on equity nor on universal accessibility, Brophy and Hladki write that "bodies are made to appear/materialize, or are barred from doing so, within a field whose boundaries are constituted by what is presumed to be outside its sense of material reality, aesthetic value, affective and epistemological legitimacy, and ethical concern" (7). Focusing specifically on the question of "affective legitimacy" that Brophy and Hladki highlight here, I identify in the "I Am Mzanzi" films – and the films *Made in China* and *Where Is the Love?* in particular – a distinctive "mood of expectation" that serves as the affective atmosphere within which fantasies of success and future happiness are both sustained and foreclosed. To understand these messy affective climates, I first offer a brief overview of a recent flurry of international scholarly activity on the topic of mood.

Mood

There are many reasons for this increased interest on the part of cultural and social theorists in mood, including the view that attention to its workings might help to "circumvent the clunky categories often imposed on experience: subjective versus objective, feeling versus thinking, latent versus manifest" and that mood serves as a good barometer of "our experience of being with others" (Felski and Fraiman vi, vii). Questions about public mood have long been of interest to those who try to measure and influence voting decisions and consumer spending, concerns that in themselves make visible the porousness of the boundary between the private and the public. Mood may also determine the extent to which an individual is deemed to belong to a (national) community (Hemmings, "In the Mood" 528). What's more, there is no escaping mood, and an analysis of its ebbs and flows is therefore required for making sense of some of the subtleties of social habitation and habituation.

Much of this work derives specifically from Martin Heidegger's understanding of mood, or *Stimmung*, which means both mood and attunement. According to Heidegger, "*mood has already disclosed, in every case, Being-in-the-world as a whole, and makes it possible first of all to direct oneself towards something*" (176; emphasis in original). By this Heidegger means that moods are the precondition of our situatedness in the world, and precede how we register and structure affective intensity and sensory stimuli; moods are neither internally generated nor shaped exclusively by external forces but in fact undo these very distinctions. Moods, in other words, are both public – in the sense that we are necessarily given over to a world which prestructures how we attune ourselves to people and things, and which delimits how entities come to matter to us – and private, in that we have the limited capacity, "through knowledge and will" (175), to shape our own moods, or to counter certain moods with others.

As Charles Guignon explains, Heidegger identifies three structures that enable our everyday Dasein (our being-in-the-world): "understanding, which opens a field of purposive activities in which equipment comes to appear in its functionality; discursiveness, which articulates our shared ways of encountering things; and situatedness (*Befindlichkeit*), which discloses our mode of being contextualized at any given time" (Guignon 183–4). The last of these, namely situatedness, "is always manifest in some mood or other" (183), and, it follows, is more than simply an inward psychic state; it reflects the relationship we have with the social contexts that we inhabit and to which we are, to a large extent, given over. In our situatedness we are, in other words, both the vessels of social mood and the agents through whom certain aspects of the world become enlivened and differentiated by way of their embeddedness in mood. The moods in which our situatedness manifests itself make it possible for us to encounter everyday life as more than simply a blur of structureless sensory data: "Moods enable us to focus our attention and orient ourselves. Without this orientation, a human would be a bundle of raw capacities so diffuse and undifferentiated that it could never discover anything" (186). How we focus our attentions and attune ourselves are, further, a result of our shared or communal Dasein – of a publicness found in "the kind of Being that belongs to the 'they'" (Heidegger 178). Yet as Guignon points out, "as we grow up in the social world into which we are thrown, we also become the masters of a determinate range of possible moods that are 'accepted' in our world ... Our moods are always regulated and generated by a shared attunement to public 'forms of life' in our culture" (187).

Guignon's point about learning to inhabit or "master" a determinate range of socially accepted moods deserves consideration in terms of the relationship between the coming-of-age process and mood. If mood enables us to "tune in" to "a highly determinate cultural world" (186), then it stands to reason that we are not born attuned but that achieving attunement is tied to larger processes of social incorporation and differentiation that mark the passage into adulthood. In other words, negotiating the coming-of-age process involves not only claiming a space of belonging in relation to intimate and larger publics or national communities, it also requires navigating and "tuning in" to the moods within which these larger communities are necessarily embedded. In the "I Am Mzansi" films, this process of tuning in to shared mood is conveyed via a range of generic formats, not least of which the genres of the *Bildungsroman* (about which more below) and the autobiography as a genre of self-projection. Both these genres are complicit in the process of socio-cultural and national incorporation at issue here, and both reflect and shape the kinds of group mood that create the atmosphere for certain modes of social belonging and exclusion.

To be in tune with national or group mood requires that one shares certain orientations towards the objects and symbols that inspire feelings of (national) belonging. To not be moved to pride, for instance, by events that heighten feelings of national exceptionalism – including sporting events or other markers of national achievement – is to be misattuned to national mood. These forms of misattunement get consolidated via technologies of othering whereby feelings of animosity are projected onto those whose moods are read as out of tune (Ahmed, "Not in the Mood" 17). As Hemmings phrases it, "being out of sync with the 'national mood,' for example, may result in individual marginalization, or rage on the part of others who more closely reflect national sentiment" (528).

In the 2014 special issue of the journal *New Formations* on "mood work" a number of theorists write about the labour involved in shaping mood and enabling possibilities of attunement. The work of Arlie Russell Hochschild in particular is referenced in this special issue as a touchstone for thinking about the labour of shaping and maintaining certain moods for the benefit of others (particularly in a commercial setting). Hochschild writes, for instance, about how flight attendants have to manage their own feelings in order to achieve the mood of friendly, warm hospitality that the airline company promises to offer its passengers. While Hochschild is concerned in her much-cited study specifically with the coordinates and costs of what she calls "emotional labour" (*Managed Heart* 11), special issue editors Highmore and Taylor suggest that expanding the terms of analysis to encompass mood "might provide new insights about our social worlds that might be harder to grasp if the focus is entirely on emotion" (6). They explain that while the emotional labour of individuals is an important contributing factor to mood, one needs to pay attention to how the situation as a whole, and the numerous factors shaping this situation, contribute to the overall orchestration of the mood that prevails in any given context. These factors include "individual and collective feelings, organic and inorganic elements, as well as contingent, historical and slow changing conditions" (6). They highlight particularly the social and historical determinants involved in the shaping of mood, which they explain via a slightly altered version of Marx's famous maxim on history: "people make their own moods but they don't make them just as they please; they do not make them under circumstances chosen by themselves, but under circumstances directly encountered, given and transmitted from the past" (8).

When returning the discussion to mood and youth self-narration in contemporary South African visual culture, one might similarly identify a range of historical and social factors – not to mention the social and aesthetic genres within which these factors are embedded – that variously demand and limit possibilities for attunement. If "mood is the form that attention takes" (9), then highlighting some of the concerns that command youth attention in the "I Am Mzansi" films will begin to give tone and texture to the "material moods that knit together culture on the ground: the endless array of social forms that are lived out with various degrees of intensity and boredom" (Highmore, "Finding" 431).

I suggest that for young people in contemporary South Africa, there are a range of historical and social factors that contribute to what I define as the "expectant mood" that orients group attention in these films. Ernst Bloch distinguishes between what he calls "Gefüllte Affekte" (filled emotions) and "Erwartungstaffekte" (expectant emotions) (*Das Prinzip* 82). Filled emotions, which include envy, greed, and admiration, are "those whose drive-intention is short-term, whose drive-object lies ready, if not in respective individual attainability, then in the already available world" (Bloch, *The Principle* 74). In contrast, expectant emotions – such as anxiety, fear, hope, and belief – "are those whose drive-intention is long-term, whose drive-object does not yet lie ready" (74). Expectant emotions are distinguished from filled emotions "by the *incomparably greater anticipatory character* in their intention, their substance, and their object. All emotions refer to the horizon of time … but the expectant emotions open out entirely into this horizon" (74; emphasis in the original). Comparable to the anticipatory structure of the promise or the "political ontology of threat" (Massumi), considered respectively in chapters 1 and 3 of this book, expectant emotions thus take shape in relation to anticipated futures that structure subjective engagements with the present.

The term "expect" (along with its variations "expectant," "expectation," or "unexpected") is key here. Derived from the conjunction of the Latin roots *ex-*, meaning "out," and *spectare,* meaning "to look" – that is, "to look out for" – the term "expect" connotes forms of deferral or waiting (*Erwartung*) that exert a variety of affective pressures in our daily lives. To expect something is generally to invest our visions of the future with feelings of anxious or eager anticipation. Expectation, furthermore, involves not only the anticipatory character of someone's own engagements with their world – what they themselves expect of the world; the expectations of others also have to be accommodated in the daily structuring and self-imagining of a person's present and future lives. For young people, the expectations of others can be felt as a particularly suffocating marshalling of their behaviours and choices, and are frequently experienced – in both conscious and less considered ways – as at odds with what seems attainable, and indeed desirable. The youth visual autobiographies that I analyse below reveal these pressures of expectation and the latter's social moods to be felt in particularly persistent ways in the post-rainbow South African economic and cultural climate. In short, expectant emotions are both shaped by and constitutive of the larger mood of expectation that orients youth attention in the context of both the (broken) post-apartheid rainbow promise and contemporary aspirational capitalism – what Deborah James, in her study of debt and aspiration in post-apartheid South Africa, calls "the long-term expectations (and hoped-for consequences) of upward mobility" (8).

Expectant Mood and Social (Im)mobility: Sarah Chu's *Made in China* and Evelyn Maruping's *Where Is the Love?*[7]

The film *Driving Force*, one of the seven documentaries included in the "I Am Mzansi: This Is My Story" films, offers viewers a success story of sorts. It features Mawande Stemela, the young protagonist and co-producer of the film, whose coming-of-age story is set against the competing pressures of crushing rural poverty and the unrealistic demands of old-school patriarchy. Growing up in a small village called Ezingcaceni near Queenstown in the Eastern Cape, Mawande is expected, from an early age, to fill the shoes of his absent father – a migrant labourer – and to help his mother brew and sell beer to the local community in an effort to make ends meet. Mawande's inability to live up to these expectations leads him down a path of youth violence, crime, and incarceration, a trajectory that ultimately informs his decision to undergo initiation. Once he returns from initiation school, he decides to join his father in Hermanus in the Western Cape, where he starts to work for a local wine-exporting company. The contentiousness of Mawande's decision to join his father as a migrant labourer in light of the impossible burden placed on rural communities by this system is emphasized in the documentary to the point of overstating its case. Yet

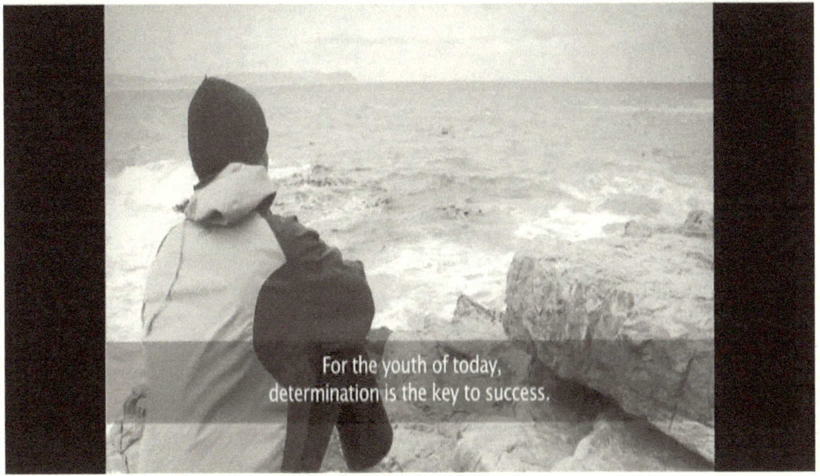

Figure 2.1 Video still from the film *Driving Force.*

ironically, the film ends with Mawande summing up his story with the following line: "For the youth of today, determination is the key to success" (figure 2.1).

Varieties of this strained reference to success can be found in each of the seven films in the "I Am Mzansi" series and serves as a useful access point into the moody tenor of youth experience and the pressures of expectation conveyed in these films. The word "success," which pops up with remarkable frequency in almost all of the seven "I Am Mzansi" films, comes to justify a range of socially sanctioned aspirations that are at once overdetermining and conspicuously vague. As a catch-all for what young people are supposed to aspire to, the term references desires that are experienced as deeply private even as they require public validation and are shaped by larger social forces. The Online Etymology Dictionary significantly emphasizes the centrality of public confirmation to recent definitions of the term success. The term thus embodies the complex fusion of private feeling and public culture that characterizes the films that I analyse here, and that has come to define the intimate public sphere in present-day South Africa. The expectations attached to the achievement of success throughout these films serve as a powerful force for orienting youth attention, and highlight many of the contradictions faced by young people who try, but more often than not fail, to align their own feelings with those promised by

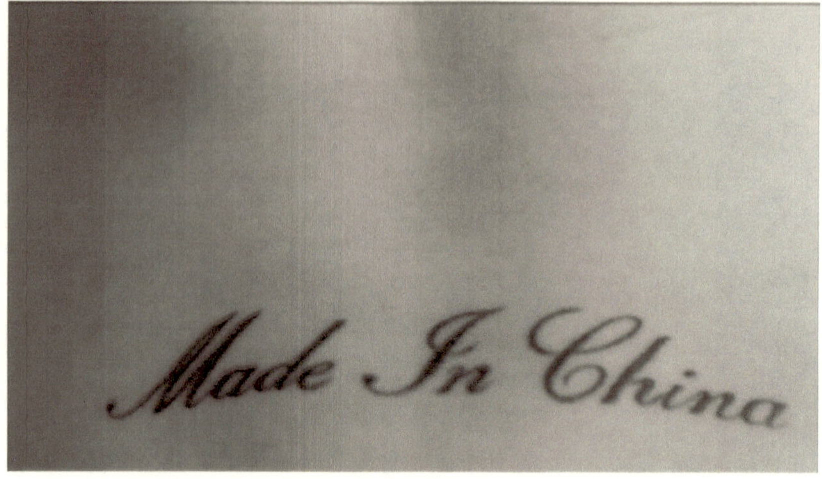

Figure 2.2 Video still from the film *Made in China*.

contemporary consumer capitalism and rainbow myths of racial reconciliation and achieved democracy.

The aspirations referenced here are articulated via a range of semi-confessional stories that suture together dreams of legitimation or success (whatever that means) and the emotional toll exacted by the repeated failure to have these dreams realized. The films *Made in China*, produced by and starring Sarah Chu, and *Where Is the Love?*, co-directed by and starring Evelyn Maruping, reveal these tensions in particularly pertinent ways. *Made in China* presents an anxious autobiographical account of Sarah Chu's experiences of emotional and cultural alienation as a result of her parents' decision to immigrate to South Africa when she was only five years old, leaving her with her grandmother in China for five more years before they came to get her. Here, the everyday dramas of strained familial intimacy are played out on the stage of citizenship's unrealized promises. In its very title, tattooed also onto Sarah Chu's lower back (figure 2.2), truncated citizenship registers as bodies trademarked and conscripted into global capitalism's depersonalizing circuits of commodity exchange, even if in Sarah's case the inscription serves her uniquely wayward brand of rebelliousness. *Where Is the Love?*, in turn, investigates the affective pull of fantasies of social belonging and shared love and care at the heart of unplanned pregnancy in Homevale Township in Kimberley, the historical centre of South Africa's once booming diamond-mining industry, now in a state of economic decline. Through a series of interviews with teenage mothers, the film reveals a world in which the socially alienating and laborious rituals of childcare have come to crush the possibility of a different life even as desires for such a life have as a result been amplified.

Like the film *Driving Force, Made in China* and *Where Is the Love?* both offer viewers a documentary sketch of the difficulties of attunement for the youth subjects of these films. The films provide multiple angles on the prolonged experience of feeling bad, and the expectations and disappointments that generate these feelings for young people in post-apartheid South Africa. The filmmakers of both films expertly manipulate filmic elements such as music, nonmusical sound, colour, lighting, and a range of other cinematographic, mise-en-scène, and editing components to craft the moods that, in turn, shape the "inner orientation" of viewers (Zettl 30).[8] Mood is also registered in these films via a range of cultural signifiers and recognizable signs, geographies, and histories, as well as the generic conventions that comprise the "aesthetic structure of affective expectation" (Berlant, *Complaint* 3). Both of these films use an array of these generic conventions, including a mix of those specific to the genres of the *Bildungsroman* and collaborative visual (auto)biography and of the expository documentary and reality television, all of which are entangled, in turn, in the more prosaic social genres of life narration, self-projection, and the coming-of-age process.

Made in China offers a remarkably well-crafted mood journey through the multiple scenes of childhood and familial trauma that culminate in Sarah Chu's negotiated integration into her familial, social, and national communities. Recipient of two awards at the sixth South African Film and Television Awards (SAFTA) in 2012 – one for Best Factual, Educational Entertainment and one for Best Short Documentary – the film gives aesthetic form, texture, and tone to both the material and more abstract human losses that accompany the process of transnational migration for diasporic families. Sarah Chu's visual autobiography is told in snapshots and moving images of things, spaces, and bodies laden with affective intensity and resonance, stitched together with an assortment of sounds and musical fragments.

The film's opening scenes present multiple angles on Sarah's exterior and interior lives: a sequence, shot in fast motion, of Sarah in a crowd of young bodies rhythmically bouncing to the loud, frenetic performance of a rock band; a series of extreme close-ups of the grooves, scars, and colours carved into tattooed skin; a moving black silhouette of Sarah's body against a bedroom curtain, lit in warm reds; a montage of intimate selfies and polaroid snapshots of Sarah's many colourful tattoos – an embodied archive of experience told in skin and ink; Sarah turning doll-like beside a biometric chart listing her name, age, place of birth, and current location – a body subjected to the classificatory technologies of the state; a visual vignette of the activities and interests that command Sarah's attention, including a rapidly edited succession of superimposed photographs of cameras, dancing bodies, artwork, Sarah holding a turtle, and an image of a woman being tattooed; and, finally, a string of snapshots of Sarah with friends and family. These visuals are given tonal ambience via a range of sonic elements, including an aural script of rock music, the sounds of a clicking camera, and the following voice-over commentary delivered in Sarah's recognizable Joburg accent: "What do you perceive when you are faced with a tattooed individual? What is your first impression? Do you perceive a hard-face, a don't-give-a-fuck attitude, and a tough shell? But do you ever ask what path they took to become who they are?"; and "I'm a freelance photographer and an aspiring filmmaker. I'm passionate about photography, filmmaking, tattoos, music, animals and art. I cannot survive a day without any of the above; I feel it and I breathe it. My family and friends mean the world to me, BUT, it hasn't always been this way."

These scenes and words set the mood for the coming-of-age story that follows. It conveys an inner life attentive not only to the rhythms of the subcultural world of tattooing and rock music to which Sarah was first drawn while she wrestled with multiple forms of alienation and misattunement growing up; she is shown in this opening scene also to have achieved forms of partial harmony – after a long personal struggle – with the familial and national communities from which she felt excluded during her troubled adolescence. Socio-cultural and affective incorporation into these communities – one subcultural, the other more mainstream – is set up from scratch as the success story that the coming-of-age testimony offered in most of the rest of the film will chart for viewers. The burden of expectation that Sarah bears while she grows up is presented, in other words, as having yielded not just disorientation but, more importantly, attunement (even as the latter continues to be negotiated and incomplete in certain ways).

Having said this, the modulations of self and body that Sarah testifies to in the film hint at the labours involved in achieving attunement for those whose bodies are read as out of sync with shared mood: "For those deemed to lack attunement, attunement might become a form of affective labour. In order not to cause non-attunement they have to become attuned" (Ahmed, "Mood" 21). Sarah's early experience of almost idyllic domesticity and emotional security in China – presented to the clichéd tune of traditional folk music via a series of snapshots of Sarah as a baby and a toddler in the loving arms of her mother and father – is shattered by her parents' move to South Africa, which she mistakenly and with devastating psychic consequences reads as them deciding to permanently leave her with her grandmother in order to replace her with a boy (China still had a one-child policy at the time). This deep personal pain fundamentally shapes her emotional life until her parents come to fetch her to join them in South Africa. Here, a new set of traumas awaits her as she must learn to adapt to a foreign cultural environment and school, in a language she does not understand. The agonizing experience of being culturally and linguistically out of step is compounded by the racism and xenophobia she finds herself exposed to at school, where she is mocked and subjected to finger pointing accompanied by a range of racist taunts. She describes this as "probably the time that I cried the most in my whole life. I'd hide in the bathroom, too scared to go out." The entangled processes of growing up and national incorporation for Sarah thus comprise both the experience of deep and abiding psychic pain and the difficult intercorporeal mood work of making her body fit in ways that are undisruptive to shared feeling: "Closing the gap between how one does feel and should feel can thus also aim to achieve a shared mood" (Ahmed, "Mood" 21).

The strategies for visual self-portraiture chosen in the sequence documenting Sarah's entry into South Africa are particularly telling of her unique brand of aesthetic responsiveness and of the labours of affective attunement she undertakes within herself and in terms of the mood she conveys and orchestrates for viewers. The filmmakers are remarkably adept at engineering the generic conventions typically used for conveying intimate distress, and at shaping the inner orientations of viewers as a result. The visual and aural details that accompany Sarah's testimony of her painful entry into a new cultural environment offer multiple clues here: Sarah shot in slow motion behind the wire fencing surrounding what is presumably her former primary school grounds, a place where she endured some of the most hurtful acts of exclusion and hostility; the haunting sounds of cello and piano music, slowing down the aural tempo found in the earlier and later parts of the film; Sarah's superimposed image, gradually fading in and out of view, shown to be slowly crossing the school grounds; her looking in through a window on a primary-school classroom, eerily empty and containing some of the well-known symbols of South African national belonging, including a series of "rainbow nation" flags stuck to the classroom walls; the use of grainy film reel footage with barely visible white lettering seen vertically scrawling across the screen – a well-known convention in documentary engagements with the past. Sarah's own aesthetic hypersensitivity to her social environment, and the psychic consequences of her deep awareness of her own difference, are further conveyed via a series of childhood photographs screened with slowly bulging and distorting perspectival relations, not only signalling Sarah's own disorientation but also subjecting viewers to minor feelings of vertigo. These elements all combine to transmit sensations to viewers that would align their own affective experience of the scene with that of Sarah and her memories of growing up.

Sarah's subsequent embrace of the subcultural world of tattooing speaks, on the one hand, to the extent of her estrangement from her parents at the time (her mother talks about the stigma attached to tattooing in China, especially for girls, saying, "We are traditional Chinese people. In China only criminals and bad people have tattoos"). She is shown repeatedly to wrestle with the burden of having failed to meet her parents' expectations of gendered embodiment and conduct, a failure which in turn structures her aspirational self-narrative throughout the rest of the film (as Karin Barber points out, aspiration is "founded upon lack" and "a sense of personal inadequacy" [5]). On the other hand, her retreat into the world of tattooing also reflects her attempt to take charge of the meanings imposed on her body: she literally scripts into her skin an account of self that defies the racist terms within which her body came to be cast in the xenophobic cultural imagination she has to navigate in her new national home. Perhaps unsurprisingly, she chooses the line "Made in China" as one of her first tattoos. As she explains, many people were saying that "everything that was produced or made in China was crap," yet as she puts it, "I was made in China, and I want to prove, prove it to them that, you know, that's not it."

Sarah's justification for becoming such a "naughty teen," as she phrases it, is revealed in part in the following lines: "I think part of the reason why was because I was trying to be different, because I spent so many years trying to be the same, trying to fit in and be normal." Here the effort required for Sarah to fit in is clearly conveyed in her expression of emotional fatigue – her prolonged moodiness – and her defiant turn, in response, to a subcultural world into which she found easier access. Yet the autobiographical account offered here is not simply one of defiance. One might read it instead as being in line with the generic and narrative formats used in the film as a whole, which ultimately charts a familiar course from hardship towards incorporation and overcoming. When Sarah starts to decode for viewers the autobiographical archive grafted onto her skin, the affective trajectory of the film noticeably shifts from the repeated visualization of traumatic memory towards a more didactic account of resolution and assimilation.

This shift is articulated in a number of ways, including via a tale of subcultural domestication apparent in the accounts given of tattooing's gradual transition from sub- to pop-cultural form, and its reduction to simply another technology of body commodification.[9] This transition is reflected in the film in part, for instance, in an interview with tattoo artist John-Scott Henderson, who recasts tattooing as an artform and reflects on the extent to which, as such, it has become increasingly mainstream. Henderson's account coincides fittingly with Sarah's own aspirational dreams of emotional attunement and the larger social successes that such attunement might bring. They also bring to mind Dick Hebdige's well-known work on the ways in which subcultural forms "hide in the light" and thus do not always operate in clear opposition to the dominant culture but instead engage in forms of exchange and negotiation with this culture (*Subculture* 35). While for Sarah the ambition to maintain a degree of separateness from mainstream culture that the tattooing scene offered continues to comprise a significant part of her self-portrait, her account of her membership to this world also clearly feeds into the larger conscription of her personal pain into predictable generic formats and a coming-of-age narrative of incorporation and assimilation into national culture.

The process of bringing the individual into harmony with the state through human *bildung* and its attendant domestication of young lives and drives into capitalism's normative values has been well documented. In *Human Rights Inc.* Joseph Slaughter, for instance, writes about these processes in terms of the formal emplotment or narrativization of young lives via the genre of the *Bildungsroman*, which he reads as linked to the discourse of universal human rights whereby human rebellion has been historically managed and subjected to technologies of state legitimation. The idealist *Bildungsroman*, for instance, which has "historically supported not only the sociocultural forces of nationalization but also those of imperialism and the 'civilizing mission'" (Slaughter 95), has been a particularly useful force for the incorporation of the wayward individual into normative citizenship (even as some forms of the genre have also worked to critique ways of blocking access to substantive and participatory citizenship).

The autobiographical representation of Sarah's *bildung* is cast in a range of affiliated generic and narrative formats that serve to lighten the film's mood via an ending that focuses on the successes of personal triumph and attunement. My analysis of these formats draws inspiration both from scholarship on the management of suffering in talk-show television – a genre I believe these documentary films to be indebted to – and from a conversation between US theorists Lee Edelman and Lauren Berlant about the kinds of optimistic social attachments that yoke people to life-worlds within which they are unlikely to thrive. Using the example of the talk-show genre to think through the global mass mediation of suffering, Rita Barnard writes, for instance, about the ways in which media mogul Oprah Winfrey's talk-show empire set itself apart from the traditional fare of daytime television in the United States – which "[elicited] more and more sensational public revelations of American lives gone wrong" ("Oprah" 23) – by making stories of personal pain into the source material for parables of individual empowerment and overcoming:

> To distinguish herself from the fray, Winfrey decided to turn her back on what she herself termed "trash TV" and to devote herself, with great earnestness and intensity, to the more uplifting aspects of life (Travis 13). The transformation was staged – as is so much in Winfrey's diligently examined life – as a psychic event of sorts. As she confessed to interviewers, the subject matter of the show (school violence, teenage substance abuse, dysfunctional families, and the like) was starting to get her down, and she resolved to stake out a new course: to lighten the mood of day-time television, to have more fun, and, most importantly, to do good. (23)

This project of "lightening the mood" has become a global staple of the self-help and wellness industries and their televisual and social media genres, reflecting what critics such as Barbara Ehrenreich have described as a tendency to preach individualized responsibility and prescribe positive thinking as a compulsory cultural attitude.[10] While the theorists whose work I draw on here write primarily about the management of feeling in the context of the United States and the Global North, these affective imperatives, as Barnard indicates, have leaked onto screens around the world and are reflected also, as I explain shortly, in the ending of *Made in China*.

In his conversation with Berlant, Edelman reflects on these forms of psychic alleviation specifically by highlighting the "problem of story" (Berlant and Edelman 3), a problem he suggests arises out of story's unassailable directionality, its momentum "toward some payoff or profit, some comprehension or closure, however open-ended. This leading *toward* necessarily entails a correlative 'leading *from*,' 'the leading from' or 'out of' at the root of 'education'" (3).[11] Much like the prolepsis

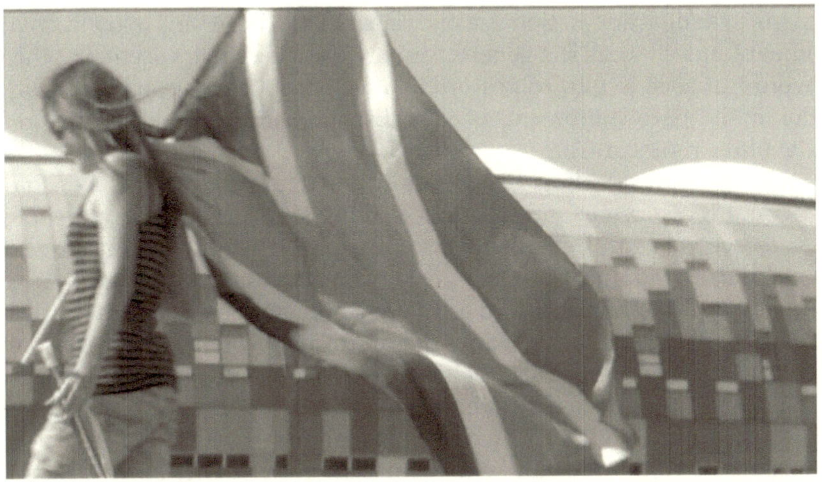

Figure 2.3 Video still from the film *Made in China*.

of the promise, the anticipatory temporality constitutive of all acts of storying necessarily inflects future-oriented fantasies of the good life of which Berlant so persuasively writes, and takes on the shape of a disciplinary technology – what Edelman, with apologies to Foucault, calls "panoptimism" – when "conceived as bestowing a value on life by way of the future anterior, by way of the life one *will have lived*, conceived, moreover, as justifying this refusal to live it *while one could*" (3; emphasis in original).

Edelman's assessment of the disciplinary mechanisms that emerge from story's future-directedness chimes with a reading of youth aspiration and expectation. The ending of *Made in China* is particularly revealing in this regard. After traversing the scenes of childhood and familial trauma already discussed, the film arrives at an ending tidily wrapped in the South African rainbow flag (positioned against the backdrop of the iconic Orlando stadium in Soweto) (figure 2.3) and conveyed through statements such as "I want to be successful, to be someone and to make my family proud"; "I'm surrounded by people that I love and care about"; "I work hard and party hard"; and "This is my story, and my life's journey lies ahead." The proleptic fantasies of success that percolate through the film culminate here in what one might call a "panoptimistic" slippage between success and succession, where the latter signals familial and national social reproduction's generic and affective lines of inheritance. The generic formats used in the film seem, in other words, at least in part to gesture to affective states that pre-emptively confer the assumed rewards of capitalist and national expectation upon the film's protagonist.

Yet the film's ending also needs to be recast slightly to take into account the survival and meaning-making strategies of young people who face structural inequality's impossible demands. In response to Edelman's reading of the foreclosing directionality central to all acts of storying, Berlant points to a difference in emphasis regarding their respective takes on the workings of optimism as a life-structuring force. Berlant explains that while Edelman "focuses on 'story' as *always* enacting negativity's drama of expectation and refusal," the concern is more with the middle ground "where survival and threats to it engender social forms that transform the habitation of negativity's multiplicity, without necessarily achieving 'story' in his terms" (5). Unlike Edelman, Berlant views optimism not simply as "'fantasy' in the negative sense of resistance to the Real" (5). Berlant is interested, instead, in "optimism as a mode of attachment to life" and declares commitment "to the political project of imagining how to detach from lives that don't work and from worlds that negate the subjects that produce them" (5).

This subtle but important distinction is especially useful for making sense of Sarah Chu's struggles with affective integration where expectation – much like the rainbow promise – functions as the default mood and mode of youth narration. My argument about the disciplinary force of the imperatives of positive thinking and happy endings notwithstanding, Sarah Chu's movingly optimistic and creative engagement with personal and familial hardship in *Made in China* might also be read as in line with what Berlant defines as "the affects of aspirational normativity" (164). In the chapter of their widely cited book *Cruel Optimism* titled "Nearly Utopian, Nearly Normal," Berlant considers how the atomizing conditions created by the regulation of labour, leisure, and life under contemporary capitalism have yielded aspirational attachments to less-than-ideal ways of living that are nonetheless desired by virtue of their supposed capacity to deliver even just temporary and tenuous forms of social belonging. In their discussion of the films *La Promesse* and *Rosetta*, Berlant explains, for instance, how ordinary life in the context of structural inequality

> is organized around the solicitation of children to the reproduction of what we should call not the good life but "the bad life" – that is, a life dedicated to moving toward the good life's normative/utopian zone

> but actually stuck in what we might call survival time, the time of struggling, drowning, holding onto the ledge, treading water – the time of *not-stopping* ... In these films, citizenship's dissatisfaction leads to reinvestment in the normative promises of capital and intimacy under capital. The quality of that reinvestment is not political in any of the normative senses, though – it's a feeling of aspirational normalcy, the desire to feel normal, and to feel normalcy as a ground of dependable life, a life that does not have to keep being reinvented. (169–70; emphasis in original)

It is this sense of normalcy that a lightening of the mood towards the ending of *Made in China* offers viewers. For while Sarah Chu's life choices are arguably nowhere near as grim as those of the young people in the films that Berlant discusses, Chu's attempts at aligning her own fantasies of success with the life that she does inhabit – conveyed in particular by the film's optimistic ending – could be said to reflect "not the achieved materiality of a better life but the approximate feeling of belonging to a world that doesn't yet exist reliably" (166). The tension between the optimistic futurity within which the film packages bad feeling, on the one hand, and the ongoing pull of long-standing structural precarity belied by the film's hygienic rainbowist ending, on the other, emerges perhaps most clearly in its brief reflections on realities of anti-Asian racism and xenophobia that Sarah and her family continue to experience in post-apartheid South Africa.

The film *Where Is the Love* negotiates similar tensions and temporalities, yet what sets it apart from the other films in the "I Am Mzansi" series is the evident inability of most of its young interviewees to convey a convincing sense of proximity to the kinds of aspirational normalcy that *Made in China* manages to conclude with. *Where Is the Love?*, instead, is a film that cannot help but dwell on the tears and regrets brought by youth pregnancy and parenthood, and the immobilizing weight that the social scripting of these experiences places upon youth subjects. Even though the "panoptimistic" conventions that translate bad feeling into fantasies of overcoming cannot fully be circumvented in the film, its ending offers no attempt at neutralizing the affective surplus produced by its visualization of negative feeling. The reasons for this failure are not necessarily innocent, given the risks that sadness be instrumentalized in a film about teen pregnancy simply to warn young women about the dangers of youth sex. To be sure, Evelyn Maruping openly states that she uses her own experience of unwanted youth pregnancy to highlight its many painful consequences, yet the film does more than indulge in facile moralisms about teen sexuality. As the recipient of other people's disappointments, Maruping does not simply dole out scorn and shame, but allows viewers to witness the range and complexity of experience that colour gendered economies of affective and sexual exchange and attachment in poverty-stricken communities.

The film presents the self-styling testimonies of eight young women living the repercussions of youth pregnancy in Homevale Township: Evelyn Maruping, Lee-Anne Burger, Bianca Seekoei, Juanita Appolis, Ronel Hoogstander, Zayleen Elwing, Geraldine Corner, and Deadre Moseki. In collaboration with the filmmaking team, each of these women engages in audio-visual forms of self-projection as they try to figure out what constitutes life-sustaining and reciprocal – perhaps even joyous – forms of sexual and maternal intimacy at the scene of thwarted expectation. Throughout the film, the expectant female body – explicitly pronounced moody by interviewee Juanita Appolis – is the terrain through which the film's titular search for love is charted. Moodiness and expectation, in other words, take on many complex and unpredictable shades here.

These complexities have much to do with the representational history of unwanted youth pregnancies in places that continue to battle the discursive and affective legacies of colonial occupation. Studying early reproduction in the South African context, Catriona Macleod suggests that we need to rethink the very category of adolescence if we are to move away from the persistently negative and stigmatizing languages within which early reproduction is invariably conveyed. She suggests that the "discourse of adolescence" as a transitional stage is tied to the colonial pairing of individual maturing and civilizational development, which in turn feeds into a range of prejudicial assumptions about youth pregnancy. Within this representational framework,

> the less developed, in the form of young people, are depicted as posing a threat of degeneration to the more developed, in the form of adults, through their careless and risk-taking behaviour – through engaging in sex, through not taking contraceptive precautions, through requiring additional health and psychological care during pregnancy or during and after the termination of pregnancy, through engaging in inadequate mothering practices and producing the next generation of problematic youth, and through relying on welfare and not being economically active. (5)

These assumptions can be clearly seen to shape the mood in *Where Is the Love?* and to weigh down the approach to the subject matter that Maruping takes. If motherhood is already one of the most heavily regulated social practices within patriarchy – compounded, in turn, by the effects of racism and other forms of social discrimination – early reproduction is subjected to even more extreme forms of social control. Youth pregnancy is the site, for instance, of extreme negativity, shame, and disillusionment in the testimonies included in the film, most notably perhaps in those by Maruping herself, as well as by Lee-Anne Burger, Bianca Seekoei, and Geraldine Corner. All four women are shown to encounter their pregnancies through the prism of the pervasive script of stigma and negativity of which Macleod writes. In fact, the failure on the part of these women to follow the conventionally sanctioned script of reproduction seems to mandate the performance of sadness and regret as prolonged emotional states or moods. The film's very first frames – positioned prior to the title sequence that gradually directs the viewer's attentions from Kimberley's most recognizable geographical, historical, and commercial landmarks towards the dusty discomforts of everyday life in Homevale Township – consist of close-up shots of Maruping attesting to the consequences of falling pregnant as a result of having had unprotected sex. The viewer is then taken into the intimate spaces of domestic childcare and its relentless labours via scenes, for instance, of Maruping washing and dressing her young son. As the image-track then slowly moves across snapshots documenting Maruping and her son during the early years of his life – scenes conventionally cast in the sentimentalities that consign reproduction to what Jack Halberstam has referred to as "family time" (153),[12] namely a heteronormative temporal trajectory involving birth, childhood, adolescence, marriage, reproduction, and death, in this order – the soundtrack tunes in to Maruping's affectively contrapuntal testimony. In this short confessional account, the word disappointed/ing features no less than three times:

> When I looked at myself in the mirror, I was not proud of myself. I couldn't face myself for a time and I couldn't deal with it. I was very *disappointed* in myself, and every day of my life during my pregnancy I just wished that I could do it over. When I told my boyfriend about this he was not happy at all. The first thing he said to me was, we have to have an abortion, and I didn't want to do that because it was against my beliefs and it was against my principles. My friends, they were all very supportive but they were all very *disappointed*, cause most of my friends they looked up to me and, you know, for someone seen as a role model by your friends and doing that, it's very *disappointing*. (emphasis added)

The film then proceeds to a slow-motion sequence of Maruping and her friends playing a ball game with her son while she narrates having her dreams of studying and going into the arts and filmmaking crushed.

Maruping's testimony sets the affective tone for the rest of the film and offers a prism of sorts for the testimonies to follow. As she frames it by way of introduction to the rest of the film: "Through my eyes, you will see the harsh reality of life experienced by teenagers in my community."

The scene of Maruping's testimony is significant for the contrast that it sets up between the emotional labour that she performs for her child, and the feelings she testifies to on screen and in voice-over. The contrast between an image track that conveys an affectionate mother who engages in joyful play with her child and the film's overall emotional arc reveals an ongoing state of tension between what is expected of Maruping and mothers like her, on the one hand, and what they experience, on the other. The "moodiness" conveyed by the emotional testimonies of the women interviewed in *Where Is the Love?* is significant insofar as it not only echoes clichéd assumptions about the pregnant female body as emotionally volatile, but also because it contributes to the overall mood evoked in the film. In addition to Maruping's own testimony, talk of suicide, and/or abortion features in a number of the testimonies, such as that of Geraldine Corner, who spends two weeks in hospital being treated for depression after learning of her pregnancy, or of Bianca Seekoei, who chooses not to terminate her pregnancy because her mother accepted her, hinting at the fact that her mother's own pregnancy was less than perfectly timed.

The sociality of teen pregnancy and parenthood is felt here as exacting a heavy toll on young mothers who have failed to meet the demands of conventional upward mobility and now find themselves having to negotiate the pressures of maternal childcare and its emotional labours. Emotional labour is frequently defined as the self-management of emotion and emotional display in the workplace in order to shape the feelings of others for the sake of generating a profit (Hochshild, *Managed*; Grandey, Diefendorff, and Rupp 6–7). While the care work done by mothers in the film is unpaid and not clearly regulated within the confines of a workplace culture in the conventional sense of the word, forms of emotional self-regulation and display attendant upon the management of the feelings of others are central to the institution of motherhood and the experience of maternity, which in turn confine mothers to a social and emotional script that they have only limited – if any – power to rewrite.[13] Throughout the film, the disappointments that attach to youth pregnancy and parenthood stand in ongoing tension with the social expectation to perform the emotional labours particular to childcare.

What kind of mood, then, do these testimonies evoke? What, furthermore, is it about mood that is useful as a frame for making sense of the audio-visual self-stylings found in *Where Is the Love*? In his work on mood and melancholia, Jonathan Flatley highlights Heidegger's point that we necessarily "find ourselves in moods that have already been inhabited by others, that have already been shaped or put into circulation, and that are already there around us" (5). Mood, he explains, can be taken to refer to a kind of "affective atmosphere ... in which intentions are formed, projects pursued, and particular affects can attach to particular objects" (19). As I have also noted above, mood as a concept then offers a generative way of thinking about the social and historical situatedness of feeling, a situatedness that a focus exclusively on emotion does not fully encapsulate, and, as such, proves particularly useful for understanding how forms of affective attunement between a mother and a child are historically and socially embedded.

If the kinds of emotional labour that mothers do more often than not constitute what Daniel Stern, in his work on the social and emotional lives of infants, calls "the intersubjective sharing of affect" (141) between mother and child, the maternal forms of emotional or affective labour that I discussed above might in fact be better defined as mood work. For Stern, affective attunement frequently serves a didactic purpose and is achieved, for instance, when a mother aims to match the quality of a child's inner state of feeling through the performance of a set of external behaviours. This is accomplished not simply by way of behavioural imitation, but by tuning in to the child's feeling state, and finding behavioural ways of signalling such attunement to the child. "Attunement behaviors," Stern writes, "shift the focus of attention to what is behind the behaviour, to the quality of feeling that is being shared" (142). Jennifer Carlson and Kathleen Stewart describe mood work in similar terms in a different context as creating "moments of interiority and co-noticing as feelings are folded inward and outward around persistent and emergent objects of attention and attachment" (115). If, as Flatley explains, the formation of *Stimmung* or mood involves focusing "attention on what kinds of affects and actions are possible within an overall environment" (27), the work of affective attunement that a mother engages in with her child constitutes a form of affective pedagogy that helps a child tailor its inner life to the regulative order of an affective sociality that is historically situated, an order that sets limits also on what a mother who is considered "premature" is expected to feel and do. It is unsurprising, therefore, that the juxtaposition of oral testimony and image track in the film so frequently yields scenes of affective dissonance, as young mothers must balance the mood work they do for their children against the demand for their own moods not to be out of sync with the emotional script to which they are confined.

The difficulties resulting from these complex tensions are conveyed most forcefully, perhaps, in the tearful testimony of Bianca Seekoei, in relation to whom Maruping tells viewers that "being a mother while still young is hard work. For some, dreams don't become realized." Seekoei explains that her relationship with the child's father, eighteen years her senior, was one defined in large measure by material considerations: "He gave me money; sometimes he would buy me luxuries. I drank juice and I ate chocolates."[14] Far from reproaching Bianca for her reliance upon an older man for material favours, the filmmakers are careful to position her choices within a larger social and cultural framework: the systemic gender-based inequalities at the root of patriarchy and capitalism's historical intersection are shown also elsewhere in the film to shape interaction across gender divides (as in interviews Maruping conducts, for instance, with a group of openly misogynist men at a local tavern, who testify to lying about their age to younger women whose attraction to these men is claimed to be largely reliant upon the conspicuousness of the latter's displays of commodity wealth). Seekoei's testimony is filmed alongside that of her mother as she walks around the cluttered yard beside their house, the visuals clearly conveying the consequences of sustained material hardship: cracked walls, barbed wire, old paint, rusted metal drums, corrugated iron sheeting, and shoddily laid bricks enfold a small, dusty courtyard. Central to the film's slice-of-life documentary aesthetic, these scenes attune viewers to the emotional dissonance at the heart of the experience of premature parenthood so powerfully expressed in the figures 2.4 and 2.5 below.

The super-imposition of the subscripts "Now I am stuck with being a mother" and "It is not nice being a mother" onto the child's delicate fingers offers up a snapshot of some the affective contradictions widely documented to be at the very heart of maternity.[15] Yet unlike women deemed to have followed the conventional script of heterosexual reproduction, the experience of maternity for this young mother holds few of the emotional rewards assumed to be delivered for mothers on the opposite end of the approval spectrum (for whom, incidentally, the expectation to derive joy from reproduction and childcare frequently emerges as an equally crushing demand). The filmmakers' decision to film Seekoei while still wearing her curlers might further be read as signalling their own complicity in scripting their subject into attendant forms of social and symbolic immobility, though Seekoei may very well have had her own agency in this scripting.

The testimony of Zayleen Elwing, who became pregnant at the age of seventeen, represents a noteworthy departure from other testimonies in the film even as it remains steeped in affective ambivalence.

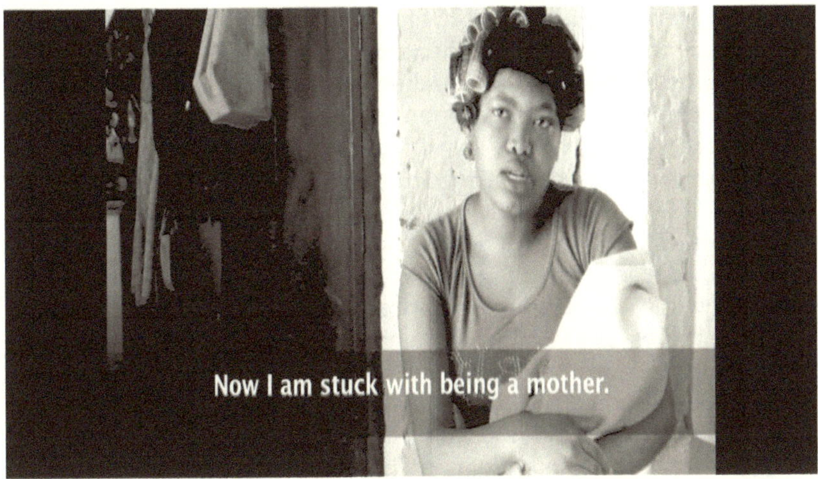

Figure 2.4 Video still from the film *Where Is the Love?*

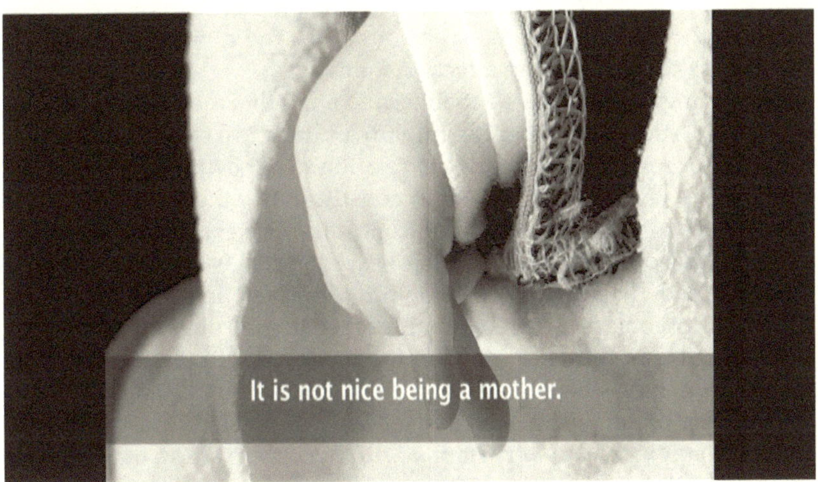

Figure 2.5 Video still from the film *Where Is the Love?*

Elwing is the only young mother interviewed who is unapologetic about her decisions, insisting "I was happy and it was my plan to have a baby." Significantly, no mention of paternal involvement or absence – featuring in most of the other testimonies – is included. Elwing's feminist agency here bears out Catriona Macleod's point about the need to reject the blanket category "teenage pregnancy": "Instead we should concentrate on unwanted pregnancies, a move that undoes the artificial separation between young and older women who find themselves in the predicament of a conception that is severely problematic for a variety of reasons, and allows us to concentrate on the conditions under which pregnancies become a burden for women" (131).

Though Elwing's pregnancy is declared not to have been unwanted, the conditions under which her decision to get pregnant was made are shown to have been anything but ideal. As the image track follows her daughter while she plays and gets dressed up, Elwing's initial declaration of happiness is placed within a history of trauma and disaffection. She explains to Maruping: "I wanted to have a child because there were so many people in my life that I felt didn't love me. There were so many things that went through my mind, like I wanted to kill myself. I did try, many times. I had a knife in my hand. I held it against my head to kill myself and I've taken pills and ended up in hospital. But then I told myself I would never do that again; it nearly destroyed me." It is not coincidental that, as Elwing mentions a history of suicidal feeling, the camera zooms in on her child. Here, yet again, affective dissonance is folded into film form, as the scene straddles the divide between life-affirming and life-negating affective states.

For Elwing, a child offers a lifeline, a relation that may well be read in psychoanalytic terms as her longing for a return to a state of fullness or unity she experienced in infancy in relation to her own mother – a state that Jacques Lacan characterized as constitutive of the imaginary stage of psychosexual development and that Julia Kristeva, in turn, viewed as distinctive of the semiotic realm of experience. Lisa Baraitser's point that "mothers do draw on their own internal relation to an idealized fantasy of union with a preoedipal mother in their love for their children" (94) helps to make sense of the workings of maternal love for Elwing here, who states "Love for me is … to love people and them loving me … and that we must all live together. Now I have the child and I am very happy … I am very happy with her. There are so many things we do together, she laughs with me, she loves to laugh. She is very friendly." Whereas for most of the women in the documentary expectation takes more conventional forms of youth aspiration in the context of contemporary capitalism, for Elwing aspiration finds expression in maternal longing. The burden of expectation – put plainly, of Elwing's search for love – is placed onto the child (a form of maternal love ripe for a psychoanalytic reading as at once narcissistic and idealistic). Yet as many theorists of the maternal have shown, the subjective singularity of the child inevitably presents the mother with the *un*expected.[16] As

Baraitser goes on to explain, "the particular alterity that is the child also presents a mother with an enigma that throws her into a certain disarray, that disorganizes her internal world with the potential for new configurations of self and other to emerge" (94). Nonetheless, Elwing's testimony points to some of the unforeseen dimensions of youth agency, claimed even against impossible odds.

The film concludes with a number of scenes that reassert its bleak affective tenor. Maruping's friend Deidre Moseki's unbridled sobbing is filmed, for instance, in prolonged and extreme close-up shots as she testifies to her sister's pregnancy and her unemployed mother's optimism and love for them amid the many hardships that they face. In the absence of a father, Moseki finds in her religious faith a source of strength: "Everything goes hand in hand with faith. They must just believe, even if it looks impossible. With God everything is possible." The filmmakers then return to a brief statement by Bianca Seekoei about her plans to still try to return to school and find employment, before it concludes with Maruping herself talking to a group of schoolgirls about her own journey and the perils of early pregnancy (in the segment, schoolboys are not shown to be included in these didactic exercises). Though this final scene offers viewers a brief reprieve from despair as Maruping converts her narrative of hardship into one of overcoming – as she uses her experience to educate younger women – the overall affective tone of the film remains unchallenged. Throughout the film, "objects of attention and attachment" (Carlson and Stewart 115) come into emotional view for the young women via a "mood prism" of disappointment, despair, regret, and downright depression. This prism is one overwhelmingly shaped by what their pregnancies are taken to mean by family, friends, and their broader social circle, as well as how their own circumstances of hardship have shaped their desire for the promises of parenthood, as in Zayleen Elwing's case.

The film is not without its shortcomings, including a tendency to individualize particularly female responsibility. Yet the critical strategies that produce such clinical readings are, to my mind, unhelpful here. When dwelling on the bad feeling left to linger in this film, as Evelyn Maruping compels her viewers to do, we might notice the difficulties with which the young mothers in her community fold severe social stigma and economic pressure into daily strategies of survival. With this in mind, we might begin to see the film as part of the larger political project, referenced earlier, of detaching "from lives that don't work and from worlds that negate the subjects that produce them" (Berlant and Edelman, *Sex* 5), even if this project remains compromised by the scripts of normative sexual and gendered intelligibility handed to young South Africans like Maruping. For while the didactic thrust of the documentary film could, on the one hand, be said to serve the biopolitical project of bringing teen sexuality in line with national trajectories of success and succession, the affective force exerted by young interviewees who have little chance of successfully managing away psychic pain calls for very different of styles of viewing, listening, and feeling.

Surviving Disappointment

I introduced this chapter with a reference to Kopano Matlwa's landmark novel *Coconut* in an effort to convey some of the affective complexities of youth expectation under conditions of contemporary racial capitalism. The description provided on the opening page of *Coconut* of the "chocolate" girl's hair as "plastic, shiny, cheap synthetic strands of dreams-come-true" hints at the false allure of consumer spending as a way out of difficult lives, yet also gestures to some of the ways in which girls claim symbolic and cultural capital in constrained surroundings. As Jessica Murray puts it in her reading of the complex entanglements of race and beauty in the novel, Matlwa's description of the child's braids "highlights both the artificiality of hair and the aspirational value with which hair is invested" (92). Aspiration is key here as a long-term *Erwartungsaffekt* that directs youth attention and mood.

I have been interested in this chapter not simply in expectant, aspirational youth mood as suffocating, but also in the possibilities it offers young people as an affective climate within which complex modes and means of social survival are negotiated daily. Nthabiseng Motsemme's work on forms of "flawed agency" ("Loving" 78) enacted by women amid the HIV/AIDS epidemic in South African townships in the mid-2000s, read alongside Dia Da Costa's study of "cruel pessimism" (3) in postcolonial India, offers some insights here by way of conclusion.

In an effort to stretch the terms and frameworks within which HIV/AIDS in South Africa had been discussed up to the time of her study, Motsemme insists on reading the everyday sexual lives of women in ways that extend beyond discussions of the pandemic only. She points to the need to reflect on the range of quotidian ways in which young women craft their own agency in relation to sex, love, pleasure, and intimacy, and manage to exert control in remaking their social worlds. She suggests that young women's daily navigation of economic insecurity and social immobility (in large part corollaries of apartheid's enduring post-rainbow afterlife), not to mention the difficulties of living intimately with illness and death, have yielded complex forms of self-fashioning best described in terms of "flawed agency." Writing, for instance, of survival strategies such as *ukuphanda/ukuphanta* – namely ways of "getting by" in conditions of extreme economic hardship that include illegal practices such as shoplifting, microeconomic ways of earning an income within the informal township economy, or wielding sexuality for the sake of both economic and emotional survival (or simply as "a way of sustaining a sense of meaning in the face of meaninglessness" ["Loving" 83]), Motsemme highlights the importance of layering our understanding of young women's agency. For while it is crucial to applaud the ways in which women enact survival strategies that might transcend the material and social conditions to which they are confined, the latter conditions must remain in focus (84).

Though the women in the films I discuss in this chapter are not shown to be contending with the repercussions and risks of the HIV/AIDS pandemic, they inhabit similar genres of social regulation and escape. In the case of Sarah Chu, as well as of Evelyn Maruping and the other women in *Where Is the Love?*, Motsemme's understanding of flawed agency chimes with my reading of wayward feeling throughout this book, particularly given the unpredictable ways in which these women draw on cultural, aesthetic, and emotional resources to which they have been given only restricted access. When trying to understand the wayward agency of these women in specifically affective terms, Dia Da Costa's challenge to some of the theorizations of affect that have taken Western historical, economic, and political contexts as their centre point is particularly apposite.

Da Costa concentrates specifically on Lauren Berlant's work on cruel optimism in contexts of "shrinking possibilities" (Da Costa 2). Whereas Berlant is concerned mainly with the lives of people living under neoliberal conditions who have fairly recently come to experience their vision of the good life as under threat, Da Costa's work on activist theatre by the Chhara in India – a group historically designated criminals under British colonial law – highlights a context "where the loss of vision of a good life is not new under neoliberalism, but rather, reworks long-standing violence and inclusion/exclusion of colonial capitalism and nation-state histories" (1). For those "born into a pervasive and intractable sense of marginality, insecurity and exclusion" (2), the affective experience of time takes on different forms. Da Costa identifies affective structures such as sentimental optimism, cruel pessimism, betrayal, and ordinary regard as alternatives to Berlant's cruel optimism and its psychosocial temporalities, suggesting that those who navigate the "uneven global histories of colonialism, development and neoliberalism" (2) often find themselves "vacillating among competing affective structures" (3).

She is interested particularly in the sensual present of those inhabiting the *longue durée* of thwarted expectation, for whom optimism itself starts to become a "source of survival, utterly dissociated from expectations of actual gain" (11). The temporality of prolonged disappointment, she suggests, eventually causes a split between optimism and expectation. How long, she asks, "after such an eventual split can people wait for belonging before the lack of expectations and actual gains humiliates, even batters, sensual intelligence towards other modes of belonging?" (11).

In the South African context, disappointment certainly has a long historical legacy. In her 2016 book on Charlotte Maxeke, South Africa's first Black woman to obtain a university degree (in 1901 from Wilberforce University in the United States), journalist Zubeida Jaffer, for instance, chronicles the devastating shrinking of access to opportunity that characterized Black South African experience in the many decades following Ms. Maxeke's remarkable feat. In reference to the near absence of schooling[17] opportunities for Charlotte and her sister Katie in Kimberley, where they both lived for some time, as well as for the many women to subsequently face similar restrictions, Jaffer writes, "For more than a century, dreams had to be discarded and talents largely suppressed. It was a time of tight control of the pecking order of privilege" (37). The political moods that historically shaped a person's sense of the future in South Africa have long varied along lines that include race, gender, age, and class positioning, but for most of those disenfranchised under colonialism and apartheid, an affective loop of repeated disappointment was the norm until at least 1994.

Within this longer historical continuum, closer examination may well reveal the recurrent splitting of optimism from "expectations of actual gain" of which Da Costa writes. In fact, to cast the emotional culture of disappointment that marks the South African present as a strictly recent phenomenon is to overlook these extended and often conflicting psychosocial temporalities at the heart of South Africa's apartheid and colonial histories. These tensions and temporalities are particularly pronounced in my reading, in the next chapter, of extractive capitalism's prolonged history of exploitative violence, and of the crisis management strategies it has more recently implemented in response to the demands for a living wage by some in the mining industry, for whom 1994 delivered the hope of greater economic justice. The horizons of possibility opened up by the end of apartheid continue to shape the actions and expectations of those – including the labour, student, and feminist activists discussed in the three chapters that follow – who continue to invest in the possibility of a more socially just future, though unfortunately often with the kind of devastating outcomes that the striking Marikana miners had to face.

In the case of the young women whose visual autobiographies I examined in this chapter, the optimism brought by apartheid's legislative demise likewise provides an important affective horizon within which expectation came to be shaped. Yet for mothers such as Zayleen Elwing, the deferred temporality of expectation and attendant forms of affective dissonance have inevitably yielded forms of wayward agency by means of which unconventional and unexpected forms of belonging and meaning-making have been taking shape. If optimism becomes, towards the end of the film, a social and affective genre within which Chu articulates her life narrative in *Made in China,* and sadness and regret are mandated for young adult mothers in *Where Is the Love?,* Elwing's decision to find a version of happiness in the bonds of love she forges with her daughter offers an example of waywardness as a daily strategy of defiant endurance. Strategies such as these are not necessarily progressive or even sustainable, but their role in helping to make difficult lives bearable for South Africa's expectant teens cannot be undervalued.

3
Managing Public Feeling

The sixteenth of August 2012 is widely regarded as a turning point in the post-apartheid South African political and activist imagination. On this day, thirty-four miners were killed and seventy-eight were wounded by police, while only a single police officer was wounded (and discharged from hospital in less than a day) – clearly indicating the level of force used by the police to have been entirely disproportionate to that used by the miners. Despite these statistics, police spokespersons, company management, and government officials repeatedly stressed that police acted out of self-defence and that the striking miners were armed, militant, and "concertedly attacking" (qtd. in De Wet). The then national police commissioner Riah Phiyega, for instance, insisted that "the militant group stormed towards the police firing shots and wielding dangerous weapons … Police retreated systematically and were forced to utilize maximum force to defend themselves" (qtd. in De Wet). Roger Phillimore, Lonmin chairman at the time, in turn described the events as the result of "violence between competing labour factions," saying that though they deeply regretted the loss of life, the incident was "clearly a public order rather than labour relations associated matter" ("Lonmin"). Both then president Jacob Zuma and commissioner Phiyega, in their respective statements delivered on the day following the massacre, were quick to declare it too soon to apportion blame; both called for a time of national mourning instead. Zuma, for instance, used this occasion to announce his decision to institute a commission of inquiry, headed by Justice Ian Farlam, to investigate the incident, and stated that "today is not an occasion for blame, finger-pointing or recrimination … It is a day for us to mourn together as a nation. It is also a day to start rebuilding and healing" (Zuma, "Statement").[1] Commissioner Phiyega presented her response in almost identical terms, maintaining, in spite of her assertions about the alleged militancy of the miners, that "this is no time for blaming. This is no time for finger pointing. It is a time for us to mourn a sad and dark moment we experience as a country" (qtd. in "Police").[2]

These declarations by former president Zuma and Phiyega are used to frame a documentary on the massacre entitled *Miners Shot Down*, released in February 2014 and directed by Rehad Desai. The film, which garnered several prestigious awards, including an international Emmy Award for best documentary, forms part of an ever-growing body of countercultural texts, audio-visual activism, artwork, films, and academic articles that contest the version of events that dominated the national media in the aftermath of the event, and that bring to light some of the long-term consequences of this massacre on the surrounding community.[3] In this chapter, I explore some of the ways in which the massacre has been mediated in both this documentary and in the dominant media at the time, in an effort to expand some of the work done in the previous chapters on the post-rainbow affective-aesthetic afterlives of colonial and apartheid dispossession. Whereas the previous chapter turned to young women's visual autobiography to consider how the psychosocial temporalities of prolonged South African disappointment inflect the present-day moods and modes of teen aspiration, I am interested here in the conflicting timelines of racial capitalism, and in the enduring violence perpetrated by South Africa's extractive industries in particular. To this end, I trace some of the ways in which public feelings surrounding the event were managed in the run-up to and aftermath of the massacre, and suggest that the affective and temporal dimensions of current attempts at containing perceived threats to financial and political stability on the part of South Africa's business and political elite are key to understanding securitization and crisis management strategies that continue to take on remarkably violent and repressive forms.

I start this chapter with Zuma and Phiyega's official statements about mourning because they open up a range of questions about the ways in which spectacles of structural precarity under late capitalism have come to be recomposed in South African public culture. Like Desai, I am curious, for instance, about why this emphasis is placed, one day after the shooting, on the imperative to mourn, rebuild, heal, and overcome. Could this be read simply as an expected and harmless palliative offered in moments of crisis? Or is there something else at work here? To what extent might it be possible to situate these sentiments within the larger context of affective containment that characterized public culture, for instance, in the immediate aftermath of apartheid, when nation-building initiatives such as the Truth and Reconciliation

Commission were put in place in an effort to manage the difficult emotional legacy of apartheid?[4] Might these strategies be read as in line with efforts to temper rising levels of frustration and disappointment on the part of post-rainbow South African publics? How are we to read the injunction to mourn in light of the competing temporalities that characterize the experience of mourning and melancholia respectively? How are South Africans to conduct this work of mourning in the absence of an account of the events that privileges the experience and feelings of workers, and that historicizes the massacre beyond the ephemeralities of the journalism of sensationalism, spectacle, and distraction?

One of the troubling findings to have emerged from analyses of early press coverage of the massacre is that the version of events that initially circulated derived primarily from business and mine management sources.[5] In her detailed study of newspaper articles published both immediately prior to and following the massacre, Jane Duncan demonstrates, for instance, that the almost complete absence of miners' voices in these news reports, accompanied by a tendency to represent miners in biased terms, amounted to "what George Gerbner has termed 'symbolic annihilation' through under-representation or non-representation" ("South African" 72). In spite of Zuma and Phiyega's contention at the time that the immediate aftermath of the massacre was not a time for recrimination, a very clear trend to stigmatize and scapegoat miners emerged in these early representations. The latter can be found, for instance, in initial reports inaccurately characterizing the conflict simply as the result of inter-union rivalry; the inclusion of value-laden language portraying miners as implicitly violent and superstitious (as did a widely circulated narrative alleging that miners who charged at police officers were under the influence of "muti"[6] and had therefore come to view themselves as invincible); an emphasis in many reports on the impact that the strikes might have on investor confidence and the company's financial viability, invoking some of the stock anxieties of the post-apartheid neoliberal order; and the failure on the part of journalists to provide the contextual information that might have explained not only the source of the miners' grievances but also the reasons why they went on an unprotected strike and decided to arm themselves in the first place (73–5).[7] The representations emerging from these journalistic blind spots "created the general impression that the miners were predisposed to illegal conduct, including violence (rather than as reacting to violence, albeit at times with excessive violence themselves)" (74–5).

If, as Imogen Tyler suggests in her analysis of public protest in contemporary neoliberal Britain, social abjection involves "a spatializing politics of disgust, which functions to create forms of distance between the body politic proper and those excluded from the body of the state" (41), the widespread mis- and underrepresentation of the striking miners, not to mention their treatment at the hands of the security forces of the state, amount to a clear case of them being abjected from the dominant social order. The technologies of exclusion that Tyler identifies in contemporary Britain are apparent, in this case, not just in a range of spatial imaginaries demarcating insides and outsides, but also in the temporal framing of the conflict by those invested in managing the potential financial and political risk generated by prolonged labour unrest. In fact, a look at the competing temporal dimensions of this particular conflict within the larger post-apartheid context reveals the relationship that South Africans are urged to develop with the miners – who figure as "revolting subjects" (Tyler, passim) in the dominant social imaginary – to be structured by fear, threat, and other forms of affective distancing.[8]

The chapter proceeds in three parts, each concerned in some way with the relationship between temporality and public feeling. First, I take a detour through scholarship on time and globalization in an effort to make sense of the temporal politics of securitization that led to the massacre in the first place. I then consider the difference between psychic and social forms of mourning and melancholia respectively, particularly in light of what these differences reveal about the technologies of sovereign control and affective containment implied by each. I organize my analysis in each of these parts broadly around two central moments featured in Desai's documentary: (1) a series of emails exchanged between Lonmin management and Cyril Ramaphosa, then non-executive director and shareholder of Lonmin mining company and current president of South Africa, and (2) the aforementioned statements made by Zuma and Phiyega in the immediate aftermath of the massacre. Finally, I conclude by offering a more detailed reading of the formal organization of the documentary as a whole, and of those rhetorical and stylistic filmic elements that contract the temporal and affective distance that exists between the miners and South African viewing publics. In short, I argue that the form of counter-affective labour found in *Miners Shot Down* constitutes a particularly compelling example of the capacity for affective conversion inherent in certain forms of audio-visual activism, functioning, by extension, as an example of the kind of politically wayward aesthetics that might become the ground from which to think more expansively and sensitively about justice and the politics of decolonization.

Pre-emptive Securitization

Investigations into the circumstances surrounding, and causes of, the massacre have uncovered a number of details that indicate that police intervention was much more premeditated and pre-emptive than initially indicated, and that Lonmin officials exerted considerable political pressure to ensure hasty police intervention at Marikana.[9] Emails sent, for instance, on 15 August to Lonmin Management by Cyril Ramaphosa make plain that police were being strong-armed to act firmly to address the situation. In these emails, Ramaphosa asserts the importance of characterizing the events not as a labour dispute but as "dastardly criminal," telling Albert Jamieson, Lonmin's then chief commercial officer, that he is "absolutely correct in insisting that [then minister of mineral resources Susan Shabangu] and indeed all government officials need to understand that we are essentially dealing with a criminal act" (qtd. in Desai). Ramaphosa further states that, during a conversation he had with minister Shabangu, she promised to brief the president and "get the Minister of Police Nathi Mthetwa to act in a more pointed way" (qtd. in Desai).[10] In light of these pressures, the fact that on the morning of 16 August, the striking miners were met by 648 police officers, 4,000 rounds of live ammunition, and four pre-ordered mortuary vans (each with the capacity to transport eight dead bodies) seems less surprising. These facts reveal what advocate Dali Mpofu, representing the arrested and injured mineworkers at the time, refers to as "the toxic collusion between the SAPS and Lonmin, at the direct level; at a much broader level it can be called a collusion between the state and capital" (qtd. in Desai), and reinforce Achille Mbembe's point "that these extrajudicial executions" served not only as "a grave instance of discrimination and inequality before the law" but as "an indictment of the state" ("SA's Death").

The obsession on the part of Jamieson and Ramaphosa with convincing government officials of the inherent criminality of events reflects their implicit understanding of the emotive value of language in manufacturing public consent. The latter is urgently needed to justify state intervention in industrial and other forms of mass action, particularly given the reality of growing class polarization and attendant forms of dissent that have plagued South African politics of late, and that the Economic Freedom Fighters have placed at the centre of their resistant political theatre. The pre-emptive characterization of the miners as criminal casts these men as threats to national safety and taps into widespread moral panics about crime and social disorder that render the social abjection of the miners palatable. The language of threat used here takes on added significance if read in terms of the ways in which imagined future perils that have come to populate our present with dread have been invoked to bend political will and to shape public feeling in both South Africa and other global contexts of neoliberal governance (Massumi). Echoes of the kinds of affective manoeuvring at issue here are evident in both the haste with which violent police intervention at Marikana was orchestrated, and in the speed with which a time of national mourning was subsequently declared.

A number of scholars of the temporal politics of globalization suggest that attempts at governing time have become one of the key ways in which political power has come to be exercised by late-modern (neo)liberal democracies. In the post–9/11 global political climate, for instance, anxieties about the unpredictability of possible future terrorist attacks have significantly reconfigured securitization strategies in the United States and elsewhere. In the face of security threats framed as largely unknowable and incalculable, state interventions have become increasingly pre-emptive. The Bush-era "War on Terror" constitutes the most widely discussed example of this form of political decision-making, because it was premised not on irrefutable evidence of, say, the existence of weapons of mass destruction to justify the invasion of Iraq, but on much less tangible but no less affectively forceful fears about imagined future terrorist attacks (Massumi 53; see also Aradau and van Munster). The same logic has been used, for instance, by the post-2016 Trump administration in the United States to justify the implementation of increasingly xenophobic, Islamophobic, and racist domestic policy.[11]

The interventions in question here are centrally concerned with the governance of an unpredictable future felt to be a threat in the present, and therefore constitute what scholars such as Brian Massumi and Liam Stockdale have theorized as an attempt to control time itself. Stockdale writes, for instance, that "the overriding imperative to govern time by precluding the future emergence of even a potential threat enables sovereign authorities to invoke the ever-present spectre of imminent catastrophe to legitimate otherwise illegal interventionary acts" (22). Stockdale warns that these forms of pre-emptive securitization "can quite easily descend into a manifestly illiberal paradigm of government" (22) (a caveat which, I suggest below, has particular salience in relation to state intervention in the unprotected strikes at Marikana). Massumi, in turn, writes in particularly affective terms about the "political ontology of threat" as it operates in relation to violent pre-emptive securitization strategies: "Threat is not real in spite of its non-existence. It is superlatively real, because of it ... What is not actually real can be *felt* into being. Threat does have an actual mode of existence:

fear, as foreshadowing. Threat has an impending reality in the present. This actual reality is affective" (53–4; my emphasis). In certain ways, the South African government's highly militarized enforcement of its 2020 COVID-19 quarantine measures stemmed from the same affective logic. Though the implementation of strict lockdown measures arguably helped to curb the spread of the virus, the government's decision to deploy nearly 3000 soldiers – primarily in townships – resulted in the number of deaths at the hands of security forces to initially exceed those caused by the pandemic, President Ramaphosa's call for police and military restraint notwithstanding. In this instance, the health threat posed by the virus is shifted pre-emptively onto the citizenry itself.

When bringing these insights to bear on the events at Marikana, one can recognize a tendency on the part of Lonmin management, the police, and a number of voices from the ANC government to advocate pre-emptive intervention in order to contain a perceived threat presented as precipitating manifest disaster not only in terms of the potential lives that might be lost at Marikana itself but also in terms of the wider financial and political outcomes to which a prolonged work stoppage might lead. Public fears about these perceived threats were in turn instigated and then leveraged to rationalize pre-emptive action. To be sure, the situation at Marikana prior to the 16 August massacre was volatile, and violent acts committed on all sides had already taken the lives of at least four miners, two security guards, and two police officers ("Marikana Inquiry"). But the claim that deploying "maximum force" against the workers was the only feasible course of action under the circumstances has been shown to have been patently untrue.[12] Instead, such action might be read as a means of shoring up the political power of those who perceived that power to be under attack. In his analysis of nationalism in contemporary France, Alain Badiou offers the following words that may well be extended to the South African context (and indeed, to the United States, the United Kingdom, and other contexts where authoritarian populisms have been on the rise, though, unlike in South Africa, these shifts are driven primarily by state-emboldened white nationalisms): "Fear of foreigners, of workers, or the people … marks the subjective situation of dominant and privileged people who sense that their privileges are conditional and under threat and that their domination is perhaps only provisional and already shaky" (8–9).

Fears about the threat that the striking miners were said to pose were fuelled in a number of ways, including via the aforementioned rhetoric of criminalization put to widespread use by journalists, politicians, and Lonmin management; the refusal on the part of Lonmin to meet with striking workers and the concomitant dissemination of inaccurate claims that the striking rock drill operators (RDOs) had no list of demands to present (thus feeding into fears about unregulated, random, and uncontainable labour unrest); widespread characterization of the strike as illegal when in fact the right to strike is constitutionally safeguarded, whether these strikes are protected, or unprotected, as in the case of the strikes at Lonmin platinum at the time; the portrayal of miners as swept into a suicidal and violent frenzy by sangomas plying them with traditional medicine, effectively relegating them to premodern time; failures to provide detailed information about the causes of the violence and the extent of the miners' grievances, or, for that matter, to give a public platform to the views of the miners themselves, thus exacerbating middle-class and racist anxieties about the miners' perceived propensity for lawlessness and irrationality; and via reports circulated particularly in the business press about the risks that the strikes pose to market stability and, as a result, the need to placate the fears of foreign investors.[13] In this script, national fear finds an easy target in the figure of the striking miner. These fears were exploited both in the run-up to the massacre and in the subsequent shaping of public opinion about the respective behaviours of the police and mine workers during and subsequent to 16 August 2012.

The work of building consent for managing the threat to national financial health and the rule of law said to be posed by the striking miners relies heavily on a larger master narrative of overcoming and achieved democracy at the core of post-apartheid myths of nation and economic access discussed in earlier chapters. This narrative justifiably celebrates the successes of the anti-apartheid struggle but was also mobilized to different effect, as my discussion of the spectacle of the promise in chapter 1 indicates, to pre-emptively authorize the fiction of a reconciled nation and to distract South African publics from the conditions whereby cheap Black labour continues to be exploited in the post-apartheid era, "especially on farms and mines, where migrant wage-seekers face quasi-permanent adverse economic contingencies as they try to leverage their way out of poverty and insecurity" (Mbembe, "Class"). That these myths of financial stability and national conquest have always been haunted by the spectre of persistent if not growing social and racial inequality does not lessen their affective and symbolic purchase in terrains of national securitization and crisis management. These myths are evident also, for instance, in Zuma's address one day after the massacre when he declared this a time of national mourning and stated: "We have gone through painful moments before, and were able to overcome such challenges together as a nation, regardless of race, colour, creed or political affiliations. We must use that national trait again during this difficult period" ("Statement").

To make sense of Zuma's call for a time of national mourning, one needs to assess the divergent temporalities that characterize acts of mourning and melancholia respectively, and to ask how we might distinguish between state-driven and individual attempts at coming to terms with loss. To pursue this line of inquiry, I briefly consider what theories of productive melancholia might bring to a discussion of contemporary South African public culture, and trace some of the parallels between Zuma's post-Marikana address and the rhetoric of national reconciliation that emerged from South Africa's Truth and Reconciliation Commission.

Accelerated Mourning

The distinction between mourning and melancholia is explored most famously by Sigmund Freud in his 1917 essay on the topic. As is widely known, for Freud, the act of mourning constitutes a healthy way of dealing with loss in that attachment to a lost loved object is gradually relinquished and displaced onto a substitute. Melancholia, in turn, is considered a form of "pathological mourning" ("Mourning" 587) in which the process of grieving remains both unfinished and relentlessly debilitating. As a clinical condition, melancholia is distinguished from mourning by the fact that it pertains to an inability to know and acknowledge that which is lost as a result of the death of a loved one. Melancholia further produces self-punishing and incapacitating feelings of worthlessness brought about by the narcissistic withdrawal of the lost object into the ego and by feelings of hostility towards this lost object, which have come to be internalized. As Freud puts it, "The patient represents his ego to us as worthless, incapable of any achievement and morally despicable … This picture of a delusion of (mainly moral) inferiority is completed by sleeplessness and refusal to take nourishment, and – what is psychologically very remarkable – by an overcoming of the instinct which compels every living thing to cling to life" (584).

Melancholia thus constitutes an incapacitating psychic condition that effectively amounts to those affected by it being at war with themselves. This clinical state of protracted, self-abasing suffering differs from the melancholically inflected forms of identification that Freud elsewhere characterizes as central to the formation of the ego (Hook, *(Post)apartheid* 152–6). In *The Ego and the Id*, Freud explains, for instance, that the disavowed losses yielded by the process of psychosexual development are incorporated into the ego, and that melancholic attachments thus become constitutive of the ego itself (a fact that Judith Butler fruitfully extends to explain how the primary homosexual passions of early childhood are incorporated as disavowed losses into the very fabric of heterosexual adulthood).[14] Freud writes that "when it happens that a person has to give up a sexual object, there quite often ensues an alteration of his ego which can only be described as a setting up of the object inside the ego, as it occurs in melancholia" ("The Ego" 29). As Butler phrases it, what this amounts to is that "melancholic identification permits the loss of the object in the external world precisely because it provides a way to preserve the object as part of the ego and, hence, to avert the loss as a complete loss" (*Psychic* 134).

Though Freud's formulations here pertain specifically to the psychodynamics of individual grieving and ego formation, they have inspired a still-growing number of cultural theorists in fields such as critical race studies, postcolonial cultural studies, and queer theory to reassess collective modes of engaging with the inheritance and experience of loss.[15] Many of these conversations stray from Freud's original discussion of the distinction between mourning and melancholia, as will become apparent below, yet they bear consideration here for highlighting some of the tensions that frequently emerge in postcolonial contexts between, on the one hand, state-driven projects of affective management in the aftermath of mass violence (of which both state-sponsored violence during the apartheid era and the Marikana massacre count as examples) and, on the other, the heavy psychic toll exacted on individuals personally affected by this violence.

In their influential edited volume on this topic, titled *Loss*, David Eng and David Kazanjian call for a rethinking of melancholic attachments to the past as simply pathological. Diverging somewhat from Freud, Eng and Kazanjian read melancholia as a politically defiant response to dominant culture's distorting amnesia about the losses suffered as a result of colonialism, racism, and other forms of historical injustice. Underlining specifically the temporal dimensions of the distinction as they view it, they write, "Unlike mourning, in which the past is declared resolved, finished, and dead, in melancholia the past remains steadfastly alive in the present … [M]elancholia might be said to constitute … an ongoing and open relationship with the past, bringing its ghost and specters, its flaring and fleeting images, into the present" (3–4). Melancholia's temporality, its stubborn attachment to histories of loss and its remains, they argue, "generates sites for memory and history, for the rewriting of the past as well as the reimagining of the future" (4).

Similar lines of inquiry can be found in other works, such as Anne Anlin Cheng's *The Melancholy of Race: Psychoanalysis, Assimilation, and Hidden Grief.* Cheng writes, for instance, about the ways in which dominant understandings of collective psychic health in the United States are predicated upon the reluctance to analyse present state and social formations as historically shaped by racial discrimination and the labour of oppressed populations. Mainstream myths of democratic inclusion and citizenship rely upon the sublimation and disavowal of the psychic injuries historically suffered by racialized minorities in the United States. Cheng suggests that a melancholic refusal to relinquish attachments to historical losses yet to be acknowledged by mainstream culture can serve the larger political project of advocating for social justice for racialized subjects for whom histories of sorrow live on. While cautious about the risks of talking about the "'melancholia' of racialized peoples, especially since it seems to reinscribe a whole history of affliction or run the risk of naturalizing that pain" (14), Cheng nonetheless emphasizes the costs of pre-emptive attempts at resolving the traumas historically caused by racism.

Ranjana Khanna, likewise, recognizes in melancholia "an ethico-political gesture" that holds onto the past for the sake of imagining alternative futures; in fact, she reads the very field of postcolonial studies as melancholic. Khanna highlights Freud's usage of the language of ingestion in his explanation of the formation of the ego by way of melancholic incorporation, which she expands to the terrain of postcolonial state formation. Through a similar logic of ingestion, the postcolonial state imbibes the violent history of colonialism as the disavowed but self-constitutive loss that it cannot acknowledge or mourn. For Khanna, "melancholia's temporality is dragged backwards and forwards in ways that force an understanding of the weight of the loss of ideal. Affect weighs against the palliative of newness, which is often alibi for conducting politics in a compromised vein. An incipient future oriented hope manifests itself textually in remainders, in dissonance, in untimeliness." The untimeliness of melancholia as it is conceptualized here, in other words, makes visible the historical wounds and exclusions at the centre of postcolonial sovereignty, and exposes the insincerity of the anaesthetizing impulses that fuel the state apparatus's rush to forget.

Though Khanna's reading of the differences between mourning and melancholia raises some concerns, as I indicate shortly, her overall critique of the postcolonial state's more sanitizing engagements with historical trauma could well be directed at the panaceas offered in recent years by a range of sovereign authorities in response to painful histories of social injustice that remain a challenge to social and political relations in the (post)colonial present. Examples include the national apologies presented in countries such as Canada and Australia to Indigenous groups who continue to battle to have their historical grievances and land claims honoured by the colonial state. As I argue elsewhere (Strauss, "Interrupting" forthcoming), initiatives such as these – which in the Canadian context includes a public apology delivered by then prime minister Stephen Harper in 2008 to Indigenous peoples for the horrors of the residential school system – could be read as part of the "closure drive" that characterizes the work of governments heavily invested in managing embarrassing pasts without having to substantively account for these pasts in ongoing structural or material terms. (Harper's 2008 apology, for instance, made no reference to ongoing land claims.)

In the South African context, one might be tempted to include the Truth and Reconciliation Commission in this list of postcolonial palliatives, yet it arguably emerged at least in part from a different governing impulse, particularly given that the process was driven by the concerns of a historically subjugated constituency that had since assumed political power (unlike, for instance, Indigenous communities in Canada and Australia). Though the TRC had numerous shortcomings, not least of which the speedy manner of its completion and its failure to fully grapple with the quotidian psychological – not to mention material – inheritances of apartheid, its management of national feeling was premised upon what many consider a sincere attempt at challenging apartheid's "proscription on mourning, specifically of the other" (Sanders 35). One of the strengths of the TRC hearings was precisely that it created opportunities for survivors and family members of the deceased to undertake the painful labour of mourning through public testimony, which the full or partial disclosure at the TRC of events surrounding the torture and/or loss of survivors and loved ones was meant to facilitate.

That the TRC hearings made possible the processing of loss for some of those who testified brings into view certain shortcomings of theories of productive melancholia.[16] In her work on diasporic citizenship and the materiality of melancholia, Lily Cho explains that analyses of racial melancholia, while important for helping to "recuperate the psychic for discussions of race and difference" and for "tak[ing] up seriously the collectivity of grief, the modes of its transmission and its emergence out of formations which extend beyond the individual psyche" (116), nonetheless run the risk of abandoning the grieving subject to an endless cycle of unresolved sorrow. Focusing specifically on the Asian diasporic subject in North American contexts, Cho takes issue with the "temporality of grief" within which this never-ending cycle of melancholia is produced:

> If we follow the logic of racial melancholia, where agency is to be found in the refusal to be cured, then the diasporic subject is doomed to the endlessness of melancholia. If we do not, then the diasporic subject appears to be lured by assimilation into becoming a healthy subject whose losses have been successfully mourned. I find this polarization of the temporality of grief deeply unsatisfying. (123)

Daniel Coleman draws similar conclusions in his work on the tensions between theories of productive melancholia and alternative approaches to healing not beholden to the epistemological inheritances of the Western academy (psychoanalysis being the central culprit here). As he puts it, "this theory which provides a powerful criticism of the status quo, can too easily become a powerful re-citation of the status quo. At its best, the theory of melancholia exposes and explains the pathologies of the existing system of power relations, but at its worst, it does this at the expense of those who suffer" (59).

The blind spots that Cho and Coleman recognize in much recent postcolonial theorizing on melancholia can be ascribed in part to a widespread misreading of Freud's writings on the topic. The distinction that Freud makes between melancholia as a psychic pathology and the melancholic attachments central to the formation of the ego in fact disappears in much of this work. As Derek Hook explains, a careful reading of Freud reveals

> the importance of distinguishing between *forms of identification* which have a melancholic character and the pathological *condition of melancholia* in and of itself ... On the one hand we are concerned with melancholia as a diagnostic structure, a pathological assumption of the place of the dead which consigns the melancholic to a state of purgatory. On the other we have in mind a *mode of identification* in which lost objects are retained as a way of building the ego. Although this may sound like a small qualification it is vital, separating as it does a psychotic condition from an everyday modality of identification present in each and every ego. (154–5; emphasis in original)

What most postcolonial theorists of productive melancholia seem to be concerned with are perhaps not so much the psychic condition of debilitating self-castigation theorized originally by Freud than the ways in which the experiences of loss, dispossession, and racialized violence on the part of historically subjugated populations seem to get conscripted into the often disingenuous agendas of (post)colonial nation-building and forced forgetting. Ranjana Khanna, by highlighting the work of mourning's relegation of "swallowed disposable bodies to the garbage can of modern nationalism," ("Post-palliative"), seems to object first and foremost to the temporal dimensions of state-driven initiatives of mourning. By Khanna's account, the latter tend to be out of step both with the psychic singularities of grieving and with the complex intergenerational transmission of suffering and social injustice that render any attempts at devising timelines for the processing of pain presumptuous. Under these conditions, the hasty declaration of a time of national mourning following incidents of mass violence – especially if what is mourned is not fully known or acknowledged – runs the risk of simply feeding into the collective dis-acknowledgment of and disidentification with those who were lost. While it is crucial to remember that mourning "is not tantamount to forgetting" (Hook, *(Post)apartheid* 155), the conditions under which mourning – as both an initiative of collective commemoration and a process of psychic healing – takes place can certainly impact its efficacy.

To bring these insights back to the South African context, one might say that, on the one hand, the TRC avoided the pitfalls outlined by Cho and Coleman by prioritizing the achievement of a sense of psychic detachment from the pain caused by apartheid-era gross human rights violations for those who testified at its hearings. The work of mourning facilitated by the TRC hearings brought into focus both the weight that grief places on the individual psyche and the intimate collectivity of historically transmitted racialized suffering under apartheid. Having said this, one of the unfortunate side-effects of the TRC's functioning as a mechanism for promoting nation-building has been the consolidation of a discourse of reconciliation and rainbowism in which continued conflicts are downplayed and attention has been diverted from, for instance, gender, race, and growing class inequalities (see, for instance, Cock and Bernstein 177, 179, and Terreblanche 444). The TRC commissioners acknowledged many of these shortcomings, and warned that the process should be read as only the beginning of an ongoing engagement with the past. Nonetheless, in light of the enormous symbolic significance that the public spectacle of the TRC took on both locally and internationally, this ongoing project is often subsumed in an overinvestment in the work done by – and the rhetorical vocabulary flowing from – the TRC itself. As scholars such as Nahla Valji have pointed out, corporatized and commodified varieties of the TRC rhetoric of reconciliation have at times been invoked to consolidate the political and economic status quo to the detriment of those yet to benefit materially from the political transition. The potentially liberating political work of postcolonial melancholia – defined in the qualified sense by scholars such as Khanna, Cheng, Eng, and Kazanjian – could be said to have been stymied as a result.

That the language used by both Zuma and Phiyega after the Marikana massacre clearly borrows from the script of accomplished national mourning sanctioned and normalized by the TRC, substantiates some of the risks identified above. When Zuma states that "we have gone through painful moments before, and were able to overcome such challenges together as a nation" ("Statement"), he enlists the widely resonant narrative of national overcoming as an affective counterpoint to the images of cruel bodily suffering that dominated South African TV screens in the immediate aftermath of the massacre. The narrative that Zuma appeals to here in fact belies the realities of stuckness that miners interviewed in Desai's documentary express, for instance, when they speak about having been locked into poverty for generations. For miners such as Mzoxolo Magidiwana, one of the strike leaders shot by police, time stands still, in part because the gains of democratization have thus far done little to improve the quality of their daily lives. As he puts it, "Poverty forces you to forget your ambition, leave school and work as a rock driller at the same mine where your boss will be the son of your father's boss." Magidiwana's reality is one that is frequently invisibilized in democratic myths of economic stability and substantive citizenship because these hardships are an uncomfortable reminder of an earlier time; they disrupt "the chronology of imagined progress" (Hook, *(Post)apartheid* 6) upon which prevailing myths of overcoming rely.

The mandate of the Farlam Commission – which, unlike the TRC, was tasked not with helping the victims of violence come to terms with their loss but with investigating "matters of public, national and international concern arising out of the tragic incidents at Lonmin Mine in Marikana" ("Proclamation") from 11 to 16 August 2012 – further supports a cynical reading of the purpose and substance of Zuma's narrative of achievable national healing. When taking into account that, at the time, the 279 striking miners who were arrested at Marikana were still being charged with the murder and attempted murder of their colleagues who were shot by police – a charge justified via the notorious apartheid-era "common-purpose doctrine," which extends criminal liability to all participants in an enterprise deemed unlawful – one has to wonder to what extent the surviving miners were in fact included as participants in the work of national mourning, or alternatively, whether their slain colleagues were considered truly worthy of public grief.[17]

What, precisely, was being mourned when the deceased miners were, by implication, being held accountable for their own deaths?

In short, the narrative of national mourning peddled by Zuma and Phiyega seems to be synchronized, as Rob Nixon (6–8) might argue, to the timelines of fast capitalism and its corporate media, attuned only to the fleeting spectacles and superficial closures that our increasingly short-lived attention spans demand. In his work on the shortcomings of the temporalities of turbo-capitalism and the latter's fixation on violence in its most spectacular, immediate, and newsworthy forms, Nixon suggests that we start paying attention to violence that "is neither spectacular nor instantaneous, but rather incremental and accretive, its calamitous repercussions playing out across a range of temporal scales" (2). Nixon is concerned here with the kind of violence that is temporally dispersed over years, decades, or millennia – as is the case, for instance, with poverty, post-traumatic stress, or environmental catastrophes that have been long in the making. Slow violence is less visible to a culture in the media-driven grip of the spectacle's immediate demands, yet the consequences of this violence are frequently cataclysmic and generally affect those lacking resources disproportionately.

One of the key challenges to making slow violence perceptible, writes Nixon, "is representational: how to devise arresting stories, images, and symbols adequate to the pervasive but elusive violence of delayed effects" (3). In what follows I consider whether Desai's *Miners Shot Down* can help to disrupt the temporalities of threat and crisis management that shaped events both prior and subsequent to the Marikana massacre. Following Nixon, I am particularly interested in how the work of shifting attention – to attend is to be consciously present in time – can make visible some of the longer histories of slow violence that affect the mineworkers and will continue to affect them long after public interest in events surrounding the massacre has subsided. In line with my discussion of the "thick present" (Haraway 1) of post-apartheid disappointment in the preceding chapters, I suggest, in short, that we reconceptualize postcolonial melancholia as a temporal strategy of wayward, counter-affective lingering that might open the violence and temporalities of spectacle to the otherwise obscured pasts, presents, and futures of slow violence, and that so might enable better conditions for the work of mourning.

Counter-Affective Lingering

To reiterate Judith Butler and Athena Athanasiou's question cited in this book's introduction, how might aesthetic responsiveness translate into political responsiveness? Might *Miners Shot Down* facilitate this translational work? To what extent does *Miners Shot Down* enable the intimacy of being moved and having one's attention captured by lives beyond the confines of one's own experiential world? A brief look at certain aspects of the film's rhetorical and formal organization, and in particular at the temporal relations between shots in a film – namely the manipulation, through editing, of the order, duration, and frequency of events or story time (Bordwell and Thompson 306–10) – offers some clues here.

The film consists of a detailed rundown of the days leading up to the massacre, bookended by visual and verbal accounts of events on the day of 16 August itself. Aside from the title sequence and a number of flashbacks, interviews, and testimonies throughout, the events are presented in broadly chronological order starting on 10 August. The film is divided into eight sections, each introduced by an intertitle signalling the days leading up to the massacre. The last sequence is subdivided in turn into time slots that stretch across the day of the shootings. This sequence is by far the most extensive of the eight parts, roughly three times lengthier in duration than the longest of the preceding parts.

The film's title sequence provides, in capsule form, a key to the film's overall affective and rhetorical register. It opens with a number of blurry images cut together in quick succession, accompanied by the spoken soundtrack of conflicted police officers saying, among other things, "We didn't follow instruction. We did but it was impossible to." The filmmaker then cuts to footage of the police officers rapidly discharging their weapons on the oncoming miners, as the haunting isiZulu words "where's the work?" crescendo into an aural backdrop (a musical refrain that recurs throughout the film).[18] Against the visual background of police violence and the graphic images of injured and lifeless bodies, the filmmaker then offers the following words in voice-over:

> It's the 16th of August, 2012. Outside the Lonmin Platinum mine Marikana, South Africa, a hundred and twelve striking miners are shot down by police. Thirty-four die. Like many South Africans, the shooting shook me to the core. Events like these took me back to the massacres of apartheid: Sharpeville, 1960; Soweto, 1976. Killings like these led South Africans to support Nelson Mandela and his struggle for freedom. But today, these miners are being shot at by our new government to ensure that it's business as usual. We could see that lives were now being sacrificed for money, and that the young democracy we had so much hope for was under threat.

When Sharpeville and the Soweto uprisings are mentioned, archival footage of these events is edited into the visual stream. Immediately following these words and their accompanying visuals, the camera cuts to the aforementioned statements about mourning by Zuma and Phiyega, both framed in medium to extreme close-ups. These statements are then followed by an image of an incredulous-looking woman – presumably a family member of one of the miners – shaking her head.

A number of things can be discerned from this sequence. First, the temporal organization of the massacre alongside references to the history of apartheid-era violence places it on the longer historical continuum of the ongoing fight against spectacular injustice, as such conveying precisely the kinds of bewildering post-rainbow affective timelines referenced in earlier chapters. Though the focus on spectacular forms of violence here risks obscuring the slow violence of which Nixon writes, placed within the context of the details that emerge later in the sequence as well as elsewhere in the film, this emphasis is arguably used strategically precisely to highlight the longer-term, slower histories of structural racial and economic injustice that culminate in events such as these. The final part of the sequence, for instance, includes a scene from the Farlam Commission during which advocate Dumisa Ntsebeza, representing the families of deceased miners, slowly reads the names of these men. As he gradually moves down the list, the visual backdrop transitions from shots representing openly distressed family members witnessing events at the commission, to scenes of rock drill operators working in the cramped tunnels of the mines, to visuals of the informal settlements and township homes within which impoverished miners and their families reside. These images bring into focus forms of "violence enacted slowly over time" (Nixon 11) by exposing Lonmin Platinum's business model as "socially thin," a phrase James Ferguson uses to refer to a type of mineral extraction – increasingly typical across African contexts – which "depends ever less on wider societal investments" (*Global* 36). Similar representations surface later in the documentary, such as when the filmmaker provides a sketch of the history and global context of platinum mining and states that "mining companies such as Lonmin view higher wages as the biggest threat to the continued health of the business."[19]

The second key feature of this opening sequence is the unapologetic partiality of the filmmaker. This is evident, for instance, in Desai's moving statements about having been shaken to the core by the shooting. Here, the filmmaker functions as an intimate mediator who leverages personal feeling as a point of access for viewers into a larger social terrain. The filmmaker's partiality and feelings are transmitted also less overtly in the editing choices made in this opening sequence. The placement of Zuma and Phiyega's respective statements between Desai's own expression of shock and the shot of a woman's incredulous head-shaking is a deliberate eschewing of "balance" and "objectivity" as widely accepted ideals in news reporting. In her assessment of the South African media's handling of the massacre, cited earlier, Duncan highlights some of the shortcomings of "balance" as an unqualified concept regulating journalistic practice. She explains, for instance, that this type of reporting is usually presented as value-free when in fact it more often than not privileges the point of view of the powerful. Her take on this deserves being quoted at length:

> In the early reporting on Marikana, many journalists clearly assumed that a limited number of sources were needed for the story to be balanced, and that the workers' voice was "covered" through interviews with union officials, when clearly it was not. The problem with "balance" is that it can lead to very superficial reporting, where a story is considered to be complete when the two "sides" in a particular story have been canvassed, and both have been given roughly equal attention (McNair, 2001: 69). In fact there may be a right and a wrong side to a particular story and, as a result, both sides may not deserve equivalent attention. In such cases, not only is neutrality an inappropriate journalistic response, it is unjust for journalists who may consider it their professional duty to speak truth to power. In the case of Marikana, journalists' emphasis on balance mitigated against them undertaking a proper investigation, and arriving at appropriate responses. ("South African" 81)

In light of this critique of neutrality – which could well be directed also at the faux objectivity of Zuma and Phiyega's respective responses to the massacre – the formal organization of *Miners Shot Down* seems particularly fitting as a means of encouraging more ethical ways of responding to injustice. Desai's explicit and emotive articulation of his film's partiality is typical of political documentaries that use a rhetorical style to persuade viewers of a particular point of view. In the words of documentary scholar Bill Nichols, "documentary work does not appeal exclusively to our aesthetic sensibility; it may entertain or please, but does so in relation to a rhetorical or persuasive effort aimed at the existing social world. Documentary not only activates our aesthetic awareness … it also activates our social consciousness" (104). Nichols's overall point applies well to *Miners Shot Down*, though I would qualify it by insisting that aesthetic responsiveness is anything but disconnected from our social worlds, as Nichols's somewhat narrow reading of both the social and the aesthetic suggests (even, or perhaps especially, in the case of narrative films that present themselves simply as "entertainment"). Rhetorical strategies work because they draw on our aesthetic embeddedness in a larger social world and on "our responsiveness to a world of feelings" (Highmore, *Ordinary* xi). The kind of political responsiveness that rhetorical filmmaking hopes to activate is premised, to echo Athanasiou and Butler again, upon one's capacity to be moved by another, a capacity which the normative political privileging of reason over passion fails to fully grasp.

Throughout the film the points of view of miners are privileged, either via the inclusion of interviews with miners such as Tholakele Dlunga, Mzoxolo Magidiwana, and Sipete Phatsha themselves; the foregrounding of events as these miners might have experienced them; the use of slow-motion and long-take cinematography obliging viewers to linger, for instance, on the suffering of the injured miners in the aftermath of the shootings; or by imagining into being a sympathetic public sphere where justice for survivors – or genuine acts of mourning for the deceased – might be part of a future to come. While forms of political pedagogy found in documentaries such as these cannot necessarily be expected to bridge "the constitutive gaps first between knowledge and action, and second between aesthetics and politics" (Szeman 38), the representation of details otherwise hidden from view, and the appeal to forms of intimacy that place viewers and miners within shared emotional time, seem at least to gesture in this direction.

Much of this can be discerned from studying the film's first and final parts. I read the fact that the shootings themselves feature in two different contexts in the film – first in the opening and then in the extended final sequence – as a challenge to the "spectacular time" (Nixon 8) characterizing the corporate media's spasmodic and decontextualized representation of the shootings. (As Franny Rabkin puts it, media interest has waned and public outrage about the massacre has dulled for reasons that include the fact that "we often confuse what is immediately capturing the attention of readers with what is really important.") Whereas the film's opening sequence presents the shootings only briefly and without much contextualizing detail, the extended final sequence is placed after much previously obscured information about events leading up to the massacre, and about the ongoing struggles of miners to have their grievances heard, has been conveyed. The shock value of the opening sequence is thus made to linger not simply for its own sake, but for the purpose of pulling viewers into an investigative project that delivers factual and durational heft to the plight of the miners.

A few scenes included in the final section are worth highlighting. The first features an interview with advocate Ntsebeza in which he comments on the decision of the police to order four mortuary vans prior to the massacre. Ntsebeza voices his feelings about this in the following statement, delivered with slow emphasis: "The most foreboding indication of the intentions of those who placed an order for four mortuary vans – vans from the morgue … What else are you anticipating? It's a statement of anticipation of what is to happen." Ntsebeza's expression of outrage offers viewers a counter-affective take on the pre-emptive reasoning that led to the massacre (similar expressions of shock are articulated in interviews included throughout the documentary). The temporal logic whereby the unactualized threat assumed to have been posed by the miners withholding their labour hardened into not only the anticipation but subsequently the reality of a substantial death toll is here recast. The threat that Ntsebeza reflects on is, however, a threat that has come to pass not for the police, the South African business community, or national financial health, but for the miners. Unlike the pre-emptive reasoning whereby police action came to be legitimated "by the affective fact of fear, actual facts aside" – a form of anticipatory action that "produced the object toward which its power is applied" (Massumi 54, 56) – the threat that Ntsebeza foregrounds is not based simply in affective fact but in the reality of the death and injury to miners that has come to pass. Viewer outrage, in turn, can thus be anchored in an archive of actualized threat that has more than just an affective, anticipatory mode of existence. What is called for, then, is a different form of political alignment than that harnessed by the discourse of pre-emptive securitization: whereas the latter aligned publics along axes of collective fear derived from "fantasies of the other" used to "justify violence against others" (Ahmed, *Cultural* 64), the film exposes these fantasies and so brings viewers into affective-temporal proximity with the fear that must have been felt by the miners themselves.

The rest of the final section uses a range of formal strategies to bring the concerns of the miners into the foreground, and to expose the conditions within which their thoughts and feelings, not to mention their entitlement to civic protections, ceased to matter. The most moving of these representations are the scenes of the shootings themselves, prefaced by an emotional plea to the mineworkers by Joseph Mathunjwa, president of the Association of Mineworkers and Construction Union (AMCU), who asks them to disperse and places their struggle within a history of colonial and capitalist slow violence. Mathunjwa's speech, which takes on devastating significance in the aftermath of the shootings, includes the words "Comrade, the life of a black person in Africa is so cheap. They will kill us, they will finish us ... and then they will replace us." The scenes that follow serve as a chilling validation of Mathunjwa's prescient words. These scenes include visual footage of both sites where police shot miners: the first shows miners being shot down as they move towards the militarized tactical response team of the police – seventeen miners were killed here; the second – which has come to be known as "scene two" – includes footage of the scene where the seventeen additional miners were shot execution-style at the small koppie several hundred metres away from the first scene. Whereas some of the images included in the first scene were circulated by the visual news media in South Africa and internationally immediately following the massacre, footage of scene two was not. Both these scenes, however, convey material and use a representational style that viewers would not have been exposed to prior to the release of the film. There are significant representational risks to the visualization of violence and the attendant spectacularizing of bodily suffering, particularly in African contexts, as my reading in chapter 5 of Gabrielle Goliath's work on the ethics of audio-visualizing gender-based violence for instance indicates. Yet Desai does manage to mitigate some of these risks to the extent that he recasts already widely circulated and decontextualized imagery of the miners' suffering into alternative representational formats – bolstered by previously unavailable supplementary evidence – aimed in turn at rendering the experience of the miners more affectively complex and contextualized, and so less prone to distortion by the techniques of aesthetic distancing deployed by the mainstream media.

The editorial and cinematographic style chosen for the first of these two scenes, for instance, differs in important ways from the truncated and hurried representation of the shootings included in the film's opening. In the final scene of the shootings at "scene one," the filmmaker stretches temporal duration by way of techniques such as slow motion and zoom-in cinematography; the repetition of key scenes from more than one angle (known as "overlapping editing" [Bordwell and Thompson 308]); a soundtrack with a slow sonic tempo; and the inclusion of shots that are extended in duration via a slow editing style. The filmmaker is unrelenting in his use of techniques of temporal expansion particularly in the scenes representing the miners who were shot, and whose suffering is shown to be wholly ignored by police manhandling them in spite of their injuries. For these officers, the miners have clearly ceased to be fully human (the filmmaker mentions, for instance, that ambulances were barred from entry to the scene of the massacre until an hour after the shooting).[20] These scenes are delayed also via the inclusion of the testimony of Mzoxolo Magidiwana, who was shot by police, reflecting on his thoughts at the time: "Death … I thought I was dying. I was facing death and I realized the only thing I was dying for was money. But it's all for nothing … without saying goodbye to my family."

The techniques that I highlight here work collectively to agitate thought and feeling. By leaving viewers with no choice but to linger on the dreadful experience of suffering conveyed, the film challenges the dissociational forces whereby dominant modes of feeling came to be uncoupled from the experiential realities of the miners. A similar pattern emerges in the filmmaker's representation of the shootings at scene two, but here viewers also get a clearer sense of the militaristic machismo culture that shaped the behaviour of police officers and that contributed to the ease with which they dismissed the pain of the miners. Viewers are shown footage, for instance, of a police officer bragging about one of the miners he shot and a colleague congratulating him with the words "Ah, you fucked him up, you fucked him up." Upon finding what they believe to be *muti* on this miner, one of these police officers taunts him with the words "That doesn't work eh, baba. You pussy." While the inclusion of this footage is clearly meant to expose the nakedly cruel conduct of these particular police officers, it also brings to light an emotional culture within which the social abjection and stigmatization of these workers have become normalized, a culture that obviously predates this spectacular scene of violence. As the foot soldiers of the state, the police are at the forefront of the state's daily consolidation of its own power through various disciplinary, affective, and discursive acts of exclusion.

In light of the filmmaker's unapologetic privileging of the perspectives of the miners thus far, it is unsurprising that the damning evidence presented here should be followed by a visual recording of the following speech made to police officers by commissioner Phiyega four days after the massacre:

> Let us take note of the fact that, whatever happened *represents the best of responsible policing*. You did what you did because you were being responsible. You were making sure that you continue to live your oath of ensuring that South Africans are safe and that you equally are a citizen of this country and that safety starts with you. (emphasis added)[21]

The voice-over narrator's response, spoken alongside a montage of still frames of Zuma and then deputy President Ramaphosa in their ANC garb, smiling and clapping hands, is telling: "But who looked out for the safety of our lowly paid miners? Surely it should have been those who worked so tirelessly for our struggle for freedom. Those who now hold the reins of political power."

The filmmaker's anger here is palpable, and constitutes a form of wayward, counter-affective labour aimed at both heightening and sustaining public outrage about the treatment of the miners at the hands of the state. Much has been written in recent years about forms of labour variously referred to as immaterial, affective, or emotional – akin to what I consider in the previous chapter as "mood work."[22] My choice of the phrase "counter-affective labour" constitutes a somewhat tangential response to this body of work. I suggest that counter-affective labour – particularly within the ambit of aesthetic activism – might serve as an oppositional response to the ways in which affective and other forms of labour in the context of late capitalism function to simultaneously reproduce and mask the latter's alienating effects. In short, I argue that the form of counter-affective labour found in *Miners Shot Down* constitutes a particularly compelling example of the capacity for affective conversion inherent in certain forms of audio-visual activism, functioning, by extension, as an example of the kind of politically wayward aesthetics – theorized in chapter 1 – that might become the ground from which to think more expansively and sensitively about justice and the politics of decolonization.

Throughout the documentary, the filmmaker conducts this counter-affective work on at least two fronts: first, he provides a platform for the expression of the feelings of those involved in events, and of his own feelings in response to these. Second, he invites viewing counter-publics into shared emotional time with the miners through the use of the formal strategies outlined above. To be clear, I use the phrase "counter-affective labour" here not to suggest that the feeling of those who were wounded be made to do political work in a film such as this. I share the sentiments of Neville Hoad, whose "imagination breaks on the question of the ethical and political uses of despair" ("Three" 136). Instead, I read the work of giving aesthetic form to some of the affective experiences of the miners as the subjective counter-affective labour of Desai and others involved in the making and dissemination of this film, leveraged in turn to call on viewers to put their own opinions and feelings to work politically.

Creative Activism

That *Miners Shot Down* aims to exert an affective force on viewers is clear, but this is not the sum total of the work that is done here. As Clare Hemmings ("Invoking Affect"), Lauren Berlant, and others have suggested, the celebratory character of some of the work coming out of the recent turn to affect in social theory, manifest in a tendency to overstate the transformative political capacities of the supposedly autonomous energies of affect, does not necessarily lead us into revolutionary theoretical and social terrain. As Berlant phrases it, "shifts in affective atmosphere are not equal to changing the world" ("Cruel" 116). In the fields of literary and cultural studies, the potential of works of the creative imagination to bring about political change tends at times to be similarly overestimated. In his paper on the representational power of poems written about the HIV pandemic, for instance, Neville Hoad cites W.H. Auden's memorable claim that "poetry makes nothing happen." Yet he qualifies this reminder by insisting that while this may be the case, the poems he analyses "all register with considerable emotional power that something happened, and is still happening" ("Three" 136).

A similar claim can be made about *Miners Shot Down*, yet its activist reach may arguably stretch significantly further than that of the poems Hoad discusses, the readership for which "is demographically insignificant" (136). I share with Rob Nixon an interest particularly in the activist and political potential of works of creative non-fiction, a field frequently overlooked within literature departments concerned primarily with the signifying capacities of texts that qualify as "Literature." Nixon, who is "drawn to nonfiction's robust adaptability, imaginative and political, as well as to its information-carrying capacity and its aura of the real," takes "seriously its adaptive rhetorical capacities, the chameleon powers that make it such an indispensable resource for creative activism" (25).

Miners Shot Down functions as such a form of "creative activism" on multiple fronts. As a work of political pedagogy openly invested in the search for emotional, material, and other forms of justice for the miners, the film invites its viewers to join a space of counterpublic coalition and collective action. It does so in at least three ways. Firstly, the film contests, via a range of strategies of aesthetic mediation, the misinformation about the shootings that has powerfully shaped the public imagination subsequent to these events. *Miners Shot Down* conducts, in other words, the politically important work of disseminating information previously obscured and thus of deepening public understanding of the circumstances surrounding the labour dispute and the massacre itself. Secondly, as already indicated, it draws viewers into shared grief with the miners, thus nourishing the grounds of postcolonial melancholia upon which genuine mourning for the loss of life might be possible. Finally, it challenges the accelerated temporalities of global capitalism by offering multiple temporal trajectories and affective timelines for the framing, staging, and recollection of events surrounding the shootings.

The last of these functions takes shape, again, in a number of ways. Viewers are called upon to linger on the experiences of the miners not simply via the alternative and expanded timelines that unfold within the confines of the film itself. Rehad Desai, Anita Khanna, and others involved in the making of this film have been conducting their activist labour on multiple additional fronts, ranging from an energetic film dissemination and discussion schedule undertaken both nationally and internationally since the film's release, to a remarkably robust social media presence by means of which events at the Farlam Commission, as well as other significant details pertinent to the struggle for better wages and social justice for South Africa's working poor, have been documented.[23] At film screenings, Desai, Khanna, and others were more often than not present to address questions from viewers, and to extend the impact of the film beyond the parameters of the viewing experience itself. This work is particularly valuable given the fact that the South African Broadcasting Corporation has, to date, refused to screen the film on any of its channels (though the channel e.tv finally agreed to broadcast the documentary in January 2016). It also helps to address the unequal distribution of media attention at the time to events such as the Oscar Pistorius trial and the Marikana massacre respectively. Writing in part to encourage viewers to attend a screening of *Miners Shot Down*, Christy Kelly reflects on this as follows:

> If I Google the words "Marikana platinum mine" there are 274 thousand hits in comparison to the 13 million for "Oscar Pistorius trial." This though the Marikana strikes kicked off the year of greatest protest in South Africa since Apartheid. This though two years on no policeman has faced jail for the use of live ammunition on fleeing crowds. This though the strike marked South Africa's "first post-apartheid massacre."
>
> It appears that the mass murder of black workers in South Africa and the most important event in the country's recent history deserves a week of coverage – as much condemnation of the strikers as sensible analysis – while the violent "indiscretion" of one of the country's ex-"darlings" several months. Sadly this balance will not be redressed through the major media channels. There are, however, other ways; next Wednesday the documentary film "Miners Shot Down" which follows the events at Marikana is showing at the Hackney Picturehouse. It would be an irenic fantasy to expect this to bring about greater parity, but the more people who are aware, the more can be made aware.[24]

Though I disagree with Kelly's trivializing assessment of the importance of attending to Oscar Pistorius's killing of Steenkamp (as I point out in chapter 5, South Africa's pandemic of gender-based violence requires sustained attention), her point regarding the distribution of media attention nonetheless bears noting for what it reveals about public concern for the miners at the time.[25] In our contemporary "attention economy" (Davenport), where the stakes of capturing attention are high, the visual representation of spectacular forms of violence often becomes the means by which affect and attention are channelled and directed (though as a comparison of media interest in the Marikana massacre and the Oscar Pistorius trial reveals, spectacular violence in and of itself is not enough to command attention in a world in which the distribution and intensity of public outrage tends to vary depending on the race, gender, sexuality, or fame of those involved). My reading of *Miners Shot Down* in this chapter may well be accused of having overvalued the film's potential to shift the attention of viewing publics beyond the grip of the temporality of spectacle. This is, after all, a film that mediates the occurrence of the most spectacular and harrowing form of state-sponsored violence seen since the end of apartheid. The film could no doubt have done more to convey forms of slow violence that have historically been central to the mining industry's exploitation of both mineral and human resources. (This work is done particularly well, for instance, in the documentary *Strike a Rock* [2017], directed by Aliki Saragas, that I analyse elsewhere [Strauss, "Energy"].)

Yet there is, to my mind, no question that the film fuelled the growth of a counterpublic sphere within which outrage about post-rainbow structural injustice came to find activist expression, most notably in the student and feminist activisms that I address in the two remaining chapters. As I point out elsewhere, "the outrage and shock that accompanied the massacre have arguably been at the heart of a post-2012 public sphere reinvigorated by increasingly robust opposition politics and inventive new forms of popular resistance" ("Affective Return" 222), a reality to which the widespread circulation of Desai's film no doubt contributed. In this context, as Ronit Frenkel and Pamila Gupta phrased it in their introduction to a 2019 special issue of the journal *Social Dynamics* dedicated expressly to "thinking South Africa after Marikana," "modes of protest seemed to be taking on new forms: from the use of excrement as political protest to the EFF's violent removal from parliament, the #RhodesMustFall movement, #OpenStellenbosch movement and the (trans)national #FeesMustFall, escalating corruption scandals and constitutional crises, the ideologies of the struggle era past were appearing in new forms in a context of escalating risk post-Marikana" (2). In the next chapter, I consider specifically what some of the "wayward commemorative activisms" associated with the 2015–17 hashtag student protests reveal about this post-Marikana affective landscape.

4
Feeling the Fall

The rise of the hashtag student protest movements in South Africa since March 2015 saw Black pain being placed squarely on the national agenda. Though the years subsequent to 1994 did occasion an engagement with the legacy of trauma central to the historical experience of racialized dispossession in the country, initiatives such as the Truth and Reconciliation Commission, as I indicate in earlier chapters, have recently faced renewed criticism for their promotion of a skewed version of reconciliation weighted in favour of South Africa's apartheid beneficiaries, as well as for deflecting attention from the ongoing experience of material deprivation and other forms of discrimination that live on in the everyday, psychic lives of Black South Africans. One of the primary criticisms of the TRC raised by student activists is that it resulted in reconciliation standing in as an alternative for justice, when the latter should have been its prerequisite.[1] Apartheid and colonialism's complex affective afterlives thus continue to have profound implications for the entangled projects of decolonial activism and material redistribution in contemporary South Africa.

This chapter maps some of the intersections of feeling, history, and public and visual culture that recent student activisms have brought into focus. In one of the first edited volumes to analyse the 2015–17 #FeesMustFall (#FMF) revolt, William Gumede suggests that the South African context differs from earlier uprisings in North Africa in that young people associated with the latter directed their wrath primarily at the shortcomings of current governments whereas South Africa's student uprisings were initially driven first and foremost by anger at the "symbols of apartheid and colonialism" (186). The aim of this chapter, then, is to engage seriously with the roots of this anger by foregrounding the affective archive to which students drew the attention of South African publics. Whereas the previous chapter turned to aesthetic mediation of the Marikana massacre in an effort to highlight some of the shortcomings of state-driven projects of mourning, this chapter takes recent student activisms as its starting point for a study of the historical weight that colonial and apartheid pasts continue to exert on contemporary South African psychic lives.

The chapter has two interrelated parts. I first consider the emergence, within student-led protests, of a political vernacular exemplified by the refusal to detach thought from feeling as students navigate the rocky terrain of contemporary decolonial activism (see also Strauss "Affective Return"). In mapping some of the intellectual precedents to this calculated political pairing of emotion and reason, I am invested in questioning the frequency with which student activisms came to be regarded, within pockets of the South African commentariat, as driven by emotion to the detriment of careful deliberation. The second part of the chapter reads two events that unfolded in relation to the toppling of the statue of Cecil John Rhodes at the University of Cape Town (UCT) in April 2015. The first is the act that initiated the #RhodesMustFall campaign, namely activist Chumani Maxwele's throwing of human excrement onto the statue on 9 March 2015. The second is a performance piece titled "Chapungu – the day that Rhodes Fell," staged by artist Sethembile Msezane on 9 April 2015, the day when the statue was finally removed from its plinth overlooking the UCT rugby fields. I consider these performances as what Jonathan Flatley calls "affective maps" (76–84) of a larger historical and political terrain. As acts of aesthetic mediation and transmission, Maxwele's and Msezane's performances open onto larger questions about the cultural forms adequate to the task of mediating political disappointment in post-rainbow times.

Feeling Thought, Thinking Feeling

In the many heated exchanges that circulated on both social and older media platforms following the first campus shutdowns in March 2015, questions about the relationship between rage and reason featured particularly prominently. Reflecting on the significance of the #RhodesMustFall campaign, novelist Thando Mgqolozana states for instance that the fall of the statue "represents the beginning of the recognition and acknowledgement of the Black experience, of Black pain" and of the fact "that it is possible to look at Black rage as something that is not just dismissed as violent but something that is necessary." In an opinion piece on the "unfinished business of decolonizing higher education in South Africa," and the institutional spaces within which

Black students have long felt alienated, Angelo Fick likewise explains that the "rage some folks professed at seeing swastikas on their campus is like the rage many of us have felt having to walk past symbols glorifying the extermination of people like us, at the same time as walking corridors, sitting in meetings, and attending and giving lectures and seminars with people who not only actively wished we were not there, but had no shame or reservation about telling us so."

These interventions are revealing both of the speed with which the language of "'Black pain" – what one might consider a shorthand for the many psychic traumas and disappointments discussed in previous chapters – came to dominate the national vernacular, and of the extent to which this language found deep historical resonance. Mgqolozana and Fick both implicitly reference a conversation first placed on the agenda by Maxwele in justification for throwing human waste on the statue of Rhodes. Echoing Jean-Paul Sartre in his 1961 preface to Frantz Fanon's *Wretched of the Earth,* in which he summarizes Fanon's argument as mapping the "status of 'native'" as "a nervous condition" (liv, xix), Maxwele explains, "The life of a black person in SA is contaminated with a nervous condition. This is true for all black people at the University of Cape Town (UCT) – from a high-profile and prolific professor to a first-year student who is accepted to study, but is on a waiting list for accommodation and financial aid." Here Maxwele draws on a long critical legacy of decolonial scholarly engagement with the psychic consequences of colonial violence – a legacy that both predates and, to some extent, informs the more recent turn to affect in critical cultural theory – to emphasize the predicament in which Black students and staff at UCT find themselves.

The UCT Rhodes Must Fall Collective subsequently formalized this emphasis in their mission statement. In a section titled "Centering Black Pain" they declare "the dehumanisation of black people at UCT" to be at the root of their struggle. This dehumanization, they explain, "is a violence exacted only against black people by a system that privileges whiteness" (Rhodes Must Fall Movement 6). That the devaluation of Black pain and anger on the part of the white establishment has long been a hallmark of the latter's engagements with attempts at addressing colonialism's residual violence is fleshed out later in the statement when the Collective explains, "Management is making clear that they are not interested in alleviating black pain unless the move to do so is validated by white voices. It is absurd that white people should have any say in whether the statue should stay or not, because they can never truly empathise with the profound violence exerted on the psyche of black students. Our pain and anger is at the centre of why the statue is being questioned, so this pain and anger must be responded to in a way that only we can define" (7).

This emphasis on Black pain proved unsettling to many, not least those historically complicit in its making. As these early protests escalated into larger national student movements advocating, for instance, for free, decolonized education, the insourcing of outsourced university workers, and the rights of trans, queer, and gender-nonconforming people, the charge that activism was driven to a greater extent by rage than reason became a frequent refrain. A notable portion of critical and social media commentary on these protests in fact revealed a tendency to binarize thought and feeling, reason and emotion, with the latter often being either devalued, correlated with violence, or subordinated to other critical considerations.[2]

In a piece titled "Rhodes and the Politics of Pain," Jeremy Seekings and Nicoli Nattrass, for instance, take issue with what they refer to as the "Manichean politics of pain" deployed by student activists calling for the speedy removal of the statue. Such a politics, they write, has a number of weaknesses, including (1) its closing down of "serious debate over what should be done with the removed statue" – reducing such debate to a crude stand-off between "'us' (the pained) and 'them' (racist critics)"; (2) its weakening of the educational role of the university (by failing to take up the opportunity to use the statue as part of an educational project, they write, "Senate sent a message that education is not [their] primary concern"); and (3) its insistence on the racialization of pain, which they suggest "serves to reduce injustices and indignities to race, foreclosing serious consideration of other forms of injustice and indignity."[3] Similar claims were made by a number of prominent South African public intellectuals and political commentators. In an article titled the "Politics of Rage Puts our Gains in Danger," published in the South African *Sunday Times* in May 2016 in response to the many protests that the #RhodesMustFall events catalysed, then vice-chancellor and principal of the University of the Witwatersrand Adam Habib, for instance, writes that, while the rage experienced by South African student publics is understandable given the country's extreme levels of inequality, "SA's leaders seem to have abandoned Madiba's legacy of reason in rage." His article opens with the following lines: "These are difficult days. All around us there are multiple manifestations of the politics of rage. Our strikes are violent, as are our service delivery protests. Student ferment has been on the rise, and has in many cases also turned violent" ("Politics").

These arguments, while not necessarily dismissive of the traumas that have historically attended colonial violence, are nonetheless premised on a tendency to polarize thought and feeling in their approach to contemporary student activisms and protest politics, and, in certain cases, to correlate the latter with violence. My concern here is less with the question of violence itself than to try to make sense of the continued prominence of the emotion-reason binary in South African public culture.[4] Though Habib's position is not blind to the value of rage in certain contexts, by calling on the need to temper rage with reason, he nonetheless draws strength from a Cartesian worldview requiring the subordination of the unruly passions to the "rational control of reason and the mind" (Cvetkovich, "Affect" 13). As Elizabeth Spelman explains in a volume on emotion and feminist philosophy published long before more recent proclamations of an "affective turn," "in western cultures there has long been an association of reason with members of groups that are dominant politically, socially, and culturally, and of emotion with members of subordinate groups" (264). She further writes that, "while members of subordinate groups are expected to be emotional, indeed to have their emotions run their lives, their anger will not be tolerated" (264); such anger, in fact, will more often than not be conflated with rage, "with the connotation of hysteria or insanity" (271).

When students invoked the much-circulated and sound-byted lexicon of Black rage, they were in fact responding to and acknowledging this discriminatory legacy by way of critical reclamation. Their defence of the political power and beauty of Black and "feminist rage" (see, for instance, Gqola, *Reflecting* 25–43) draws inspiration from anti-racist, feminist, and decolonial activism and theory in a range of historical contexts, most notably the civil rights and Black power movements in the United States (roughly from 1954 until the early 1970s) and, in South Africa, the Black Consciousness Movement (BCM) of the late 1960s and 1970s. The poetry volume *Cry Rage*, published by James Mathews and Gladys Thomas in 1972 and subsequently banned by the apartheid government, constitutes one of the most memorable defences of the power of rage against apartheid brutality. Many of the concerns articulated in this volume and others associated with the BCM in South Africa, as well as in a range of anti-racist writings and activisms in the United States, have been echoing through contemporary student activisms (attesting also to the transnational character of many forms of protest in the age of digital connectivity and social media). In the United States context in particular, Black rage has been historically defended by theorists and political activists such as Malcolm X, Cornel West, bell hooks, and Audre Lorde for the power it has to deliver "clarity" (hooks 18; see also Lorde 127) in the face of injustice.[5] More recently, in the era of Black Lives Matter, critics such as Mychal Denzel Smith,

Debra Thompson, and Brittney Cooper have made a persuasive call for a renewed politics of Black rage, particularly also following the killings of George Floyd, Breonna Taylor, and Ahmaud Arbery and many other Black US citizens in 2020.[6]

Much of the work of these critics is characterized by a refusal to consider rage and reason in binary terms, or to simply suggest that those drawing on the power of rage in their activisms are incapable of maintaining the divide between rage and violence. In her memorable essays "Killing Rage" and "Beyond Black Rage" bell hooks, for instance, is careful never to read rage simply as "mindless" (19). She rejects the tendency to represent Black rage as "always and only evil and destructive" (19), and while acknowledging that "rage can be consuming," she insists that it must be tempered not so much with reason as "an engagement with a full range of emotional responses to black struggle for self-determination" (19). This view is found also, for instance, in Debra Thompson's powerful essay on "Black rage" in the context of the contemporary United States, and the work of the Black Lives Matter movement, where she emphasizes that "it is impossible to conceptualize black rage as an isolated emotion" (466) and points to the importance of a combination of reciprocal emotions and shared emotions within larger contexts of social mobilization. hooks further refuses to pathologize this rage, or take extreme examples of violent rage as representative of all forms of Black political anger, suggesting that "it is useful for white supremacist capitalist patriarchy to make all black rage appear pathological rather than identify the structure wherein that rage surfaces. At times black rage may express itself pathologically. However, it also can express itself in ways that lead to constructive empowerment" (29).

Though Habib's call for "reason in rage," then, does at first glance seem to challenge the strict dichotomization of these terms, the problem lies in the implication that "student rage" – invoked here as a blanket category – was necessarily uninformed by deliberation. In framing his argument as such, Habib in effect instantiates the very binary he critiques. This position constitutes a flattening out of the complexities of student protest across a range of sites – of the conditions within which, in some pockets of student activism, rage gave way to violence – and, perhaps more importantly, of what Brittney Cooper, in a defence of Black rage in the United States, refers to as a tendency to privilege "the product of the provocation and never the provocation itself" ("In Defense").[7] The binary is evoked even more explicitly in his suggestively titled book *Rebels and Rage: Reflecting on #FeesMustFall*, where Habib declares, for instance, that understanding the challenges faced by higher education in the country "requires a *dispassionate* analysis of successes, failures and obstacles to transformation, and how these can be overcome" (94; emphasis added). He goes on to state that "we need honest deliberation, committed to the goal of transformation but *unburdened by emotion*" (94; emphasis added). Pitting deliberation, reason, and rationality against emotion in this manner, as South African scholar Raymond Suttner phrases it (evoking the epistemic legacies of feminist ethics and theology), fails to account for the fact that "both qualities are needed to understand how full human beings act." The point here is not to promote irrationality or unreasonable responses to conflict; it is rather to question the assumption that reasoned deliberation is necessarily detached from feeling, or that impassioned engagements with injustice cannot simultaneously be reasonable.

The historical association of emotion with subordinated groups arguably also informs the frequent subjection of South African protests to what has come to be known as the "protest paradigm" in journalism (Duncan, *Protest* 147), a mode of reporting characterized, for instance, by "the de-legitimisation of protests as being irrational or irrelevant" (147) and a tendency to focus disproportionately on protests considered violent (often conflating "property damage with violence, when in fact these are not the same" [143]).[8] In an assessment of protest reporting in relation to four South African sites of protest (Rustenburg, Mbombela, Blue Crane Route, and the Nelson Mandela Bay Metro), Jane Duncan found, for instance, that "many stories were framed primarily by the actions of their most extreme elements, which led to them being constructed as largely *unreasonable* responses to grievances" (151; emphasis added).

These arguments, and the calculated insistence on the part of activists that "rage and anger are powerful tools" (Dlakavu, cited in Fikeni), are fundamental to this book's refusal to detach the political from the psychic, the intellectual from the emotional. For even if "'Black pain" on occasion fell prey to "aspects of an uncritical neo-liberal knowledge economy" (Lewis and Hendricks 12), or came to be instrumentalized to prop up unacknowledged forms of bigotry (most notably as hypermasculine nationalist posturing blind to intersectional claims to access and justice, about which more below), the frequency with which the pairing of rage with unreason, anger with thoughtlessness, featured in critiques of student protest suggests a deeper critical legacy that remains entrenched in the South African public sphere. This is a legacy characterized by what Athena Athanasiou refers to as the "devaluing of passion – in all its assigned connotations of irrational sentimental femininity, uncivilized primitiveness, and an inarticulate working class"

(177). As my overview of the historical roots of the discourse of Black and feminist rage suggests, this "devaluing of passion" has long been the target of feminist, queer, and anti-racist intellectuals invested in undoing the legacies of colonialism and its violent corollaries (Ahmed "Cultural"; hooks; Jagger; Lorde; Pedwell and Whitehead; Spelman). In fact, "feminist work on bodies and emotions *challenged from the outset* mind-body dualisms, as well as the distinction between reason and passion" (Ahmed, "Cultural" 206; emphasis in the original). It is no accident that Audre Lorde – whose pioneering theoretical and activist work in the mid-to-late twentieth century fundamentally reshaped the terrains of Black feminist and queer resistance – has been one of the figures most frequently cited by feminist student activists in defence of anger as a source of "information and energy" (Lorde, 103; see also, for instance, Naidoo 6).

In an essay on some of the intersections between 2015–17 student activisms and academic feminist struggles at South African universities during the late 1980s and 1990s, Desiree Lewis and Cheryl Hendricks highlight precisely the centrality to the #FMF movement of the feminist idea that "embodied experience *matters* in determining what we know" (5; emphasis in original):

> Memories and understandings of *embodied* experience in the Fallist Movement have been central to students' efforts to articulate resistance in psychosocial terms. Of particular importance has been the surfacing and re-emphasis on the notion of "black pain" ... Like feminists in the 1990s, Fallists countered the trivializing of the psychic pain inflicted on socially marginalized groups by situating this pain at the very centre of their embodied insight into power and situated knowledge. (7–8)

Though Lewis and Hendricks pay closer attention in their analysis to the body as a site of social inscription than as affectively charged, the latter has been equally central to student theorizing. It is safe to say then that, in the vein of feminist work on affective embodiment, the activist vernacular shaping recent student organizing has been characterized from scratch by a rejection of the historical dichotomization of the mind and body, thought and feeling, particularly in the terrain of higher education, where the emphasis on objective scientific rationality has long trumped engagement with feelings, not simply as objects of analysis, but as embedded in all aspects of life and research. Historically, the very idea of the university is predicated upon the privileging of the mind and reason over the body and emotion (Berg and Seeber 2). Shose Kessi, currently dean of the Humanities Faculty at the University of Cape Town, at the time explicitly captured these concerns in a blog posting titled "Of Black Pain, Animal Rights and the Politics of the Belly." Her argument deserves being quoted at length:

> It is interesting how bodily and affective experiences are often weaved out of what is deemed "rational" theorising of current events and political talk. How can my mind operate separately from the rest of my being? Where does the separation occur? At the eyes? The nose? The mouth? The belly? The waist? Surely, that is irrational. Surely that is precisely what the work of so-called rational men concerned with scientific neutrality and objective benchmarks have brought to this world, by excluding particular bodies, experiences, and ways of being and thinking that would disrupt the logic of modern life. How can I, as a black woman in a predominantly white institution that was never meant for me think of rational solutions that I can't see, smell, taste, speak, or feel? …
>
> The idea of logical reasoned argument outside of affect is nonsensical and serves to legitimise the idea that intellectual projects and academic freedom exist outside of historical structural analyses. It serves as a smokescreen that invisibilises whiteness or white feelings. I cannot count the number of times I have been in classrooms, meetings, and committees where the feelings of white students and staff dominate the space in suffocating ways that exclude and silence – under the guise of "logical reasoned argument." The burden of black academics in these spaces is often one of appeasing and negotiation for fear of being dismissed and labelled as irrational, at best, or, at worst, for fear of the white backlash that typically spirals out of control. Black pain and anger is pathologised and condemned whereas white people's anger is cajoled, understood, and considered rational.

Kessi's reference to the experience of suffocation is echoed in the phrase "I can't breathe" that I refer to earlier, and that became a frequent refrain among student activists, invoking the anti-racist battle cry of the Black Lives Matter movement following the choking death of Eric Garner at the hands of the police.[9] As Joanna Ruth Evans phrases it in a reading of the "becoming material" of the statue of Cecil John Rhodes resulting from Maxwele's protest, "This cry is not now a metaphor, now a desperate plea for bodily survival, now a political rallying call, and now an institutional critique: it is, from the moment of its utterance, all of these" (138). Yet by exposing some of the suffocating ways in which power circulates through white feeling masquerading as dispassionate thinking, Kessi does more than confront fictions of detached deliberation with their embodied effects. She also very deliberately shifts attention from Black pain as an object of scientific or anthropological study to those modalities of thinking and feeling historically at its root.

In his comprehensive account of the historical conditions that saw the rise to prominence of Black pain in the post-#RMF popular vernacular, Francis Nyamnjoh similarly argues for the need to conceive of Black pain first and foremost as a consequence of white privilege: "Black pain and white privilege are two sides of the same coin … the pain, poverty and discomforts of the one are actively produced or co-produced by the privilege, pleasure and power of the other" (*#RhodesMustFall* 89). White privilege and its accompanying affective attachments and entitlements – to access, attention, audience, capital, gratitude, land, leisure, legitimacy, space and understanding, to name a few – in other words necessitates active unmasking and dismantling. Without doing so, not only will Black pain continue to be pathologised or called into question, but also the psychic injuries historically sustained under colonialism, apartheid and attendant forms of historical injustice will continue to be reproduced. The experiential distance from Black pain on the part of white South Africans – myself included – is at the heart of what makes it possible to doubt its legitimacy; as Sarah Ahmed explains in a different context, the experiences one is "protected from having; the thoughts [one does] not have to think" are precisely "what makes a privilege a privilege" ("Broken Bones").

What I refer to in chapter 2 as the temporality of prolonged disappointment that attended colonialism and apartheid, necessitated the repeated invention of psychic survival strategies that could dull its accompanying pain. Citing novelist Bloke Modisane's influential novel *Blame me on History* (1963), in which he writes about having to force down the pain of historically protracted racial dehumanisation, Nyamnjoh explains that, "in many respects, for black South Africans to recognize their own pain, is to have come of age … To feel pain is to have hope, and to believe that human agency can result in creative innovations" (*#RhodesMustFall* 83).[10] The explicit centring of Black pain in 2015 signals a moment of awakening from the psychic anaesthesia administered specifically by post-1994 initiatives of nation-building, which student activists have by now successfully exposed as having provided only a temporary and partial panacea, as I point out also in the introduction. Indeed, as Nyamnjoh further explains,

> Of the multiple pains blacks succeeded in freezing under apartheid, post-apartheid South Africa seems to have mitigated little more than the pain

> of political disenfranchisement. It has reawakened material desires and aspirations that had been numbed *à la* Bloke Modisane who [... describes] numbing as a survival strategy in the days when freedom was an extravagant illusion. Little wonder that the language of black pain now proliferates, especially among those who feel they have invested effort enough at schooling themselves in the values enshrined by the whiteness that has dominated them – body, mind and soul – for so long. (94)

As I argue in the previous chapter, state-driven initiatives of collective affective management of historical injustice more often than not produce distorting forms of amnesia. The acknowledgment of the persistence of Black pain close to thirty years after the end of legislative apartheid constitutes both an awakening from the apartheid-era forms of psychic dissociation addressed by Modisane and Nyamnjoh, and from the nation-building initiatives put in place in the years after apartheid. As such, the newfound call for the centring of Black pain may well be read as melancholic in that it is premised on a stubborn refusal to let go of histories of loss, injustice, and their remains. Yet to the extent that this melancholic refusal is concerned first and foremost with the continued hold of this history on the present, it can be read as less melancholic in the pathological, Freudian sense than as a seemingly paradoxical resource for antidepressive modes of political engagement.

The political forms of melancholia associated with contemporary South African student protests may well then be considered as a concerted rethinking of melancholic attachments to the past – less as regressive and pathological than as invested in the realization of a more socially just future, a future to be found in Leigh-Ann Naidoo's "hallucinated time" referenced in this book's introduction. It is precisely this form of melancholia that I find generative for theorizing some of the modes of aesthetic activism that came to dominate student politics across a range of sites. The embodied aesthetic activisms of Chumani Maxwele and Sethembile Msezane that unfolded in relation to the toppling of the Rhodes statue in 2015, for instance, were particularly resonant to resistant publics both in South Africa and internationally, and powerfully serve to undo the body-mind, emotion-reason dualisms that continue to hold sway in South African public culture, and higher education in particular. I argue that these performances, as conveyors of the intergenerational transmissions of racialized feeling, constitute archives of larger historical and political forces, the decoding of which is essential to any project of decolonial redress.

Affective Cartographies

A remarkable range of opinion has by now been tendered on these two moments in the life of recent student activisms, particularly on the performance of Maxwele, in part for its obvious shock value. As acts of aesthetic mediation and transmission, their performances exemplify a recent shift in the modalities and stylistics of South African audio-visual cultural production and activism. Their interventions convey the renewed political urgency that has come to pervade the creative public sphere, epitomized, for instance, in the work of groups such as the graffiti collective Tokolos Stencils, who started marking buildings and walls around Cape Town with words such as "Remember Marikana" in blood-red paint in the months preceding Maxwele's Rhodes protest (*Tokolos-Stencils*), as well as more recently in the inventive new modes of feminist resistance and activism discussed in chapter 5.

My aim here is not to rehearse the body of opinion on Maxwele's and Msezane's performances but rather to point to some of the affective dimensions of their work that have been largely overlooked. I am specifically interested in the extent to which these performances might serve as "affective maps" (Flatley 76–84) of the historically divergent terrains of racialized South African experience. Flatley conceptualizes "affective mapping" as an aesthetic technology "that represents the historicity of one's affective experience" (4). What he means here is that aesthetic practice – in the form of various modes of aesthetic mediation, including literature, film, art, and audio-visual or performance culture more broadly – offers a map or archive of sorts of the affective lives of those who view, or otherwise access, these texts. Writing about the workings of melancholia in the work of modernist theorists and writers such as Walter Benjamin, W.E.B. Du Bois, and Henry James, Flatley explains that aesthetic practice enables forms of affective mapping "not primarily through realist representation of a social space in the world, but through a representation of the affective life of the reader herself or himself" (80). Flatley explains that when we start to conceive of creative cultural and other forms of aesthetic production as affective archives, or as conveyors of the affective lives of their readers and viewers, we might begin to see the historical and political roots of our seemingly individualized feeling. Maxwele's and Msezane's performances chart affective maps across a range of cultural registers, including the concrete moments of their embodied presentations themselves and the near-instantaneous hypermediation of these stagings globally across visual and social media. These activist interventions are notable in particular for how they channel and direct the language of Black rage discussed above, even as their affective reach also extends beyond this specific experiential terrain.

Much has been written since 2015 about why Maxwele's "visceral excremental politics" (Robins, "Back") struck such a powerful chord across South African campuses, and about Maxwele himself as a controversial political figure at best. Few moments since 1994 have been more revealing of apartheid's stubborn legacy of affective polarization than his act of excremental insurgence. The pages of South Africa's daily newspapers and social media platforms immediately lit up with anger on both sides of the spectrum: on the one hand, those who live the psychic legacies of racial exclusion were quick to join Maxwele's cause and come to his defence (see, for instance, the opinion pieces by Mgqolazana and Fick cited earlier). On the other hand, backlash against Maxwele's method and the support he drew from many emanated from both racist and, at times, more progressive quarters. Predictably, right-wing Afrikaner groups and conservative public figures such as Sunette Bridges, Steve Hofmeyr, and Dan Roodt funnelled their reading of Maxwele's and other similar protests into a larger narrative of Afrikaner victimhood, or, in the words of Roodt, as expressions of "anti-white anger" and "anti-white hate" (Thamm; Schutte; Roodt).[11] Responses such as these reveal colonialism's and apartheid's material and symbolic legacies to have left deep psychic grooves that still tend to bifurcate along racial lines.

I am interested here in the intergenerational transmissions of racialized feeling occasioned by Maxwele's juxtaposition of human waste with the seated figure of Rhodes – intentionally placed in a contemplative pose by sculptor Marion Walgate in 1934, and deliberately imitative of August Rodin's famous 1904 sculpture *The Thinker*.[12] Maxwele's performance reveals a number of ways in which waste and "white civility" (Coleman, *White*, passim) coincide across vast historical ground. As Steve Robins phrases it – with apologies to Freud – "of all the desires to be repressed in the name of the civilizing process, anal and excretory activities and pleasures present the greatest threat to the attainment of bourgeois respectability" ("Back").

The performance features Maxwele's shirtless body in a bright pink miner's hardhat wearing a white sign in the front that reads, "EXHIBIT WHITE @ ARROGANCE U.C.T." and at the back a black sign inscribed with the white letters "EXHIBIT BLACK @ ASSIMILATION U.C.T." (figure 4.1). The juxtaposition of the Rhodes statue with human waste is thus explicitly framed in terms of the history of colonial plunder that saw the relegation of Black South African bodies to the margins of South

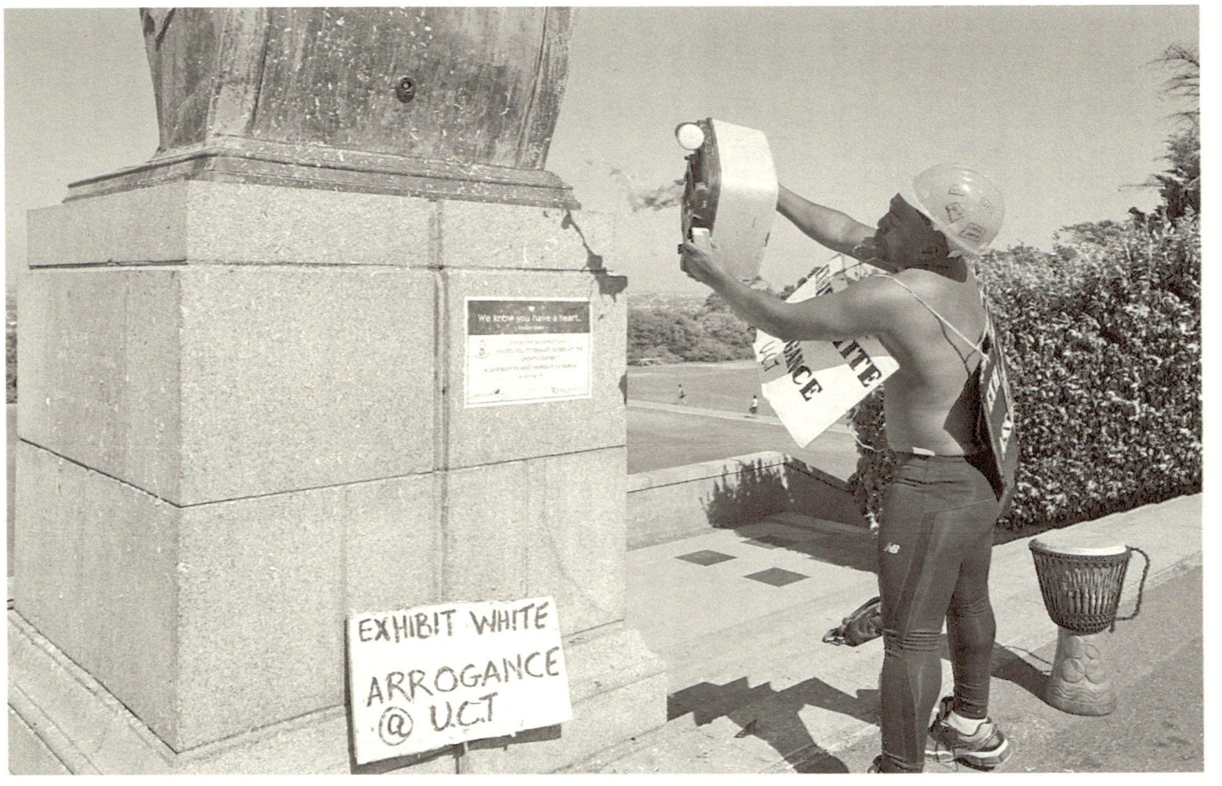

Figure 4.1 © David Ritchie / African News Agency (ANA).

African economic and academic life, and that, more recently, prompted the "Toilet War" in Cape Town over the appalling state of sanitation services in the region (Robins, "Poo Wars," "Back," and "How Toilets"; Jackson and Robins). The latter started when, in the run-up to the 2011 Cape Town municipal elections, the ANC Youth League destroyed portable flush toilets and substandard toilet enclosures in a number of townships in Cape Town in a bid to draw attention to the manner in which inadequate access to sanitation violates the rights of local residents to privacy and dignity. In May 2013, similar protests were staged as a result of a labour dispute between the city of Cape Town and a sanitation services company they hired to collect waste from portable toilets in townships, whereas in June of the same year, dissatisfaction with sanitation provisions led to a group of protesters, for instance, covering the steps of the provincial parliament as well as the entrance of the international terminal at the Cape Town airport with faeces.

Situated within this larger terrain of activism, then, Maxwele's protest forcefully exposes some of the affective, political, and material afterlives of colonial and apartheid sanitation policy and infrastructure planning. As Shannon Jackson and Steven Robins explain, protests such as these point to a historical mismatch between infrastructural developments and democratization, which in the South African context take shape not only in the historical regulation of access to sanitation provisions along racial lines (a historical reality far from having been fully addressed), but also in the sensory and emotional relationships South Africans have to contemporary citizenship.[13] As they phrase it, "cultural histories of waste and odour … reveal the role of infrastructural technology in the objectification of modern bodily boundaries and a *felt* sense of political belonging" (72; emphasis added). Indeed, as Jay Pather and Catherine Boulle read it, Maxwele's was "an act of calculated political significance that was also a searing physical manifestation of emotional overflow" (2; see also J. Pather).

Openly defiant of the boundaries that separate racial capitalism's beneficiaries from its abjected African body politic, Maxwele's performance unapologetically thrusts intimate corporeality into public culture and politics. Here scatology serves as the affective modality for refusing to conceive of privilege and precarity, aesthetics and politics, in binary terms. As such, Maxwele's protest confirms Joshua Esty's point in a much-cited article titled "Excremental Postcolonialism" that, in a post-independence African context, "shit has a political vocation: it draws attention to the failures of development, to the unkept promises not only of colonial modernizing regimes but of postindependence economic policy" (32). Specifically, by bringing human excrement onto the sites of higher education and colonial commemoration, Maxwele very deliberately references the stubborn historic reach of colonial urban sanitation politics that saw the displacement of the Black poor from urban centres in South Africa and elsewhere, and of the ongoing reality of Black domestic labour upon which the sanitation of white homes has historically depended. (As the son of a domestic worker and a miner, these associations would not have been lost on Maxwele.)

More to the point, the contrast reveals the harm done by the weaving out of "bodily and affective experiences" from "what is deemed 'rational' theorizing," as Shose Kessi phrases it in the blogpost cited earlier. Interestingly, Maxwele himself expressed impatience with those who refer to his protests as driven by anger: "Anger equates to irrational and emotional in the white world. So when black people do something it is not seen as rational or intellectual. I would not describe it as anger but passion. We are very passionate" (qtd. in Fekisi and Vollenhoven). While his point does at first glance reveal the extent to which the emotion-reason binary has shaped even the terms of protest, his substitution of anger with passion does undo some of these assumptions, at least to the extent that he views passion as compatible with intellectual deliberation. Though his statement does not fully chime with the activist rhetoric of Black rage, in effect Maxwele points precisely to the pain inflicted by a system that historically relegated those deemed "emotional" to the sidelines of academic life.

By bringing the visceral intergenerational experience of poor sanitation as a site of shame, disgust, and quotidian racial humiliation into intimate, olfactory proximity with the contemplative white body, Maxwele's "poo protest" explicitly shifts attention onto that which, as Nyamnjoh explains, is at the core of Black alienation and pain, namely white privilege and its accompanying affective attachments parading as dispassionate, logical thought. The historically exploited, labouring Black body that Maxwele stages, then, is both self-referential – in initial interviews on the protest he made it clear that he had thrown the "contents of a portable flush toilet container at the statue to highlight his [own] feelings of shame" at having to use these toilets (Robins "Back") – and accusatory, in that he draws the privileged white viewer sensorially into the experience of both disgust and shame, thus pushing this viewer beyond the impulse to pathologize and anthropologize Black pain towards the discomfort of confronting the past and present roots of this pain in whiteness. Subsumed into the contemplative pose of Rhodes and its attendant invisibilization of white feeling, then, is a history of subjugation predicated upon the regulation of Black life and feeling for the sake of enabling white comfort.

This history of bodily and waste regulation is explored on a global scale by Dominique Laporte in his famous 1978 book *The History of Shit,* where he reveals the relegation of human waste to the private realm of the household to have been central to the globalization of colonial capitalist modernity, the formation of modern notions of the (white) self, the organization of urban infrastructure, and even the regulation of language.[14] As he explains it, "to touch, even lightly, on the relationship of a subject to his [*sic*] shit, is to modify not only that subject's relationship to the totality of his body, but his very relationship to the world and to those representations that he constructs of his situation in society" (29). Laporte's choice of the word "shit" is one that is echoed by most contemporary theorists on the subject for political and rhetorical reasons (Phillips 173), particularly given the historical links between human waste management and the so-called cleansing of the human language of references to a range of bodily functions and parts. The matter of shit – in both its physical and linguistic forms – is above all charged affectively: ostensibly vulgar language is as likely to express and arouse strong feelings as are more material encounters with shit.

It further bears noting that as an affective resource, shit is profoundly gendered. The historical confinement of human waste to the realm of the home was fundamentally tied to the depoliticization of domestic life and the attendant dichotomization of the private and the public, feminine and masculine, feeling and thought. Citing European political theorists such as Hannah Arendt, for whom "private household matters such as defecation, toilets and sanitation did not qualify as 'political,'" Steven Robins ("How") explains that, in the context of South African sanitation activism, poo is political in explicitly gendered ways for reasons that include the threat of rape to women using public toilets (see also Phillips 179) and the fact that the burden of navigating the health consequences of poor sanitation so often falls on women (a burden amplified by the COVID-19 pandemic).

I highlight the centrality of gender to excrement in part in light of Maxwele's own contentious relationship with South African gender politics (Mthonti; Xaba in Isaacs; Lujabe). The UCT Trans Collective and a number of feminist commentators have, for instance, described Maxwele's brand of student leadership as being characterized by what Fezokuhle Mthonti calls "insidious formulations of violent, heteronormative masculinity that are oppressive to queer identities" and that show "deep commitment to mechanisms of Rape Culture." Writing at the time of the 2016 protests, Mthonti contends, for instance, that

> despite claims of being representative of an intersectional revolutionary praxis, the kind of political action displayed at the moment is one that is consistent with the brutalisation of a queer woman named Khwezi by our country's number one and his supporters. It is reminiscent of the ways in which Maxwele and others violated black queer women at Witswatersrand University after they had questioned the legitimacy of a secret #FeesMustFall meeting that was almost entirely made up of men. It is also reminiscent of the ways in which Maxwele silences the UCT's Trans Collectives' bold statement about him allegedly being a rapist and a routinely violent male in his private life.

That Maxwele's Rhodes performance received such heated national and international attention is ironic in part given similar work that a number of Black feminists, artists and cultural workers had been doing to contest the erasure of Black women from South African public culture prior to Maxwele's explosion onto the scene. One of these artists, Sethembile Msezane, had been contesting the absence of Black women from the South African commemorative landscape since 2013, when she first started to articulate her own feelings of alienation and dislocation from South African public space through live performance art. Msezane subsequently joined a collective called iQhiya,[15] made up of eleven women who came together to contest the under-representation of Black female artists on the South African art scene (Jayawardane, "Bad").

Msezane's work is remarkable in many ways, not least for the affective pathways it opens up into colonialism's commemorative archive – what Rahul Rao suggestively refers to as the "psychic life of statues." Following in the footsteps of artists and visual activists such as Zanele Muholi, Mary Sibande, Nandipha Mntambo, and Berni Searle, Msezane makes her own body the stage for visual cultural critique. Her first performance on Heritage Day in 2013 outside of Parliament in Cape Town featured her in full Zulu regalia in front of the statue of Louis Botha, the first prime minister of the Union of South Africa (1910–19). Subsequent performances have extended these initial commentaries by bringing Msezane's embodied renditions of historically marginalized Black women onto a number of other sites of public remembrance. For instance, on 27 April 2014, the public holiday that commemorates the first democratic elections held in 1994, Msezane portrayed a version of Lady Liberty in Zulu dress, whereas on 1 May of that same year, as part of the Workers' Day commemorations, she performed as Rosie the Riveter in the iconic blue workers' uniform, again coupled with Zulu motifs (Msezane, "Public").[16]

Her performance of "Chapungu" (figure 4.2) at the removal of the Rhodes statue features an embodied conversation between herself and the historical figure Chapungu, a Zimbabwean spiritual medium considered to have been a messenger of God and the ancestors (Msezane, "Living"). Chapungu is arguably best known as the Great Zimbabwe bird: an intricately carved soapstone sculpture looted from the Great Zimbabwe ruins in 1889 by European hunter Willi Posselt and subsequently sold to Rhodes, who mounted it in the library of his Grootte Schuur estate in Cape Town. The figure of Chapungu, which rises with wings outstretched as the statue of Rhodes falls, serves as an especially apposite symbolic counterpoint to the long history of colonial plunder preceding this day in April 2015. It is significant particularly given the perverse interest Rhodes took in the soapstone sculptures and the city of Great Zimbabwe in the late 1800s: aside from decorating the stairwell of his Grootte Schuur estate with five wooden replicas of the soapstone birds and erecting massive stone reproductions at the gates to his house near Cambridge, England (Kuklick 135), Rhodes commissioned James Theodore Bent to inspect and document the Great Zimbabwe ruins and investigate the possible existence of additional soapstone sculptures. Bent concluded that there had been at least eight more of these birds and incorrectly credited the ruins and sculptures to an ancient non-African civilization, believing the ancestors of local Shona residents to have been incapable of such an impressive architectural and artistic feat (Kuklick 137–8; Maylam 85).

The significance of the Great Zimbabwe ruins and its soapstone birds lies in part for Rhodes in the proof he mistakenly thought it offered that the land north of the Limpopo had long ago been colonized by an ancient civilization, so symbolizing "the justness of colonization – a kind of archaeological legitimization of his own colonization of Rhodesia" (Maylam 74). His 1890 acquisition of the Zimbabwe bird fatefully also coincided with him gaining a royal charter for his British South Africa Company to occupy then Mashonaland; only a few years later, in 1895, the name Rhodesia was given to Mashonaland's territory south of the Zambezi (Kuklick 135). Furthermore, of the soapstone birds relocated by Posselt and Bent respectively to South Africa and Germany, seven were returned to post-independence Zimbabwe, but the one taken by Rhodes remains at Grootte Schuur to this day. This is a particularly startling fact in light of the legend that peace and prosperity will return to the land only once all the birds have come home to roost

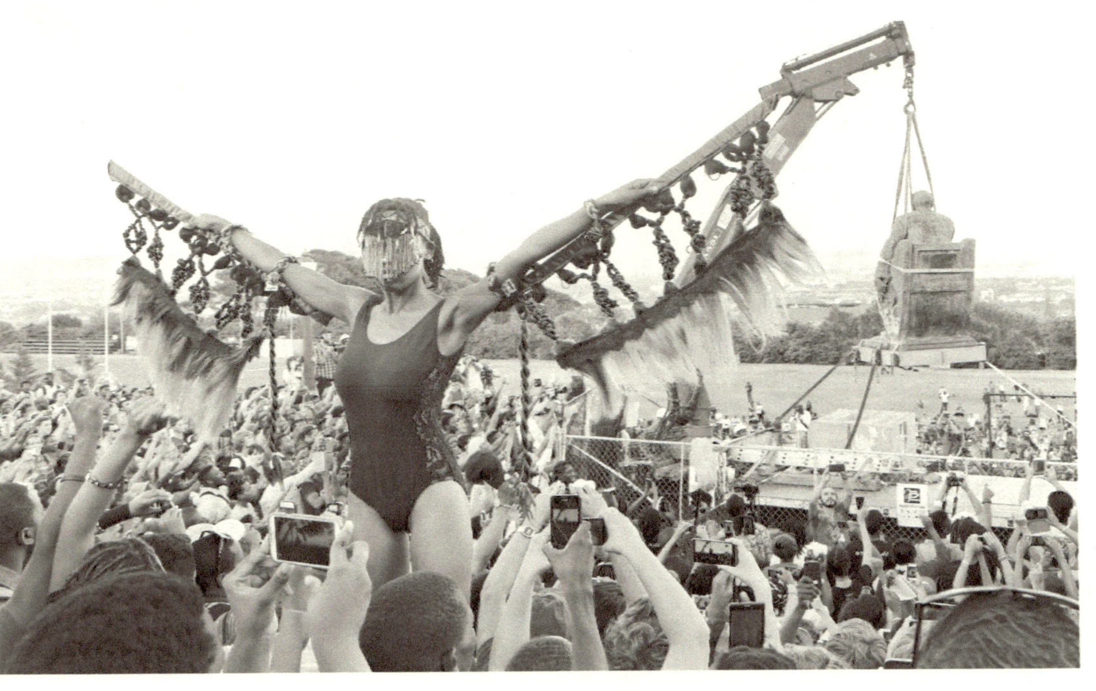

Figure 4.2 Chapungu by Sethembile Msezane.

(P. Murray 203), a legend that also explicitly informed Msezane's choice of medium at the fall of the Rhodes statue, as well as a film titled "Falling" that she subsequently made about Chapungu (Msezane, "Living").

Though Msezane's performance resonates politically across a number of platforms, for the purposes of my argument here, I briefly highlight two aspects of what I conceive of as the work's *affective* cartography. First, the juxtaposition of her living, breathing body with the statue of Rhodes powerfully shifts the focus from the archive as a fixed, institutional site of knowledge retrieval towards what Jacques Derrida might call its feverish qualities – those absences and omissions that are both produced by and paradoxically constitutive of the archive (Derrida and Prenowitz, passim). This is an archive, as Elspeth Brown and Thy Phu have shown (19), that is particularly amenable to being read for its affective granularity. For Msezane the institutional archive encapsulated by a statue such as that of Rhodes has in fact always been deeply affective in its painful obliteration of alternative accounts of South African history.

Second, the work very deliberately engages the historically dissimilar terrains of white and Black feeling. On the one hand, Msezane's performance of Chapungu, as well as her larger body of performance and conceptual art, seems to be aimed very firmly at a young, Black female viewer, who will be familiar with the exhausting psychic labour that attends inhabiting Cape Town's hostile colonial urban infrastructure (see, for instance, Msezane, "Kwasuka"; Jayawardane, "Bad"; Maroga; Lemu). Msezane references this pain and labour also as profoundly gendered as she stands on the plinth behind Rhodes in six-inch stiletto heels – a well-known signifier of women's conscription into painful standards of beauty – and as her arms shake with the effort of holding up the heavy wings of hair crafted into chains (see "Msezane Performs"). On the other hand, Msezane also invites white viewers into her performance in very specific ways. Having declared viewer engagement to constitute a key dimension of her work, she has stated, for instance, that she wants the viewer to either "identify with the work or question their discomfort," and has listed the emotions evoked by her work to have ranged "from confusion or surprise to intrigue or even anger" ("Gallery"). As Kopano Maroga phrases it, "her work creates a psychosphere of ancestral energy that is reflected in those who attend her exhibitions."

In other words, her work functions explicitly as an affective map that represents the historicity of each viewer's unique experience, and as such necessarily opens up a very different emotional landscape for me as a white viewer than it would for viewers who identify with her experience on racial grounds. Like Maxwele's intervention then – and in a way that is uniquely attentive to the unequal distribution of multiple, intersectional forms of power – Msezane's work compels white viewers to move beyond the impulse to simply fetishize Black pain. She demands instead that white viewers do the difficult labour of confronting the archive of white privilege and its accompanying affective legacies, a form of labour that necessarily requires "taking on a role in a political project that outstrips [one's] own interests" (Hook, "Threatening" 197).

This labour is tied also to the manner in which Msezane references pain both in the act of embodied narration and as a figurative echo of unresolved historical violence. Of her performance as the statue of Rhodes was removed, Msezane explains,

> I was up there for hours. I would hold up my wings for about two minutes, take a 10-minute break and then put them up again. My legs hurt, but I didn't realize how sore my arms were until I came down – they were shaking. My feet were blue, I was sunburnt; I had heat stroke and blurry vision from looking directly into the sun. ("Msezane Performs")

Msezane's experience of somatic pain here reaches well beyond the personal as it dwells in, and bears witness to, some of the macrohistories of dispossession and violence that haunt the present, and that I discuss in greater detail in relation to gender-based violence in the next chapter. At surface level, the pain and discomfort she experiences on her plinth echo the pain she experiences as a Black woman inhabiting a stifling commemorative landscape. Yet her staging of pain also extends deeper into the spiritual realm of intergenerational ancestral memory as it references the psychosomatic afterlives of various colonial regimes of bodily regulation and exploitation.

Her decision, for instance, to craft Chapungu's wings out of hair reflects a preoccupation that runs through much of her artistic oeuvre, most notably in the installation "Kwasuka Sukela: Re-imagined Bodies of a (South African) 90s Born Woman."[17] As a signifier and site of biopolitical control, hair has long been central to the bodily lives of both racism and sexism (Erasmus 380).[18] For Msezane, hair also specifically references the difficulties of disentangling colonial practices of bodily gendering from historically African cultural practice:

> Researching hair within our traditional Zulu cultural context, I found out that hair was not as gendered as it is today. Both women and men adorned their bodies with hair; men would wear it on their arms and their

> legs and women would wear it as hats or skirts. The hair thus became an object unto itself, and I was interested in turning this thing that we now think of as very feminine into an object of commemoration. Hair also has strong links with identity, alluding to both racial politics and beauty politics. ("Kwasuka")

As an object of commemoration, then, hair is heavy with history.[19] Read alongside the six-inch stiletto heels and the reality of physical pain that she experiences as she tries to hold up her wings, Msezane's use of hair is deeply attentive to the unique ways in which sexism has lodged itself in the Black female body and psyche. As creative writers such as Kopano Matlwa and Malika Ndlovu have indicated in texts such as *Coconut* and *A Coloured Place,* racism has historically settled into the hair and hair regulation practices of Black South African women in remarkably hurtful ways.[20] These texts represent young Black women who stagger under the social pressure of unrealistic Eurocentric ideals of beauty, as they subject themselves to painful chemical hair straightening regimes. Writing about Matlwa's *Coconut,* Jessica Murray fittingly states that "in hair we thus see a powerful example of the well-known feminist insistence that the personal is political and that a rigid separation between the public and private spheres is untenable" (92). For Msezane, likewise, hair straddles the boundaries between private and public as it serves at once as a performative sign of bodily suffering and of the larger political histories that brought this suffering into being.

By inhabiting this history of psychosomatic pain, Msezane's performance of Chapungu further evokes the difficulties inherent in both the representation and witnessing of pain. In her much-cited book *The Body in Pain,* Elaine Scarry writes about the ways in which pain resists signification, about how the descriptive languages available to us fail in the face of extreme bodily pain. This state of unrepresentability also complicates how others are able to respond to pain. For Sara Ahmed, the impossibility of inhabiting another's body and feeling the singularity of their pain does not render pain a private experience, nor does it negate the ethical demand placed on those who witness this pain: "The impossibility of feeling the pain of others does not mean that the pain is simply theirs, or that their pain has nothing to do with me ... an ethics of responding to pain involves being affected by that which one cannot know or feel" (*Cultural* 30). Furthermore, the ethics of witnessing pain requires moving beyond simply appropriating this pain as one's own, as so frequently happens when those in power witness the pain of others. Ahmed insists instead that the "ethical demand" of witnessing another's pain is "that I must act about that which I cannot know, rather than act insofar as I know ... it is the very assumption that we know how the other feels, which would allow us to transform their pain into our sadness" (31).

Ahmed's thinking on "how pain enters politics" (23) further offers a map for moving from what Wendy Brown calls the fetishization of the wound – that is, the assumption that pain can be translated into an identity, which may in turn feed the view that there is an equivalence between forms of injury, or that there is a hierarchy of legitimate pain – towards collective resistant action. In her work on the ways in which experience became the grounds for collective mobilization during the 2015–17 student protests, feminist theorist Amanda Gouws draws on this work by Ahmed to highlight the need to "learn to hear what is impossible to hear and to be moved [by] a pain we cannot feel" (Gouws 11). Specifically, Gouws underscores the necessity to engage the affective imprint that apartheid and colonial history left on anyone who was not white, a legacy that "the transition to democracy could not erase, not even for the 'born free' students ... whose extended families may still be exposed to poverty and social exclusion" (11). Gouws points out that, even though student activists did mobilize pain as the grounds for political action in at times exclusionary ways ("through the exclusion of those who were sympathetic, but questioned the means" [12] of activism), in effect the politics of pain neither amounted to a straightforward fetishization of the wound nor prevented constructive political action: "on the contrary – the students managed to shift, through the protests, the goal posts around funding for education and the exposure of rape cultures more, in 2 years, than in the previous 21 years after transition" (12).

To bring this back to Msezane's work, the mobilization of the politics of experience by student activists opened up new ways of thinking about the sensory, embodied afterlives of colonial and apartheid dispossession, a topic central to Msezane's body of work. As Gouws explains, oppression has a long experiential legacy that "cannot be denied for those who feel them. For the students in the protest their experience of hostile, alienating (read white) institutional cultures was causing them pain that is mediated through bodily sensations" (11). Gouws touches here on two aspects central to Msezane's performance of Chapungu. First, for Msezane, history is lodged in the body, which serves, as I pointed out above, as a living, breathing contact zone between past and present. If, as Jonathan Flatley phrases it in a different context, "our affects come into existence only when attached to the ghosts from our past" (89), Msezane positioned her hurting body as a portal through which the ghosts of the past enter the present, and by means of which viewers can navigate their own feelings in relation to this present-past. Second, by performatively centring the realm of "bodily sensations," Msezane challenges approaches to commemoration that stop at the intellectual or the psychic without also attending to the imprint that histories of suffering made on the body, the flesh, the skin, the nerves, the breath, the muscles, the hair, the senses, and the gut.

In effect, then, Msezane's intervention works precisely against efforts to fetishize the wound as a sign of equivalence between widely divergent forms of individual suffering inflicted by a shared history. By singularizing this history through her sensorial, enfleshed body, Msezane's wayward performative activism, much like that of Maxwele, highlights the need to shift from commemorative archives cast in stone towards aesthetic archives anchored in the always shifting contingencies of experiential life.

Towards a Wayward Aesthetics of Commemoration

In the first chapter of this book, I considered some of the ways in which aesthetic activity might enliven viewers to a world of sensate perception beyond the confines of dominant modes of political and social belonging. I suggested that disappointment might be put to work as a mode of wayward feeling that disrupts some of the nation-building myths circulated in the early years after apartheid. As these myths are increasingly being called into question, the manner in which Maxwele and Msezane have been mobilizing the affective potential of embodied performance has chimed with what I elsewhere describe as "a reorientation from the conciliatory force of rainbow nationalism and attendant post-apartheid nation-building projects towards a more sensorially and aesthetically heightened engagement with South Africa's terminal contrasts" (Strauss, "Affective Return" 229).

As a challenge to existing commemorative practice in South Africa and elsewhere, the interventions of Maxwele and Msezane are nothing if not wayward in their obstinate refusal to maintain the dichotomization of thought and feeling, aesthetics and politics, past and present. Both performances in fact speak to an intensification of the affective charge of disappointment into a less patient and more urgently heated political aesthetics of pain, disgust, and/or anger (see also Nuttall, "Upsurge"). Maxwele's performance, for instance, mobilizes disgust as a politically charged feeling in ways clearly responsive to the definition of aesthetics that I privilege in this book's introduction. As the domain of aesthetic inquiry shifted from the corporeal and sensorial towards a narrower focus on beauty and the artistic object, so the embodied world of shitty feelings and smells came to be confined to modernity's outhouses and its subjugated populations. As Laporte points out, the "European Enlightenment's political economy of the senses appears to favor the visual" over the olfactory (84). In the discourse of Enlightenment aesthetics – and in the philosophy of Immanuel Kant in particular – "beauty does not smell" (84). Maxwele's intervention might be read then as an "aesthetic education" (Spivak, *Aesthetic* 122) of sorts, in that it by implication counters the repression of the excremental and the embodied in Enlightenment, colonial aesthetics; in effect it reintroduces smell's comprehensive sensorial archive into the terrain of higher education. If for Joshua Esty, shit serves as a powerful "discursive resource" in the work of decolonial symbolic and political redress (25–6), Maxwele's aesthetic activism also positions it as a commanding *affective* resource, mobilized in this instance as an olfactory catalyst to arguably one of the most vigorous challenges to existing habits of commemoration, not to mention to the most widespread and successful decolonial protests seen since the end of apartheid.

Msezane, likewise, offers a mode of commemorative practice firmly rooted in the living, sensorial body, that is, a commemorative aesthetics attentive to the corporeal singularity of the experiential body. Her performative embodiment of past pain further makes explicit the affective dimensions of what Marianne Hirsch has memorably defined as "postmemory," namely the inheritance, on the part of the descendants of survivors of trauma, of memories and stories they did not witness firsthand, but that nonetheless continue to manifest in profoundly hurtful ways. What Msezane enacts in her performance of Chapungu might be described, following Hirsch, as a form of "post-pain" accompanying "present-pain," in the sense that catastrophic histories are shown to echo across generational boundaries (even as the material inheritance of racial capitalism continues to inflict new wounds). As Kopano Maroga aptly phrases it,

> Msezane's work operates as a mechanism of re-remembering both our named and unnamed ancestors. Those whom history refused to document but have lived on in the psychosomatics of their descendants. Msezane's work operates as a vindication of intergenerational memory and a love letter to all those young black South Africans who have been dispossessed of their history; an offering of return.

This work also explicitly calls on those at a remove from the pain Msezane references to attend to this pain as an alternative, other-directed mode of wayward commemoration. For white South Africans, this means making ourselves vulnerable to what Ahmed calls

> a pain that cannot be shared through empathy [but that nonetheless serves as] a call not just for an attentive hearing, but for a different kind of inhabitance. It is a call for action, and a demand for collective politics, as a politics based not on the possibility that we might be reconciled, but on learning to live with the impossibility of reconciliation, or learning that we live with and beside each other, and yet we are not as one. (*Cultural* 39)

Ahmed's reference to "attentive hearing" here is particularly suggestive, as it leads us into the next chapter's focus on "resonant listening" as a mode of engaging the pain of another. In what follows, I consider the collaborative, multimodal work of audio-visual artist Gabrielle Goliath to further delve into some of the questions regarding mourning, loss, and witnessing the pain of others raised in chapters 3 and 4 thus far, and to ask what a consideration of resonance, in its multiple significations, might bring to making sense of wayward post-rainbow feeling.

5
Feminist Resonance

As August bled into September 2019, outrage about the scourge of gender-based violence in the country reached fever pitch. South Africa's "Women's Month" – meant to celebrate the achievements of women across the country – yet again witnessed staggering levels of violence against women.[1] News and social media feeds were overflowing with reports of women subjected to some of the worst misogynist violence ever recorded in a country well acquainted with deplorable levels of hate directed at women and gender-nonconforming people.[2] "Women's Month" and the weeks that followed witnessed the shooting and killing of boxing champion Leighandre "Baby Lee" Jegels by her estranged police officer boyfriend, the rape and murder of University of the Western Cape student Jesse Hess in her Parow flat, the killing and dismemberment of Lynette Volschenk at her flat in Levestein, Janika Mallo's gang rape and murder with a concrete block in Heinz Park, University of KwaZulu Natal student Sinethemba Ndlovu's death by stabbing, the abduction and murder of bakery owner Meghan Cremer by three men in Philippi, and the rape and murder of University of Cape Town film and media student Uyinene Mwretyana by a post office worker in Cape Town.

Mwretyana's murder in particular seemed to be the last straw to women accustomed to living under siege. Her killing sparked a viral movement that registered well beyond South African borders as people voiced their fury under the hashtags #AmINext, #RIPUyinene, #NotInMyName and #SAShutDown. It also brought large numbers of people out onto the streets, once again, in protests and marches against femicide and gender-based violence. On 5 September, for instance, thousands of women, gender-nonconforming people, and allies marched across the country dressed in black and purple, wearing chains, and carrying placards with slogans such as "My Body, Not Your

Crime Scene" and "Enough Is Enough." The protesters were calling for a state of emergency to be declared, and for a considerable shift in governmental priorities and in the allocation of state resources. Rosa Lyster's assessment of these events, published in *The New Yorker* on 12 September 2019, offers a particularly illuminating barometer of the state of public feeling at the time:

> For many South Africans, the protests following Mrwetyana's death have been an indication that there are ways of responding to this crisis that go beyond *sadness* and *anger* and the state's promise to set up some sort of commission of inquiry at a vague time in the future. Confronted with the reality of how she died, and the knowledge that "the post office" must now be added to the long list of places to be *scared* of, women around the country are reaching what feels like a breaking point. At protests and vigils this week, the mood has been a combination of *fury and astonishment* at how distorted our definition of "normal" has become. This past Thursday, in Cape Town, thousands of people marched on Parliament to demand a more definitive and urgent response to violence against women. It would be easy to say that there have been so many marches just like it, with the same songs, the same posters with the faces and names of dead women and girls, many of the same slogans. But, walking up Plein Street to the parliamentary buildings, where President Cyril Ramaphosa was scheduled to address the protesters, the *mood felt different*, as if the flashover had occurred, the point when the fire in the room becomes the room on fire. (emphasis added)

Lyster's words here echo many of the terms that have shaped my reading of the affective textures of post-rainbow political disillusionment up to this point. If, following the chronology of public feeling traced thus far, the burning tire in Berni Searle's installation "Black Smoke Rising" signalled structures of feeling that were still somewhat anticipatory – still circulating, to invoke Raymond Williams again, "on the edge of sematic availability" (134) – what we are witnessing are public moods increasingly indicative of a shift from smoke to fire, to stick with Lyster's analogy. Indeed, as I intimate also in the introduction, the horizon of time shaping post-apartheid aesthetic mediation seems increasingly to be informed by the affective logics of urgency and impatience.[3]

At a time of heightened global awareness of rampant sexual assault – brought to light in part by the #MeToo and #TimesUp movements – the hope in South Africa is indeed that we are seeing a public awakening of sorts, even as we know that similar hopes have been expressed many times before. It matters that this mood is one that has a long history, deeply embedded in centuries of push and pull between resistant feminist feeling and collective mobilization, on the one hand, and efforts at affective regulation and activist containment, on the other. What Sarah Nuttall identifies in relation to recent South African student activisms as "the shock of the new old, where what was taken by some to be the past is not past but coeval with the present" ("Afterword" 280) – a wave of activism fuelled by anger over late capitalism's exacerbation of economic inequality coupled with the enduring "legacies of colonialism and racism" (280) – is similarly to be found in "new old" forms of violent patriarchy, currently amplified and accelerated globally across new media platforms alongside a resurgent "politics of white restoration" (Hage). Yet if violent patriarchy and its affective corollaries have deep historical roots, the same is true for feminist feeling, and it is to these affective resonances that I turn in this chapter.

In brief, this chapter builds on my discussion of Black and feminist rage in the preceding chapter to make explicit some of the psychosocial precursors that are resonating through contemporary feminist popular protest and aesthetic activisms. Using the example of a postgraduate course on "feminist rage and love" that I have been teaching over the past few years as a starting point, I consider, for instance, how feelings historically subjected to patriarchal restraint – feelings that elude documentation by conventional means – have come to be mediated in recent activisms and aesthetics. Archives of sexual violence are particularly resistant to such an undertaking given the secrecy, fear, and silence that so frequently accompany sexual assault. What are the forms that anger takes when it is confined to an affective loop of repeated historical dismissal and constraint? What are the affective means by which silence is manufactured in the post-apartheid public sphere, and what modalities of feminist affect might be mobilized in response?

The chapter is inspired by both inventive new forms of South African feminist organizing (including those already mentioned and, for instance, the #RememberKhwezi, #RUReferenceList, #RapeAtAzania, #MenAreTrash, #EndRapeCulture, and #TotalShutDown protests), and by award-winning artist Gabrielle Goliath's painstaking aesthetic and ethical labour to collaboratively mediate the experience of gendered, racialized, and sexualized violence in her performative installations *Personal Accounts* (2014), *Elegy* (2015–present), and *This song is for …* (2019–present). With these activisms and aesthetics in mind, I attend to the concept of *resonant listening* as a decolonial feminist rebuke to violent patriarchy and its enduring effects. In the previous chapter, I wrote about the challenge recent student activisms have posed to the subordination of sensation and emotion to reason in colonial epistemologies, and to the historical imprint of this legacy on South African public culture. In this chapter, I highlight Goliath's undoing of this dualism through her multimodal approach to the question of loss, mourning, and traumatic recall, which she approaches by way of a decolonial gesture that resists ocularcentrism in favour of a creative practice open to "other affective and sensory registers" (Goliath, "Embracing") – the sense modality of hearing in particular.[4]

My reading of the concept of resonance as a frame for understanding both historical shifts in South African feminist public culture and Goliath's multisensory feminist aesthetics draws in part from Veit Erlmann's captivating rereading of the historical trajectory of Western thought as unfolding through the tension between reason and resonance. Alongside a groundswell of cultural theory associated with the affective turn, referenced throughout this book, Erlmann's work provides a germane critique of the still-influential Cartesian assumption that deliberation can only proceed from a place of cool detachment, a critical stance that has historically led to the dominance of the sense of sight over that of hearing.[5] As Erlmann explains, "ever since René Descartes and John Locke invented an entity called 'the mind,' thinking has come to be understood as reflection. Just as the mirror reflects the light waves without its own substance becoming affected, the mind mimetically represents the outside world while at the same time remaining separate from it" (9). Erlmann departs from those who would make thought conditional upon the absence of resonance – an inheritance to be found also in certain schools of historical and anthropological thought that saw the development of historical and cultural differences "along an axis distinguishing a modern, image-saturated West from the sound-oriented, 'tribal' societies of China and Africa" (14). He unearths an alternative trajectory in Western cultural history – of which he cites Romanticism and twentieth-century phenomenology as the most prominent examples – which places reason and resonance much less at odds than has been assumed to be the case, an intellectual history that instead "refused to let go of the simple fact that truth and knowledge do not exist independently of the way in which they are acquired and that subjectivity is not merely the impure other of objectivity" (11).

Without getting sidetracked by Erlmann's journey through the bowels of Western philosophy, I find in the attention he pays to the senses – and to the ear and the generative concept of resonance – a critical impulse recognizable in much recent work in the field of affect studies, and also seen in decolonial and feminist gestures to centre the embodied sensorium in any project of decolonial and feminist redress. If resonance, in dominant Cartesian approaches to the mind-body, reason-emotion dichotomy, is conceived of as too affective – as entailing "adjacency, sympathy, and the collapse of the boundary between perceiver and perceived" (Erlmann 9), and as making a sensory claim on the body that makes detached deliberation impossible – the term in fact beautifully chimes with feminist work at the core of this chapter and book.

What follows is a two-part exploration of the concept of feminist resonance to make sense, first, of the afterlives of feminist feeling in the contemporary South African public and feminist imagination and in recent activisms, and second, of the tribute Goliath pays to these resonances in her work on the pasts, presents, and futures of gender-based, sexualized, and racialized violence. The structure of the chapter corresponds roughly to two of the interrelated meanings of the term resonance, namely, as the power of certain ideas to strike a chord – to come into affective-emotional-cognitive harmony – and to the materiality of acoustic vibrational transfer. In line with the distinction between hearing and listening made by French philosopher Jean-Luc Nancy, discussed in greater detail below, I argue that *resonant listening* – a mode of wayward listening that moves beyond conventional boundaries between past and present, mind and body, meaning and sound – is central to the work of undoing gender injustice. Following Red Chidgey's work on "feminist afterlives," namely the "materialisation of activist pasts in successive presents as they endure, circulate and intensify" (2), I start by conceptualizing resonant feminist listening, in the first section, as a method of attending to some of the gaps, silences, and erasures that haunt the multisensory affective archive of South African feminist writing and activism. I develop my argument here by way of two affectively loaded examples: (1) the apartheid-era editorial interference in Miriam Tlali's novel *Muriel at Metropolitan* (later republished as *Between Two Worlds*), and (2) the Jacob Zuma rape trial and its feminist afterlives. In the subsequent section, I consider how the works of Goliath enable modes of resonant feminist listening responsive to these multisensory and affective histories as she moves her audiences beyond the imperative to simply understand, towards the more-than-understood-of embodied testimony and experience.

Resonant Rage

The second chapter of this book concludes by considering the temporality of prolonged disappointment and its sensual present. Using the example of Charlotte Maxeke's extraordinary struggle to become the first Black woman to obtain a university degree in 1901, and the subsequent shrinking of access to opportunity for educational and economic advancement for Black South Africans, I pointed out that an affective loop of repeated disappointment was the norm for those disenfranchised by colonialism and apartheid for many decades to come. For those inhabiting patriarchy's long historical reach, frustrated expectation continues to assert itself in contemporary efforts to shape a more gender-just future.

This chapter stems in part from an honours course that I have been teaching since February 2017, titled "Archives of Feminist Rage and Love in (South) African Literature and Culture." The course conceives of a selection of theoretical and creative cultural texts, primarily from South Africa, as conveyors of gendered feeling. The aim of the course is twofold: (1) to map some of the intellectual precedents to contemporary articulations of feminist feeling in cultural theory and creative production, and (2) to read a range of literary and audio-visual cultural South African texts as affective archives. Two bodies of scholarship offer methodological and conceptual anchors for these somewhat vague and nebulous tasks, and also inform this chapter's understanding of misogyny's affective archives as "recalcitrant."

The first aim derives from the much-discussed imperative – referenced also in my discussion of Msezane's work in the preceding chapter – to re-evaluate the archive as an unreliable site of knowledge production, preservation, and mediation during South Africa's colonial and apartheid pasts, when histories tended to be filtered unapologetically through the lenses of those in power. In a volume titled *Refiguring the Archive*, published in 2002, only a few years after the Truth and Reconciliation Commission hearings were formally concluded, Carolyn Hamilton, Verne Harris, and Graeme Reid articulate this imperative along Foucauldian lines as the need to study the archive not simply in its conventional institutional locations but rather as "the system of statements, or rules of practice, that give shape to what can and cannot be said" (9). The "Apartheid Archive" project, originating in 2008 at the University of the Witwatersrand and bringing together a large group of researchers from around the globe, constitutes an important recent effort to refigure and augment apartheid's partial archive by foregrounding the quotidian experience of apartheid racisms that escaped the purview, for instance, of the Truth and Reconciliation Commission and its emphasis on apartheid-era gross human rights violations. The thesis at the core of this project is that apartheid-era racisms will continue to reassert themselves in both psychic and social ways unless this past is acknowledged and processed as an ongoing component of the everyday lives of the country's citizens. As Garth Stevens,

Norman Duncan, and Derek Hook phrase it in their editorial introduction to a volume collating some of the work to emerge from this project, "As a sociopolitical and psychical apparatus, racism proves notoriously recalcitrant and difficult to shift, precisely because a challenge to any one aspect of its system, as in the case of a change to prevailing discursive norms, can be absorbed by compensatory processes" ("Introduction" 1–2). Extending the work done in this project, my aim here is to try to think about "recalcitrance and recrudescence" (Stevens, Duncan, and Sonn 26) in gendered terms. If the TRC was tasked at least in part with addressing the traumatic legacy of apartheid-era racisms, how are we to account for the arguably longer history of trauma resulting from violent misogyny?[6] In the absence of a TRC concerned explicitly with confronting histories of gender-based human rights violations (not to mention the more quotidian experience of sexism both past and present), how are we to approach South Africa's history of gender-based trauma?

The second body of scholarship consists of work generated in South Africa and elsewhere on the affective means whereby women's dissent gets managed or coerced out of sight, and women's bodies, movement, and psychic lives come to be regulated in spaces both private and public. Ann Cvetkovich's reading of lesbian lives as archives of feeling is particularly generative in this regard, as is work by South African feminist critics such as Nthabiseng Motsemme ("The Mute") and Pumla Dineo Gqola (*Rape*; *Reflecting*) on the "feeling rules" (Hochschild, "Feeling" 563) that have historically determined whether women's trauma and anger are legible. Cvetkovich, for instance, laments "an apparent gender divide within trauma discourse that allows sexual trauma to slip out of the picture" (3), and instead approaches histories of trauma through cultural texts as an "archive of feelings, the many forms of love, rage, intimacy, grief, shame, and more that are part of the vibrancy of queer cultures" (6). Attentive to the fact that trauma "puts pressure on conventional forms of documentation, representation and commemoration" (*Archive* 6), Cvetkovich assembles an unusual archive, incorporating the genres of personal memory, testimony, memoirs, letters, performances, family photographs, and so forth, to flesh out the psychic textures of everyday lesbian experience in the US context of which she writes.

Gqola, in turn, theorizes the value of approaching women's feelings as a valid source of knowledge (*Rape* 169), particularly in the absence of reliable historical evidence. Writing about the partial historical record of women's experience of sexual violation and rape during South Africa's slave, colonial, and apartheid pasts, when Black women were largely considered "unrapable" (53) and therefore without recourse to legal protections, Gqola invokes the insights of feminist scholars such as Gabeba Baderoon, Yvette Abrahams, Jane Bennett, and Sue Armstrong to advocate for analytical methods that "read silences not as absences but as spaces rich with meaning" (171). In questioning why silences on women's history, experience, and feeling blight available documentation – why these silences "are forced and/or chosen, by whom and when" – writes Gqola, "lies a wealth of knowledge" (171). Refusing to let silence be mistaken for absence, Gqola turns to fiction and other forms of imaginative cultural production as important resources for filling in gaps, and for making sense of the means by which women's psychic lives came to be regulated through the "female fear factory" (78), namely the many "visible, audible and other recognizable cues to transmit fear and to control" (78), including "the threat of rape and other bodily wounding" (79).[7]

Our course texts span a sizeable historical landscape, ranging from creative and theoretical engagements with (South) Africa's slave pasts in works, for instance, by Yvette Christiansë, Berni Searle, and Ama Ata Aidoo; to novels and biographies that texture women's experience of racism, sexism, and sexual violation during and after apartheid, such as Miriam Tlali's *Muriel at Metropolitan/Between Two Worlds*, Lauretta Ngcobo's *And They Didn't Die*, Kagiso Lesego Molope's *This Book Betrays My Brother*, Redi Tlhabi's *Khwezi: The Remarkable Story of Fezekile Ntsukela Kuzwayo*, and Kuleka Putuma's *Collective Amnesia*, to recent imaginative contestations of toxic masculinity and feminist and gender-queer resistance in works by Angela Makholwa and Thando Mgqolozana. My students and I found in Tlali's *Muriel at Metropolitan* a remarkable example of editorial interference that amounted to the deliberate excising of feminist rage, and our reading of this text, alongside work evidencing the process of editorial intervention that led to its eventual publication, set the tone for our subsequent consideration of South African archives of feminist feeling. The editorial history of Tlali's text helps also to elucidate some of what informs this chapter's approach to the work of resonant listening as a means by which to access archives of historically excised or suppressed feminist feeling.

In brief, Tlali's semi-autobiographical novel, first written in 1969, was not published until 1975, after having been rejected by a number of local publishing houses. Ravan Press published it, as Theophilus Mukhuba explains, "only after removing certain extracts they thought would certainly offend the Censorship Board – the South African literary watchdog" (2469). These efforts notwithstanding, the board nevertheless deemed it too jarring to apartheid sensibilities and summarily banned it shortly after its publication. Remarkable here is not that the novel ended up being banned – an unsurprising decision on the part of apartheid's notorious Censorship Board – but rather the extent to which editorial intervention unfolded along affective lines. Two brief examples, cited by Sarah Nuttall in her critical excavation of this literary archive, will suffice to make the point.

The first concerns the title of the text. The original manuscript lists the title as *I Am Nothing*, with possible alternatives included by Tlali as *Them and Us* and *Between Two Worlds*. The shift in tone here is noteworthy, and demonstrates clearly the softening of sentiments assumed to be deemed dangerous by the apartheid state. As Nuttall puts it, in the editorial decision to replace these titles, "the sense of extremity … is lost, the notion of not being worth anything that is absent in the much more placid *Muriel at Metropolitan*" ("Literature" 283). Editorial changes such as these "play down the feelings of worthlessness and also the anger that Tlali often expresses in *I Am Nothing*" (285), a fact made plain also by the quote, reprinted from Sheila Roberts's foreword, chosen for the back cover of the Ravan edition:

> Muriel's story is *never strident in hatred or resentment* against those who have turned her, in Fanon's words, into an "object in the midst of other objects." There is even at times a *latent warmth in her attitude towards those "on the other side,"* a warmth which she knows they will never allow to develop … this story should *enlighten, surprise and even delight* readers, both black and white. (emphases added by Nuttall)

For Tlali to express her true feelings about racial injustice, as Roberts's words indicate, would be to come across as "strident" – from the Latin stridor, meaning a "harsh, creaking noise, [or] shrill sound" (Online Etymology Dictionary) – a term with deeply gendered undercurrents, given the frequent association of women's anger or emotional articulation with shrillness. To guard against Tlali's narrative taking on the threatening tones associated with the "feminist killjoy" (Ahmed, *Promise* 67), Roberts is at pains to present her as genial in her disposition towards her white readers in particular. In short, Black female feeling is here subjected to the affective directives of what Robin Diangelo, in the context of contemporary race relations in the United States, has termed "white fragility" (*White*, passim), namely the defensive behaviours that stem from being confronted with the truth of one's own racism, and the demands these behaviours place on those trying to challenge white supremacy.

It bears noting here that the change in title, and the editorial gutting of her manuscript, were experienced as particularly hurtful by Tlali. As she explains in the introduction to the restored 2004 version of the novel published by the Canadian publisher Broadview – this time titled *Between Two Worlds* – the initial title

> was a far cry from "Between Two Worlds" – one of the tentative titles I had preferred. And I returned to my matchbox house in Soweto, locked myself in my little bedroom, and cried. I decided later to go away to Lesotho, when the book came out. I ran away. The book was finally published, or rather what was left of it. Five whole chapters had been removed; also paragraphs, phrases and sentences. It was devastating, to say the least. (Tlali, *Between* 10)[8]

In the context of apartheid-era South Africa, one may defend Roberts's placatory editorial interventions with the observation that the editors were doing what needed to be done to try – unsuccessfully, as it turned out – to get the novel past the apartheid Censorship Board. Yet as Nuttall points out, the excised sections of the text also reflect liberal-leftist suppositions about voice, genre, and feeling that resulted in editorial decisions arguably in excess of the obvious considerations regarding apartheid censorship. Tlali's own reflections in this regard, cited by Nuttall, are revealing:

> INTERVIEWER: Let's talk about your work now. Many critics tend to find your work "modest" and "subdued" (to quote Richard Rive), yet I find an element of anger, especially in the protest of Muriel … Would you agree with this?
>
> TLALI: Yes. There is very great anger, and I'm happy that it does show. My own grandmother was a very angry woman, and my mother was. You can discover this in Muriel, for instance … There's anger in almost every one of us. (qtd. in Nuttall, "Literature" 289)

Tlali's views here show apartheid's literary archive to be incomplete not only as a result of the obvious limitations placed on publishing by the apartheid state, but specifically also on affective grounds, as Black writers – and Black women writers in particular – were subjected to a range of affective prescriptions that restricted the range of feeling deemed appropriate for inclusion in this archive. Given the historically intersectional nature of gender injustice in South Africa, these prescriptions were necessarily forged through the lenses of both racism and sexism, through which the body and its affective articulation became the object of colonial and apartheid control. The excision of the full emotive range of Tlali's narrative offers a notable South African incarnation of Elizabeth Spelman's point, cited in the previous chapter, regarding the manner in which the anger of those considered subordinate has been historically proscribed or conflated with rage by those who considered themselves racially dominant.

This history of affective excision is a central part of South Africa's colonial and apartheid archive, and percolates through the manner in which women's everyday lives continue to be regulated post-apartheid, as well as in how feminist aesthetic and political activisms have taken shape in response. In attending to these affective erasures and edits, I propose a methodology of *resonant feminist listening*, namely, a method of reading the archive of women's cultural production and activism for its multisensory, multigenerational resonances. Red Chidgey's understanding of "assemblage memory" (1) and Rainer Mühlhoff's theorization of "affective resonance" (189) help here to elucidate how women's (emotional) pasts resonate across time and space, and enable me to foreground the embodied, sensorial elements through which feminist activist pasts have been made available to present feminist reworking and amplification.

In a nutshell, Mühlhoff derives the concept of "affective resonance" from work in developmental psychology, Spinozan ontology, classical physics, and affect theory, defining it as a "process of actualization in a relational field of potentials to affect and be affected that is jointly constituted based on the affective dispositions of individuals in an affective arrangement" (194). Affective resonance as a mode of relational affective embedding, as Mühlhoff defines it, does not necessarily presuppose agreement, even if it can, under the right conditions, "contribute to the gradual and tacit emergence of empowering new forms of attachment and intimate relatedness" (198). Mühlhoff further conceives of these resonances in interpersonal terms as a dynamic flowing from the "affective dispositions" (194) of bodily co-present individuals in a particular social encounter, yet acknowledges that the concept could be extended to study the reception, for instance, of films or novels, or to understanding contexts in which physical co-presence may be digitally mediated (a reality made near-inescapable since 2020 by the coronavirus pandemic).

It is in this regard that Red Chidgey provides a valuable approach to the diachronic transmission of activist knowledges across generational boundaries in her work on the afterlives of feminist social movements. Chidgey pays attention to "the agile, contradictory, sometimes vital, sometimes banal, extensions of feminist ideas and materials into time frames not of their making" (6). To this end, she takes an "assemblage approach [that] enables the researcher to move beyond 'snapshots' of particular generations, media or single units of analysis, to see longer resonances and cross-fertilisations at play" (6). Neither Mühlhoff nor Chidgey explicitly foregrounds the acoustic dimensions of resonance, which I theorize in my reading of Goliath's work as an important element of resonant feminist listening, yet I nonetheless find in their combined approaches to resonance a generative entry point into some of the affective afterlives of South African gendered excisions and feminist activisms in digital times.

Chidgey ascribes the restlessness of activist histories in part to the increased presence of digitally mediated communicative modes through which histories of resistance have entered into the everyday lives of contemporary civic actors. The "reproducibility and transferability of digital data" account for the increased speed and ease with which memories and knowledge of feminist movements have of late been circulating "through new media ecologies," in turn "generating an unprecedented 'long-tail' of protest online" (2). With this in mind, Chidgey studies how a selection of "feminist assemblages" (4) – namely assemblages of personal and mediated memories, digital data, archival materials, cultural production, and so forth – "bring politically loaded pasts to bear in the present with new intensities" (4).

In the South African context, the "assemblage memory" surrounding the widely discussed rape trial of former president Jacob Zuma reveals similar new media-enabled resurgences of activist intensity. This trial, and the many modes of feminist writing and protest to emerge from it, fundamentally reshaped the gendered public sphere in South Africa, and cannot but feature centrally in any attempt to consider post-apartheid public culture as an archive of gendered feeling. The trial and its psychosocial aftermath – in terms of both its misogyny-bolstering and resistant feminist resonances – provides an exemplary record of feminist rage as it came to be policed during and after the trial, and subsequently excavated and amplified across protest sites. My aim, in the remainder of this section, is not to rehash the many analyses of the trial and its outcomes, but to briefly present it as an archive of recalcitrant and recrudescent misogyny and resonant feminist rage.

To summarize, in November 2005, Fezekile Ntsukela Kuzwayo, a well-known HIV-positive lesbian activist at the time, brought a rape charge against then deputy president Jacob Gedleyihlekisa Zuma, a family friend whom she considered to be a father figure. Daughter to Judson Kuzwayo – a close personal friend and comrade of Zuma, and chief representative of the African National Congress in Zimbabwe before his passing in a road accident in 1985 – the woman who came to be known to the public only as Khwezi could not have predicted the extent to which her life would be altered as a result of her attempt to hold a politically powerful man to account. Explicitly naming Kuzwayo here is significant, as her identity had to remain hidden during and long after the trial owing to fears over her safety.[9] In the prologue to journalist Redi Tlhabi's 2017 biography of Kuzwayo, who passed away on 9 October 2016, the latter is quoted as saying, "The rapist is not in hiding, why must I? Khwezi has served me well, but now it is time for her to go" (1). Made many years after Zuma's acquittal by a sympathetic judge who admitted the complainant's sexual past and prior experience of sexual assault into evidence during the trial, Kuzwayo's statement here exposes a pervasive rape culture within which victim blaming and revictimization act to silence rape survivors. It also reveals Kuzwayo's relief at finally having her ordeal made public after years in exile in the Netherlands and Tanzania, while her rapist went on to become the country's president.

A large corpus of media and academic commentary was generated by those of us who were outraged by the way in which events played out in both the legal and popular theatre surrounding the trial, about how Kuzwayo was treated throughout, and about the implications all of this had for gendered citizenship in South Africa. As I phrased it at the time, "during what should have been an inquiry into the sexual conduct of the defendant, Khwezi found herself the target of an invasive assault on her character, had to listen repeatedly to allegations that women with a certain sexual history and who dress in a certain way 'ask for it,' and had to face insults and death threats from the crowds of Zuma supporters who gathered outside of the courtroom" ("Memory" 85). The trial led many of us to take a new look at the disconnect between South Africa's progressive Constitution and the everyday lived realities of women in the country. It has resonated powerfully, and with increased force, also through feminist activisms many years after the trial. In short, Kuzwayo's treatment during this trial and the feminist activism her bravery subsequently inspired could be considered exemplary of a larger shift in the articulation and reception of feminist feeling in post-apartheid South African public culture.

The reception that greeted Tlhabi's 2017 biography of Kuzwayo when compared to that of feminist writer and activist Mmatshilo Motsei's *The Kanga and the Kangaroo Court: Reflections on the Rape Trial of Jacob Zuma*, published in 2007 shortly after Zuma was acquitted on the charge of rape, provides a good example of this shift. Unlike Motsei's book, Tlhabi's biography of Kuzwayo was met with widespread applause, garnering record-breaking audiences at its launches, and racking up enviable sales figures. Whereas Motsei's book circulated mainly among a small group of feminist scholars and activists at the time, and resulted in Motsei's subsequent "loss of income, of friends and of security" (Mbandazayo), Tlhabi's book was widely embraced. This striking contrast had nothing to do with the quality of the writing, or the eloquence of the authors' respective assessment of events surrounding the trial: both texts offer an excoriating and persuasive critique of a political, social, and criminal justice system rigged in favour of (powerful) men.

Instead, the contrast in reception reflected widespread national exasperation at the lies, corruption, and dysfunction that plagued the Zuma presidency, and that made it safe to take a public stand against him. Even Cyril Ramaphosa, then still vice president of the country, opportunistically declared, in December 2017, that he believed Khwezi was raped (Lekabe), setting off a twitter storm and outraging every feminist who had witnessed his silence for more than ten years while Kuzwayo was being brutally muzzled and pushed out of sight. As Kwezilomso Mbandazayo, the feminist activist who loaned her name to Kuzwayo, phrases it in her deeply personal, heartfelt comparative review of Tlhabi and Motsei's books, addressed posthumously to Kuzwayo, "attitudes towards you, Khwezi, have softened somewhat, and even some who counted among Zuma's staunchest supporters back then say they made a mistake in standing by him – but not because of what he did to you; because of what he is doing to the country as state president. The gall." In fact, Mbandazayo reads Zuma's waning support as the primary reason why Tlhabi's biography received such a warm public embrace.

Shifts in Zuma's public fortunes notwithstanding, there is no denying that the work of a host of feminist scholars and activists – especially the members of the "One in Nine Campaign," founded in support of Kuzwayo in her case against Zuma, who have been actively refusing to let this trial be airbrushed from public memory – contributed to a gradual build-up of feminist rage among a new generation of feminists. If Kuzwayo and Motsei were – much like Miriam Tlali – subjected to coercive misogynist censoring, their outspokenness, anger, and defiance have nonetheless been resonating with increased intensity through public culture in recent years. A similar point is articulated by feminist scholar Shireen Hassim as she ponders the reasons why Tlhabi's text found fertile public ground a decade after Motsei's was widely dismissed:

> SA has changed. In the wake of the trial, a new and assertive feminist movement seeded and grew. It began with the women's rights organisation,

> One in Nine, formed expressly to support Fezeka, but has ballooned well beyond that.
>
> Its daughters are everywhere — the four young women who held up banners during a Zuma speech at the Independent Electoral Commission in 2015 [*sic*]; the queer black feminists on university campuses who are no longer prepared to tolerate violence in the name of unity; the artists and musicians and writers who are framing experiences in new ways. They too, are part of a new moment that makes possible a new conversation.

Of the many feminist daughters of whom Hassim speaks here, the example provided by the four young women responsible for the so-called #RememberKhwezi protest, perhaps best conveys the extent to which feminist rage has been resonating intergenerationally of late. On Saturday, 6 August 2016, at what should have been an uneventful ceremony to mark the end of the municipal elections, these four young Black feminists stole the limelight. As Zuma delivered his address, Simamkele Dlakavu, Tinyiko Shikwambane, Naledi Chirwa, and Amanda Mavuso gathered in front of his podium to hold up five A4-sized pieces of paper that read "I am 1 in 3," "#," "10 yrs later," "Khanga," and "Remember Khwezi." Clearly referencing the 2006 rape trial, their silent protest served eloquently to highlight the fact that the criminal justice system consistently fails rape survivors. The protestors forcefully inserted feminist defiance into a gender-conservative nationalist narrative that would rather have kept Kuzwayo's struggle out of public view. Unlike earlier generations of women's activism (including on the part of the notoriously gender-conservative ANC Women's League), the #RememberKhwezi protesters – as well as young women associated with protests such as #EndRapeCulture, #RUReferenceList, #TotalShutDown, and #RapeAtAzania – were unapologetically feminist, and were unafraid to refer to themselves as such.

While feminist commentators applauded the women's courage, members of both the ruling elite and their patriarchal foot soldiers were quick to condemn their actions, and to decry the "disrespect" they had shown Zuma. ANC Women's League president Bathabile Dlamini, for instance, rushed to insist that Zuma had been acquitted of the charge of rape in 2006, and that "no head of state should be treated like this."[10] She took pains to suggest that the women were simply puppets of the Economic Freedom Fighters and its male leadership, who were said to be responsible for choreographing their protest (a charge that the women strongly reject, and that Gqola ascribes to the "deliberate phallic re-insertion of men who are not in the frame of reference and minimising what the women's choices and bodies communicate" [*Reflecting* 37]).

The moment has been discussed at length by South Africa's feminist commentariat as indicative of precisely the kinds creative strategies to have emerged from the "new and assertive feminist movement" of which Hassim writes. Gqola, for instance, reads the protest as a powerful example of "the beauty of feminist rage" (25). In a chapter in her 2017 book *Reflecting Rogue: Inside the Mind of a Feminist*, Gqola takes a particularly interesting example of social media–driven culture jamming following the protest to make sense of this transmission of rage across generational lines, offering, in turn, an eloquent account of the kind of feminist resonance that Chidgey identified in a different context.

The example involves an image that well-known unionist, former parliamentarian, and gender rights activist Pregs Govender posted on her Facebook page, namely of the four women staging the #RememberKhwezi protest superimposed onto an image of four of the leaders of the famous 1956 Women's March against the South African pass laws, commemorated every year during "Women's Month" (figure 5.1).[11] The black and white archival image of these women significantly serves to edit Jacob Zuma out of the picture, with all that such an excision implies. The image was widely shared on social media, and reminds viewers that the #RememberKhwezi protest not only marked ten years since the end of the Zuma rape trial, but perhaps more importantly, sixty years since this 1956 march, famously led by Lillian Ngoyi, Helen Joseph, Rahima Moosa, Albertina Sisulu, and Sophia Williams-De Bruyn. These women managed, on 9 August 1956, to organize a protest march of an estimated 20,000 women to the Union Buildings, many years before the existence of digital technologies and hashtags.

The palimpsest provided by the image also calls forth other, more recent, activist resonances. As Gqola explains, "#RememberKhwezi is in the spirit of the many marches by the 1in9 Campaign and student feminist action like #RUReferenceList, Silent Protest, #RapeAtAzania and many other forms of action feminists organise regularly across the country" (*Reflecting* 43). These are debts of which the #RememberKhwezi protesters are acutely aware. Dlakavu's articulation of these debts merits being quoted at length:

> We stand on the shoulders of a long lineage of black women doing the work of dismantling patriarchy and rape culture.
>
> They encourage us and give us the vocabulary to affirm that naming and shaming rapists is a legitimate black feminist response to patriarchal violence. An entire genealogy of black feminist resistance allowed us to stand up in Pretoria last Saturday night.

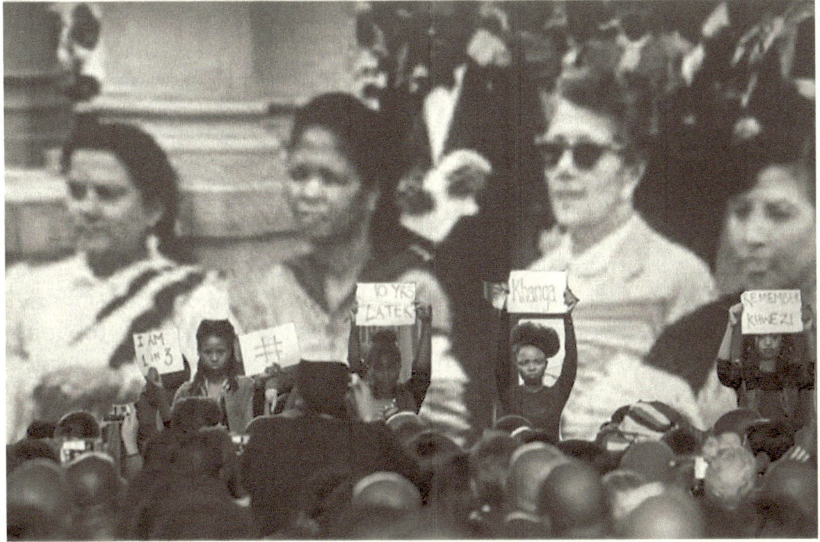

Figure 5.1 #RememberKhwezi Protest. See https://fleurmach.com/tag/lilian-ngoyi/.

What would have happened if black women did not unite to create the One in Nine Campaign? If black women at University of Cape Town had not called a rapist to account through #RapeAtAzania?

If women did not start the #RUReferenceList and organise at the university known as Rhodes?

If black women in townships and rural areas did not engage in mob justice as the only way to hold rapists to account when the law failed them?

And what would have happened if Professor Pumla Gqola had not written her book, *Rape: A South African Nightmare*? In it she writes: "We often place so much pressure on women to talk about rape, access counselling and get legal services to process rape, but very seldom do we talk about the rapists. We run the danger of speaking about rape as a perpetrator-less crime."

Throughout the week, one message has stuck with me. It was a tweet from Amanda Charles: "I was too young to understand at the time … but now. Now. I believe Khwezi."

Charles' tweet is one of the reasons we all felt it was important to engage in that impromptu protest, regardless of fear and consequence. We hope

> that one day we will live in a society that believes black women when they say they have been raped.
>
> We hope to live in a society free of rape. Until that society exists, we will continue to mobilise, protest and disrupt any space that seeks to perpetuate rape culture and erase women's histories. ("Khwezi Protest")

Dlakavu's reading here of the deep feminist pasts that sustain her own activist labours provides a poignant example of the work of *resonant feminist listening.* The unruly archives of feminist rage that Dlakavu evokes are mobilized explicitly for the sake of conscientizing a new generation of women to the work that remains to be done, and in the interest of refusing the recrudescent terms of misogynist affective coercion that would see fear override collective feminist agency.

Much of this labour is performed, as Hassim also implied in her assessment of the "new and assertive feminist movement" that grew from the trial, by "artists and musicians and writers who are framing experiences in new ways." In this regard, 2019 Future Generation Special Prize and Standard Bank Young Artist award winner Gabrielle Goliath does important work to move bodies beyond the incapacity of fear into the regenerative collaborative space of cross-generational, psychosocial feminist repair. Like Dlakavu, Goliath evokes suppressed histories that nonetheless echo affectively across generational boundaries, and that require sustained attention if the country's ongoing crisis of gender injustice is to be undone, and the traumas inflicted over centuries by violent misogyny are to be healed.

Feminist Acoustics

> The singular note that *Elegy*'s performers vocalise conveys a life – an agency, a subjectivity – that cannot be erased. That note resonates powerfully within us, long after the performers have exited the podium, and long after we leave the pavilion.
>
> Neelika Jayawardane[12]

Goliath's installations *Personal Accounts* (2014), *Elegy* (2015–present), and *This song is for …* (2019–present) speak intimately to her audiences about the costs of chronic gender-based and homophobic violence in South Africa. Harnessing the affective power of rhythm, repetition, and resonance – as acoustic and sensory technologies that make a powerful claim on the body – Goliath plots alternatives to trauma's distorted temporalities, and, by extension, conscripts her audiences into a larger project of feminist amplification. Her work is at its core motivated by a search for ethical ways of responding to violence, which in turn stems from her stated concern over the spectacularization of bodily suffering that so frequently attends the representation of gender-based, sexualized, and racialized violence. As Goliath herself explains, she seeks, in her work

> to counter the kinds of symbolic violence through which traumatised black, brown, feminine, queer and vulnerable bodies are routinely objectified. And here I am referring not only to art, but to the field of representation at large, and the ways in which we image, write, sound, speak and perform violence. My objective is to make possible alternative aesthetic encounters that allow for the commemoration as well as celebration of disavowed subjectivities. And this I see as being in itself a kind of recuperative and political work. (qtd. in Z. Jappie)

This recuperative, ethical drive informs the research-intensive, purposefully slow, and collaborative approach she takes to her work. It is also at the heart of Goliath's embrace of the multisensorial and acoustic dimensions of mourning and traumatic recall, particularly as these reconfigure the work of mediating the traumas that attend gender-based violence. In this regard, Goliath's work is deeply sensitive to what Nancy Rose Hunt, in her writings on the archive of rape in the Belgian Congo, has critiqued as the "shock of the photographic," namely the way in which the visual often distorts the complexity of experience by "blot[ting] out all else" (48). Like Hunt, Goliath engages "more fragile memory pictures and acoustic traces that tell something new and more complicated about the immediacy of violence and its duration in memory" (Hunt 48). Her feminist acoustics further chimes with Diana Taylor's point that "trauma-driven activism (like trauma itself) cannot simply be told or shown or known; it needs to be enacted, repeated, and externalized through embodied practice" (249).

Instead of attempting to render violence visually on screen, then, Goliath uses her installations to open possibilities for ethical resonance, what one might define as an acoustically inflected version of Kelly Oliver's notion of "response-ability" (*Witnessing* 5). Writing about the ethical obligation that attends the work of witnessing the pain of others, Oliver insists that the impossibility of fully knowing the experiential, emotional, epistemological, and sensory realities inhabited by another does not absolve one of the responsibility to nonetheless witness "beyond recognition" (6). (Oliver's position overlaps with that of Sara Ahmed, referenced in the preceding chapter, regarding the ethical demand placed on those witnessing – without appropriating – the pain of another.) For Oliver, subjectivity emerges fundamentally from an intersubjective space of "address-ability and response-ability" (7), a space exceeding that which can be assimilated into the already known.

Goliath's work with sound, and its capacity to resonate between bodies, eloquently conveys what Oliver, following Shoshana Felman's analysis of eyewitness testimonies of the Jewish Holocaust, conceptualizes as the more-than-known of witness testimony, namely that beyond the straightforward narration of the facts of an event – often conveyed through bodily, non-verbal cues – which both makes eyewitness testimony unique and points to its paradoxical impossibility. In other words, given that the *performance* of testimony "says more than the witness knows" (86), Goliath's use of sound, breath and other forms of non-verbal bodily communication serves as a "supplement of this more than knowledge," that is, as a gesture towards approximating the "truth of experience" (86).

By drawing viewers into an embodied encounter with the affective dimensions of experience, Goliath in effect brings to life what Oliver calls

> a repetition of an event, not a repetition of the facts of the event, or the structure of the event, but the silences and the blindness inherent in the event that, at bottom, also make eyewitness testimony impossible. In other words, *what makes testimony powerful is its dramatization of the impossibility of testifying to the event*. What makes witnessing possible is its performance of the impossibility of ever witnessing the event. (86; emphasis added)

Goliath's installations heighten precisely those elements of survivor testimony that exceed detached, disembodied recounting. As such, Goliath offers what Lucienne Bestall describes as "a holding space for our collective grief and anger … something other than statistics, than lost dockets and disbelief. Her work inspires something less ready-made than sympathy, something more immediate and bare. Call it a momentary understanding, or the raw material of empathy."

It helps here to recall Toni Morrison's insight that "language can never live up to life once and for all. Nor should it. Language can never 'pin down' slavery, genocide, war. Nor should it yearn for the arrogance to be able to do so. Its force, its felicity is in its reach toward the ineffable." Faced with the representational and ethical difficulties that Morrison gestures to here – making specifically the unspeakable traumas inflicted by violent patriarchy the focus of her work – Goliath chooses to make art, sound, and embodied performance the languages through which she reaches towards the ineffable.

Personal Accounts, for instance, mediates the politics of vocalization and silencing central to gender-based violence in tellingly somatosensory ways. The 5-channel video installation features five video portraits of survivors of domestic violence – and for some of rape – whose testimonies have been edited to include only the embodied gestures and sounds between verbal expression, that is, the inhales, the pauses, the swallows, the eye movements, and the facial modulations. Each of these portraits mutes the dialogue while amplifying the gesticulatory and the non-verbal sounds and somatics of communication, rendering each testimony "the living, breathing palimpsest of a violence of inscription and erasure" (Goliath, *Personal*). The effect is enhanced by the extended duration of each portrait, ranging from twelve minutes and thirty-nine seconds for the woman named only as "Charmaine," to fourteen minutes and thirty-two seconds for "Brenda" (only the first names of the women represented are provided, an indicator, one can assume, of domestic violence as a force of silencing, but perhaps also of patriarchal lineages enfolded, in most cultures, into surnames). Goliath's excision of the words spoken by each of the survivors, and her decision to include only these non-verbal embodied gestures, make breath and sound the gateway into the aftermath of domestic and gender-based violence for her audience. The emphasis she places on the personal here further signals the broader feminist challenge that her work poses to detached, impersonal engagements with gender-based violence, so frequently reduced to statistics and data, and subjected to scholarly paradigms derived from Cartesian metaphysics.

In a similar vein, *Elegy* brings together a group of female vocal performers to enact a long-term sonorous ritual of mourning, each dedicated to a specific woman lost to gender-based and homo-/transphobic violence. Staged multiple times nationally and internationally since 2015, each ritual involves a performance of roughly forty-five minutes, during which the performers vocally pass the note B-natural to each other and so stretch sound across a range of voices to create the impression of a single, sustained note. Each of the performers is dressed in black and emerges from the back of a darkened stage onto an illuminated podium, where she holds the note until she runs out of breath. She then steps to the right of the stage as the next vocalist moves onto the platform, in turn taking over the note from her. (The ritual is presented also as a multi-channel audio-visual installation in which up to nine recorded performances play in chorus.) This physically demanding performance draws in the audience to engage with the vocalists in a prolonged keening for the women lost, hauntingly calling forth the deceased into the presence of the gallery space.

In *Elegy*, the raped and murdered women commemorated thus far include Kagiso Maema, Louisa van de Caab, Ntombifuthi Eunice Sasha Dube, Sizakele Sigasa, Salome Masooa, Joan Thabeng, Hannah Cornelius, Camron Britz, Lerato 'Tambai' Moloi, Lekita Moore, Noluvo Swelindawo, Sinoxolo Mafevuka, Koketso "Queen," and Ipeleng Christine Moholane. The news of the passing of many of these women, though widely circulated in feminist circles, did not make it to national or front-page headlines, a tragic reality that speaks to the normalization of femicide in South Africa, and to which *Elegy* serves as an important corrective. Deeply mindful of her responsibility to the loved ones of the deceased, Goliath takes pains to contact them prior to each performance, and to include a tribute to the victim scripted by them. Eunice Ntombifuthi Dube, killed by her intimate partner on 20 September 2017 – the same day as her mother's birthday – is eulogized, for instance, by her sister Hulisile Portia Dube in a deeply moving reflection on the difficulties of coming to terms with her loss, particularly given the circumstances of her sister's painful killing. Koketso (better known as "Queen"), in turn, is lamented by a nameless "Friend," who writes in heartbreaking terms of the manner of her killing by a client, and of the shameful bungling of the investigation into her death by the police. Like "Queen" did, the friend works "at the bush" (Friend), making the fact that the killer continues to walk free particularly alarming given the ongoing threat that this presents to sex workers in the area. As she puts it, "most of us have not been interviewed by the police to give our statements" (Friend), an injustice that speaks plainly to systemic indifference to the safety of sex workers in the country.

Each of the three installations under discussion here – namely *Personal Accounts*, *Elegy*, and *This song is for …* – explicitly works with the voice and the breath as instruments of sound production, of the transmission of affect, and of the articulation of agency. The effect of inhabiting the reverential acoustic space in which these works are presented is emotionally overpowering, an experience deepened by the transmission of carefully manipulated or controlled breath and sound work in each of these installations. Journalist Hazel Kimani's reflections on *Elegy*, for instance, convey some of the installation's emotional force: "I am certain that it is impossible to shake off visual artist Gabrielle Goliath's *Elegy* performance. It has been weeks since I was part of the audience and I am still haunted by the memory." These works thus make significant emotional and ethical demands on their audiences, placing them in a relational space with the survivors, the deceased, and a community of mourners. As Goliath explains regarding *Elegy*,

> Significant to the work is how loss becomes a site for community, and for empathic, cross-cultural and cross-national encounters ... *Elegy* performances open an alternative intersectional space, wherein mourning is presented as a social and politically productive work – not in the sense of healing or "closure," but as a necessary and sustained irresolution.

The formally sparse, unadorned character of Goliath's *Elegy* belies its deep affective and ethical complexity. This is true also for *This song is for ...*, which unfolds as an elaborate meditation on the ethics of mediating the survival of sexual violence and its lingering traumatic effects. Here Goliath again works expressly with representational registers that stretch beyond the strictly visual or verbal. The privileging of the visual, writes Goliath, is a "very Western preoccupation" ("Embracing"), and its uncentring in favour of a multisensory aesthetics is thus tied to a larger project of decolonial activism. *This song is for ...* consists of eleven songs, each dedicated to – and chosen by – survivors of rape with whom Goliath collaborated closely. The songs were selected by each survivor for the way it resonated with them personally, transporting "them back to a particular time and place" and evoking "a sensory world of memory and feeling" ("Embracing"). Each dedication song is performed – again, in careful collaboration with Goliath – by a local ensemble of women-led and/or gender-queer musicians producing a new cover version.

Goliath deftly arranges the gallery space in which *This song is for ...* is staged to integrate the visual and the aural. On one side of the space, the words of each of the women expressing her experience of rape – taking the form variously of poetry, testimony, a letter, a news report, and a prayer – are printed on a purple wall in white lettering (the colour purple has a long association with feminist struggles against domestic and gender-based violence). On the other side of the space, two large television screens play a two-and-a-half-hour-long audio-visual track of each of the songs, conveying quite literally the gesture of dedication, as the songs chosen by each woman are directed at their words lining the opposing gallery wall. A few minutes into each performance, the musical score gets stuck, and the same few musical bars start to repeat in a loop, evoking the effect of a scratched vinyl record. The disruptive sonic iteration takes up the bulk of the duration of each song, and the soundtrack is only restored close to the end of each track, prolonging the installation's unsettling acoustic effect. The relief offered when the "scratch" is restored at the end of each performance is only short-lived, soon to be undone by the next dedication song, repeating the same pattern. The metaphor of the scratched vinyl record plainly signals trauma's haunting afterlives, sonically figured here as a disruptive memory that permanently threatens to intrude upon the rape survivors' present. The "stuckness" of the record conveys the temporality of trauma to render the rape survivor relentlessly tethered to the memory of her violation, yet the power of the performance lies in large part in the manner in which it alters psychic time for the listener. As trauma theorist Susan Spearey puts it, "the *listener*, rather than being permitted the stance of objective observer of the traumatised body, has to share or participate in the experience of 'stuckness,' and because of the workings of resonance, has to partake in an embodied way of this feeling of distorted temporality."

Though the visual track, featuring the musicians performing each song, also remains stuck in an accompanying loop, it is the aural that proves impossible to escape. The same is the case for *Personal Accounts* and *Elegy*, in which Goliath yields the sonics of breath, tone, and pitch to similar effect. It bears stating the obvious here: unlike the eye, which comes equipped with a lid to protect itself from unwanted sights, the ear cannot close itself off from sound by itself. Sound, in other words, is immersive. The visual, moreover, is unidirectional, and the conversion of the "real" into a filmed image involves a loss of dimensionality. Sound, in contrast, is omnidirectional, and the reproduction of sound "does not carry with it such a reduction in depth of information" (Elsaesser and Hagener 151).[13] What is more, the moving image can be frozen and reproduced in a single frame, whereas sound can only be reproduced in real time, is necessarily fleeting, and is tied to temporalities of loss (156).

Goliath's use of sound, then, is significant on multiple levels. First, her decision to mediate traumatic recall through the senses – and through embodied sound in particular – chimes with clinical studies of traumatic memory that indicate intrusive recall to proceed through a combination of sensory elements. As Bessel van der Kolk and Rita Fisler have shown, memories of trauma tend to be experienced – at least initially before the event is given semantic and narrative form – "primarily as fragments of the sensory components of the event: as visual images, olfactory, auditory, or kinesthetic sensations, or intense waves of feelings" (513). Of these sensory fragments, the aural is often dominant, a fact that is perhaps unsurprising given the dynamic nature of echoic memory, which, unlike iconic memory, resonates and is replayed in the mind to facilitate better understanding. In other words, given the fact that auditory stimuli are received by the ear only once (unlike the visual, which under conventional circumstances can be accessed and processed across a longer time span), and has to be briefly stored and replayed in order for an auditory sequence to be made meaningful, the retention of echoic memory necessarily takes a different durational shape than other modalities of sensory memory.

Second, it matters that sound is tactile and resonant, as it literally touches the body through a complex process of vibrational transfer. A brief anatomy lesson is needed here: longitudinal sound waves are collected by the outer ear or pinna, and travel through the auditory canal towards the eardrum, which then vibrates to set in motion the hammer, anvil, and stirrup bones, in turn amplifying these vibrations and transmitting them to the cochlea. Fine hair-like cells in the cochlea again vibrate and so transmit the nerve impulses to the brain, where, finally, sound is made available for interpretation. The body, in other words, is complexly affected by sound waves, resonating well beyond the cognitive and interpretative dimensions made possible once sound arrives in the brain. Breath, likewise, resonates across bodies both through the sonics of air modulation as it travels in and out of the airways, and atmospherically through the release and reception of oxygen and carbon dioxide respectively.

To return to Erlmann's rethinking of the relation between reason and resonance, referenced at the start of this chapter, Western philosophy, one might say, has been historically hostile to those elements of embodied sound not immediately tied to cognition and meaning. It is precisely the sensorially resonant dimensions of sound reception that Jean-Luc Nancy, like Erlmann, hopes to reclaim for philosophy by distinguishing between listening and hearing, a distinction that proves particularly pertinent to Goliath's affective-auditory approach to the mediation of trauma. For Nancy, to listen is to register more than one does when simply hearing or trying to understand what one hears. To listen is to attend to that which exceeds the reach for meaning so central to Western philosophy, namely the vibrational, corporeal dimensions of the acoustic experience, to be open to "the resonance of being, or to being as resonance" (21). "Every sensory register," writes Nancy, "bears with it both its simple nature and its tense, attentive, or anxious state: seeing and looking, smelling and sniffing or scenting, tasting and savouring, touching and feeling or palpating, hearing and listening" (5). The last pair in this list, he points out, has a unique relationship to "*sense* in the intellectual or intelligible acceptance of the word (with 'perceived meaning' [*sens sensé*], if you like, as opposed to 'perceiving sense' [*sense sensible*])" (6–7). In light of the primacy historically given to hearing as understanding, Nancy suggests that "perhaps it is necessary that sense not be content to make sense (or to be *logos*), but that it want also to resound" (6). To listen is to "be on the edge of meaning" (7), to straddle "the shared space of meaning and sound" (7). To listen is further to approach the self as a resonant subject, always being moved or agitated towards meaning by that to which it listens, even if the arrival at meaning is never assured. To Nancy, the shift at issue here is that from "the phenomenological subject, and intentional line of sight, to a resonant subject, an intensive spacing of a rebound that does not end in any return to self without immediately relaunching, as an echo, a call to that same self" (21). Nancy envisages this resonant subject further, "as that part, in the body, that is listening or vibrates with listening to – or with the echo of – the beyond-meaning" (31) (a "beyond-meaning" evocative of the "more-than-known" that Oliver posits, as I indicated above, as foundational to any "response-able" ethics of witnessing).

This brief summary of Nancy's redirection of philosophical inquiry from what he calls "philosophizing anesthesia" (31) – a form of inquiry numb to the entanglement of sense and the (resonant) senses – towards a renewed embrace of the embodied sensorium (in this case also specifically challenging the ocularcentric), corresponds with what I highlight at various points throughout this book as forms of wayward aesthetics.[14] Goliath's use of sound to draw audiences into a more capacious engagement with trauma's afterlives than would be possible through the visual alone likewise proceeds along wayward aesthetic lines, acutely attuned to the ethical risks that attend mediating the trauma of others, and propelled throughout, to invoke Hartman again, by waywardness as "as an ongoing exploration of *what might be* … when there is little room to breathe" (228).

It further matters that the sound in neither *Personal Accounts*, *Elegy*, nor *This song is for …* is acousmatic: bodies and sound are intimately bound in each of these works. Acousmatic sound, as theorists such as Pierre Schaeffer and Michel Chion define it, is characterized in film by the visual absence of the physical object or voice from which the sound emanates. Audiences encounter only the sounds themselves, not their originating causes. Goliath, in contrast, takes pains to situate sound in the human body, and to make visible the musicians through whom sound is affectively rendered in her installations. This is, again, an ethically grounded choice: Goliath explicitly foregrounds the collaborative nature of her projects, and is deeply responsive to and respectful of the labour involved. The embodiment of sound speaks further to Goliath's sensitivity to the embodied forms that trauma takes, and her refusal to depersonalize or objectify the traumatic experiences of her subjects through techniques of aesthetic distancing.

For audiences, this means that encountering Goliath's work can never proceed from a place of distance and detachment. In terms of its deliberate use of sound as a sensory mode that brings together a variety of contributors – not least of which the audience – Goliath's work in fact has a discernibly methexic character. As a form of group sharing that originates in Greek theatre, methexis involves audience participation and improvisation, much like the call-and-response format central to public and performative gatherings in a range of African contexts. Indeed, the participatory dimensions of Goliath's work places her along a vast historical continuum of African performance and live art. As Jay Pather and Catherine Boulle point out, "the role and involvement of the audience has been a significant dimension of African performance from classical tradition through to contemporary live art. Immersion, improvisation and participation can be traced back to the San trance dance recorded in rock art paintings dating back thousands of years" (4). The sonorous, as Nancy suggests, is furthermore "tendentially methexic (that is, having to do with participation, sharing, or contagion)" (10). Listening, likewise, constitutes "a form of participation in the sharing of a sound event" (LaBelle, "Auditory" 470), a characteristic that Goliath puts to eloquent use in her work, in which the participatory action proceeds corporeally through both sound and breath.

To make sense of the methexic reach, first, of *Personal Accounts* and *Elegy*, it helps to delve a bit more deeply into Goliath's deliberate manipulation of breath, transmitted between the bodies of the vocalists and those of her audience. The edited testimonies screened in *Personal Accounts* and the B-natural note held by vocalists in *Elegy* both engage breathing patterns known to regulate the autonomic nervous system and to be interpersonally transmissible. It is significant, in *Elegy*, for instance, that sound is carried vocally on an exhale. An elongated exhale helps to activate the parasympathetic nervous system, which moves the body towards rest and release. In order to achieve what Eddie Stern has popularized as "resonance breathing" (166) – defined as a type of breathing that helps to balance the parasympathetic and sympathetic parts of the autonomic nervous system, which in turn controls heart rate, blood pressure, digestion, respiration, and many other autonomic functions of the body (189) – an effort has to be made to focus attention on exhaling, often through the deliberate, regulated elongation of the exhale. Whereas the sympathetic branch of the nervous system works to accelerate the autonomic functions of the body, the parasympathetic branch slows it down, a detail that has important implications for Goliath's mediation of the physicality of traumatic recall in *Personal Accounts* and her embodied temporalization of the act of mourning in *Elegy*.

Whereas both installations home in on the respiratory functions of the body to make a larger claim about the workings of trauma and grief, they do so to contrasting effect. In *Elegy*, the vocal performance and breath work allow for an energetic deceleration through the resonant transmission of elongated breath and sound. Here *Elegy* differs somewhat in emphasis from *Personal Accounts*. Whereas the latter places emphasis on the inhale – the drawing in of breath between each vocal expression, thus foregrounding the sympathetic branch of the autonomic nervous system which in turn serves as an accelerant of the body's "fight or flight" impulses – in *Elegy*, the emphasis is placed on the exhale. For those inhabiting the gallery space, the haptics of aurality and breath are to be found in *Personal Accounts* in the repeated representation of breath intake, transmitted from audio-visual track to viewer as a stimulant of the autonomic nervous system. In *Elegy*, in contrast, it finds expression in the slow elongation of the melodic exhale and the extended duration of the near hour-long performance, which in turn deepens the contemplative reach of the act of mourning itself. In both installations, Goliath compels her audience to pause in protracted sensorial contemplation of another's suffering: in *Personal Accounts*, as an intercorporeal transmission of the somatic stresses that the experience of violence inflicts, and in *Elegy* as a deliberate slowing down devoted to the memory of a particular womxn lost to gender-based violence. What I referred to in the third chapter as the aesthetics of counter-affective lingering – aimed at slowing down to enable better conditions for the work of mourning – is in fact central to each of Goliath's tributes. Even in *Personal Accounts*, where the effect is that of autonomic acceleration through vibrational and energetic transfer, the impact of this anxiety-inducing affective transmission lies in large part in the elongated duration of each performance, which in turn draws audiences into an extended act of somatosensory-anchored deliberation. Each of Goliath's installations at issue here in fact refuses to engage the mind and body in isolation from one another, demanding precisely the kind of resonant listening that Nancy advocates.

To stay a bit longer with the breath in *Elegy*, the manner in which each woman is made to hold the single B-natural note on her exhale, making audible the gradual waning of breath, is in itself resonant with meaning, a meaning, it bears repeating, that can only be reached for affectively as it eludes full cognitive capture. A great deal of information can be found at the end of the exhale, particularly given the context that Goliath references. For example, the strain made audible as each vocalist runs out of breath powerfully calls forth the women lost, who were literally robbed of their last breath. To return to the parasympathetic nervous system, which regulates the autonomic functions related to rest, repair, and restoration, one might read the performance's protracted interpersonal exhale as an act at once of mourning and of feminist healing. Indeed, as a performance of wayward feminist resonance "when there is little room to breathe" – to echo Hartman again – it matters profoundly that from the loss of breath and sound at the end of each vocalist's turn on the podium emerges another woman's voice, yoked to the preceding vocals in a sonically continuous lamentation. This auditory trick highlights both the subjective distinctiveness of each singer's voice and the community through which feminist defiance, endurance, and care are sustained. The fact, furthermore, that the entire, forty-five-minute-long performance is carried on an exhale, heightens the call for feminist release and repair.

The acoustics of feminist defiance and care in fact resounds across generations: one of the women commemorated in *Elegy*, namely Louisa van de Caab, is an enslaved woman killed by her intimate partner on 20 February 1786. In her evocative tribute to van de Caab, historian Saarah Jappie tries to gently pry open the "tattered, yellowing pages" of the archive to reveal something of the fullness of van de Caab's life, and the pain of her death. Like Goliath, Jappie reaches synaesthetically to the aural as she is confronted with the absences presented by the archive: "I tried to *listen with my eyes*, to grasp the pain in [her mother's] statement. In desperation I foolishly read it aloud, and still the Official Record spat back only facts. Dates, names, times. The trajectory of the knife as it cut through you and took your life – a life of which we will only ever know one brutal, last moment" (emphasis added). Goliath's sonic deepening of the affective resonances called forth by Jappie compels her audiences to ponder the intergenerational transmission of gender-based violence, not to mention the historical links between slavery, rape, and the invention of race as entangled colonial technologies of domination. The latter history constitutes an important thread in the fabric of contemporary rape culture, profoundly shaped by the numerous "deliberate and indirect ways" in which "race was made through rape" (Gqola, *Rape* 38).

It is significant also that *Elegy* is a long-term commemorative project that continues to add women to its roster of dedicated performances staged around the globe. (Since its inception in 2015, fourteen women have been commemorated in this way.) In other words, even as the performance constitutes a gesture of feminist reparation carried through sound and breath, the project is in no way aimed at dictating closure.

As Goliath puts it, the work proceeds from "the conviction that art has, despite its capacity to re-inscribe harm, the possibility of facilitating transforming aesthetic and inter-relational encounters" (qtd. in Jayawardane, "Goliath's"). She explains further that though *Elegy* is aimed at "facilitat[ing] a certain … 'recovery' of the subject, performed in the context of absence, of loss" it does so "in such a way as to draw viewers into a more relational, and so affectively, ethically and politically-involved, encounter" (qtd. in Jayawardane, "Goliath's"). The project is melancholic, then, in the sense considered elsewhere in this book, namely as refusing prescribed timelines for coming to terms with loss, especially in a context where structural sexism and long-term rape cultures continue to render women's safety precarious. Goliath's refusal to dictate grief and recovery's timelines, in fact takes shape within a larger political project that redirects our collective psychic energies towards a clearer understanding of the *causes* of loss, grief, and feminist rage. The same "non-depressing, politicizing melancholia" (Flatley 8) structures *This song is for …*, in which the songs chosen by each of the survivors, as Lucienne Bestall phrases it, "are at once a supplication to healing and an expression of pain's persistence."

The dedication song proves a particularly fitting form for the political work of resonant listening that *This song is for…* demands. As a "memory-soaked love language" (Gqola, "Goliath"), the dedication song springs from a place of deep reverence and attention, as the etymological roots of the term "dedicated" suggest: "devoted to earnest purpose, as to some person or end" (Online Etymology Dictionary). To devote is to "give all or most of one's time or resources to (a person or activity)" (OED), which fittingly describes Goliath's long-term feminist activism, but also speaks to the kind of listening that *This song is for …* requires of its audiences.

Each of the dedication songs featured in the installation in fact cannot but capture the attentions of those within its aural reach, as they necessarily strike a powerful emotional chord not only for the ways in which many of the songs will call forth the listener's own memories of melody and lyrics (in the case of widely known songs such as Queen's "Bohemian Rhapsody," Beyonce's "Save the Hero," REM's "Everybody Hurts," or Michael Jackson's "Ben," chosen by Nondumiso Msimanga, Sinesipho Lakani, Deborah Ho-Chung, and Karen Howell respectively) but also for the way in which Goliath manipulates sonic and psychic time. My own experience of listening to each track was one of profound unsettlement, carrying me through emotions ranging from sorrow, dread, and panic to impatience and even anger. I am not alone in having been unsettled by the installation. Blogger Viwe Tafeni, for instance, likewise describes his response to the installation in these terms: "I become aware of tension in my body and the anxiety has me looking around the room and worrying about my safety."

The effort of staying with each track through the full duration of its scratch-like repetitions, while slowly reading through each of the texts provided by survivors, further proved unnerving in unexpected ways. At first, the phrases repeating in a sonic loop for most of each track had a mesmeric, entrancing effect, but as the repetitions came to register for me as increasingly relentless – aggressive, even – I started hearing aberrations, as though my ears were playing tricks on me. My first discovery of what seemed like a glitch in the soundtrack's loop left me shaken, as though a ghost had entered the acoustic space. For instance, in the powerful cover of "Bohemian Rhapsody" – reinterpreted by Nonku Phiri and Dion Monti from the version done by the band "The Braids" and dedicated to Nondumiso Msimanga – the audio-visual track gets stuck on the lines "anywhere the wind blows" at three minutes and forty-seven seconds, which goes on seemingly endlessly until a brief variation emerges at 15:33, when the "a" in anywhere is missing, and the vocalist seems to be swallowing. Picking up on this discrepancy had the effect of gluing my attention to visuals and sonics, gradually leading me to the conclusion that the musicians were in fact performing each of the scratch-like disruptions in a repetitive loop; the "scratch" was not the result of editing, in other words, as I had thought at first. This revelation was subsequently confirmed via email by the artist (as she phrases it, "The fact that this is performed, rather than mechanically reproduced or digitally manipulated, is key" [Goliath, "Re: Query"]), and brought home some of the ways in which each of the performance pieces was coded semiotically and somatically more complexly than I had initially understood.

The best way to articulate some of this complexity is perhaps through some of the meanings of the term "tone," namely as referring to either colour or sound, or, as a verb, to increasing bodily or muscular strength. First, each of the performance pieces is rendered visually through a different chromatic filter, ranging from tones of brown, sepia, and yellow to turquoise, pink, and purple, a gesture, perhaps, to the singularity of each survivor's experience as well as to the manner in which technological and audio-visual modes of mediation can shift viewer and listener perspective. Second, tone refers to melodious or vocal sound, and to the quality of that sound in terms of pitch, timbre, and volume. Each of the performances plays with sonic tone in new ways as the distinctive musical sensibilities of each musician or band are brought to bear on the original song, in turn inviting a dizzying array of interpretative possibilities from listeners when lyrics, sound, chosen survivor text, and embodied performance are studied in concert.

To provide a brief example here, the cover version of Michael Jackson's "Ben," hauntingly delivered and presented across split screens by the band "The Wretched," opens with a strangely discordant sequence featuring sound distortions seemingly rendered through feedback from an amplifier or microphone and attenuated noise, as well as vocal and other sonic echoes. The lyrics of the song – famously dedicated by the young protagonist of the 1972 film *Ben* to his pet rat, his best friend and defender from bullies – take on additional layers when placed in conversation with survivor Karen Howell's harrowing account of rape and retraumatization through what she categorizes as her "Institutional Rape" and her "Judicial Rape" respectively. The echoing sounds included in the opening bars of the song, along with the seemingly endless loop of the lines "know, you've got a place to" (from the original "If you ever look behind and don't like what you find / There's something you should know, you've got a place to go"), offer an aesthetic approximation of the experience of unbearable delay and dismissal that Howell faced in her efforts to hold her rapists to account. Howell writes at length about the ways in which she was reduced to "just another rape victim" by the many "inconsiderate, disinterested and unsympathetic men" she encountered at the police station, the hospital, and in court. Each step of the process is dragged out beyond endurance, as the following lines from Howell's account, describing some of her journey through the judicial system, attest:

> The case is extended for yet another two years, exacerbated by the incompetence and compounded by a lack of interest. Documents go missing, prosecutors are chopped and changed, the original IO has done an incompetent job and the chain of evidence is broken. I am being violated yet again. The judicial system is raping and raping me … in what is commonly referred to as secondary rape. Interpreters do not pitch, witnesses are not available, the suspect's attorney is ill, then the stenographer machine breaks down, or no stenographer is available! Postponement after postponement after postponement … (qtd. in Goliath, *This song is for …*)

What Howell articulates here disturbingly echoes the aesthetics of protraction staged in the musicians' performance of the song, heightened by the prolonged thwarting of listener expectation to achieve the comfort that would otherwise have been offered by reaching the word "go" in the lyrics. The manner in which Goliath monopolizes audience attention across sensory faculties, however, works precisely against the forms of inattention that Howell has to confront in her search for some measure of healing, again demanding of audiences to participate in the larger project of feminist dedication and care central also to the representational politics of *Personal Accounts* and *Elegy*. As such *This song is for …* demands forms of resonant listening that nurture what sound theorist Brandon LaBelle calls "engaged attention" (*Sonic* 7), given sound's capacity to relate us "to the depth of others" (7) and attendant modes of empathizing and radical care.

To tone, lastly, refers to the act of improving muscular, bodily strength. Realizing that each of the sonic disruptions in the dedication songs was in fact performed and not the result of editorial manipulation left me with a deep sense of the incredible muscular, vocal, and respiratory control that each of the performers had to exert through the extended audio-visual loop to successfully achieve the effect of a prolonged editing glitch. The fine control of bodily, facial, and vocal muscles, for instance, to convincingly repeat the same gestures – in some cases, for close to twenty minutes – must have been physically and psychically gruelling, revealing dedication that far exceeds the relatively straightforward act of dedicating a song to each survivor. Performers dedicated their bodies in an act of incredible stamina, endurance, and strength, reaffirmed also in the repeated references in both song lyrics and survivor text to the strength required of and displayed by survivors.

Toned mind-bodies are in fact on display in each of the song/lyric/text combinations dedicated to each survivor. Examples are numerous, including in the lines "But I am praying, and I am very strong and God is / going to answer me one day … / You must fight for life" offered by a woman who chose to withhold her name to accompany the traditional isiXhosa hymn "Uyesu Ulithemba," performed by the band Msaki and featuring Lebogang Ledwaba and Thembinkosi Mavimbela; in the selection by Corey Spengler-Gathercole, who refers to herself as a "strong rape survivor," of Rachel Platten's "Fight Song," performed by Desire Marea and featuring Izimakade; and in the memorable statement by survivor Pat Hutchison that "I didn't know how strong I was, until being strong was my only choice" (qtd. in Goliath, *This song is for …*). The latter lines follow Hutchison's testimony of abduction and gang rape by four men who drugged her and left her to die before she was miraculously found, and accompany the song "Unstoppable," originally by Sia and performed here by Nonku Phiri and Dion Monti. The performance of "Unstoppable" – which gets stuck on the lines "stoppable today, I'm unstoppa," – in fact compellingly reveals the tension between trauma and stuckness, on the one hand, and strength and resilience, on the other, that each of the survivors has to navigate daily.

This is a tension to which Goliath's audiences are made more than spectators, as Goliath places them in relational, tactile proximity to the pain of others. As Linda Coulthard notes, following Nancy, "sound is above all else, tactile and corporeal … it not only communicates physical presence, sensuousness or feeling, but actually moves outward to quite literally move the body of the spectator, sometimes in aggressive ways … and sometimes in thought provoking, contemplative and ethically implicated ways" (18). What Coulthard terms "haptic aurality" (18) reveals itself in the manner in which bodies are made to carry sound in Goliath's expressive testimonies in *Personal Accounts* and dedication songs in *This song is for …*, in *Elegy*'s commemorative lamentations, as well as in her wayward refusal of the kind of aural pleasure and comfort associated with mainstream listening and sound cultures. Her use of "interruptive auditory editing" (Coulthard 22) in *This song is for …*, and her relentless extension of aural temporality in *Personal Accounts* and *Elegy*, render any attempts at mindlessly immersive or escapist listening futile. Though *This song is for …* makes use of conventional musical scores to guide audience feeling, it does so in thoroughly disruptive ways, making it impossible for her audiences to be cognitively detached from the affective force of the sound, as affect and cognition, body and mind, are drawn into corresponding resonance. To be precise, audiences are encouraged to listen rather than simply hear. As Coulthard explains, "hearing might be pleasurable but listening, as Nancy suggests, can be frustrating, anxiety producing and agitating" (20).

Listen

Feminist theorist Jane Bennett, in an article published nearly twenty years ago on the importance of "'finding the ears' to understand violence against African-based women" (88), writes about the various social, institutional, historical, and psychic barriers to fully addressing and dismantling gender-based violence in African contexts.[15] As part of a larger argument about the work that needs to be done to not only tear down these barriers, but also to find ways of healing the many wounds inflicted by violent misogyny, Bennett cites the following words by psychologist and human rights activist Nomfundo Walaza, then director of the Trauma Centre for Survivors of Torture and Violence:

> The critical instrument in any healing practice is listening … Imagine that we all carry within us an African drum on which we play our own beat and rhythm. When we come together with another person, if we maintain

> our own rhythm we will be out of beat with the other's drum. The challenge as a healer is to listen to the other's rhythm, and to modify our own beat in time until there is synchronicity. Only then, when we can hear the other rhythm and respond to it, can we truly tend to another person's context and needs. (qtd. in Bennett 94)

Walaza's emphasis on healing as rhythmic attunement resonates powerfully with Goliath's wayward mediation of feminist repair in the post-rainbow South African present. Her choice of the words "tend to another person's context and needs" chimes well in particular with Goliath's dedicational aesthetics. To "tend to" means to "care for or look after" and to "give one's attention to" (OED). In other words, the work of healing requires precisely the kind of "engaged attention" that LaBelle suggests acoustic resonance can enable. Walaza's emphasis on listening as adjusting to another's rhythm points centrally to the somatosensory, energetic dimensions of experience that lie beyond the strictly linguistic as modes of communication. Such forms of listening are particularly crucial in our contemporary world of digital distraction, which, as Kate Murphy explains, "keeps the mind occupied but does little to nurture it, much less cultivate depth of feeling, which requires the resonance of another's voice within our very bones and psyches. To really listen is to be moved physically, chemically, emotionally, and intellectually by another person's narrative" (4).

To tend to another's context further demands cultivating sensitivity to the larger archives of experience and feeling pulsing through the immediacies of interpersonal encounter. This is an archive not only of disempowerment and silencing, but also of the structures of privilege complicit in its making. The work of resonant listening then entails also engaging in a larger political project aimed at uncovering the causes of loss, violation, and suffering, as Goliath and the feminist activists and theorists cited in this chapter do with such force. As Elaine Swan reminds us, to listen *from* a place of dominance is also to listen *for* dominance. For Swan, writing about the politics of white feminist listening, the "goal of political listening is the decentering of privileged white ... interests and feelings" (554), and requires turning away "from white solipsism – self-loathing and self-glorification – and towards others" (557). The same is required for modes of listening anchored in cis- and heteropatriarchal privilege. Those keeping violent patriarchy in place, as has been said many times, must learn to listen. The work of rhythmic attunement that Walaza places at the heart of healing, requires, after all, of listeners to modify their own beat, rather than impose it on others.

Conclusion: Shutting Down

Our systems are designed to promote more life.

Leanne Betasamosake Simpson[1]

When I drafted this conclusion, South Africans were preparing for a twenty-one-day lockdown as the national government tried to curb the spread of COVID-19. At the start of the journey that culminated in this book, I could not have envisioned a shutdown of the scale implemented in countries across the globe since the start of the pandemic, yet I have been thinking about the embodied and cultural politics of the "shutdown" for some time. In October 2016, for instance, as the higher education community in South Africa once again found itself in the midst of a country-wide institutional shutdown, I convened a departmental seminar titled "Shutting Down: #FeesMustFall as a Site of Affective Conversion" aimed at working through some of the epistemic and logistical implications of the politics of the shutdown for university employees supportive of dissenting students' struggle for free decolonized education, as we hoped simultaneously to reroute individualized emotional difficulty into affirmative modes of coalition, connection, and care. By way of conclusion, I turn again to the shutdown as I recast archives of wayward feeling as archives of regeneration.

At the time of the 2016 departmental seminar, I conceived of the shutdown in two interrelated ways: first, and most obviously, as the means by which student protesters captured the attention of university administrations and government; and second, as a form of emotional withdrawal in response to overwhelming or traumatizing events. Variations of these types of shutting down can in fact be found throughout the pages of *Wayward Feeling*, including in the examples of labour, student, and feminist activism discussed in chapters 3 to 5 in particular, and in the many audio-visual and aesthetic mediations of loss – of an ideal, of safe and predictable futures, of bodily and emotional security, even of life – and the varieties of grief that the subjects of these texts have had to navigate in response. Yet the writing of this book in the years since has also given me occasion to deepen these initial reflections on the shutdown in its activist and affective forms, an occasion yet again offered by a still-unfolding planetary pandemic. As a mode of shutting down, deceleration emerges at various points throughout this book, for instance, as a method towards regeneration and repair following times of heightened and accelerated tension, and as a disruption of Berlant's "survival time, the time of struggling, drowning, holding onto the ledge, treading water – the time of *not-stopping*" (*Cruel* 169; emphasis in original), referenced earlier in my discussion of Sarah Chu's film *Made in China*. As such, *Wayward Feeling* has revealed how shutting down can also be a refusal to be shut down.

It pays to briefly pause here to contemplate some of the embodied conditions of work within which this book took shape. It is hardly news that the South African higher education sector has faced significant challenges of late, not least of which those emerging during and in the aftermath of the hashtag student protests. Even as student activists managed to achieve the previously unimaginable, including a commitment by former president Zuma that the national government will fully subsidize "free higher education and training for poor and working class South African undergraduate students" (Zuma qtd. in Areff and Spies), the protests themselves and the increased securitization of campuses exacted a substantial psychic toll especially on students at the frontlines, but to varying degrees on campus staff and academic faculty as well. The long-term effects of the protests on the mental health of students are an open secret, with many choosing to delay or discontinue their studies as a result (Akoob). This was the case also at the University of the Free State, my place of work for the past nine years, where these challenges have been compounded by the ongoing food insecurity of the majority of our students (subsequent fee subsidies notwithstanding), as well as by the difficulties brought by the move to online modes of teaching and learning during the pandemic lockdown, particularly for those on the disadvantaged end of the digital divide.[2]

Recent years have further seen higher education in South Africa zealously following the global trend of increased corporatization and the attendant implementation of market-driven learning, research quantification, punishing audit regimes, and compression of timeframes for the delivery of work (further accelerated by the shift to the digital realm necessitated by the pandemic). Though the irony of corporatization masquerading as decolonization post-Fallism has not been lost on academic faculty in the humanities in particular, managerial task teams have been largely immune to such critiques. Instead, tertiary institutions across the country have enthusiastically embraced neoliberal metrics for the measurement of the performance and productivity of academic staff, even as class sizes and administrative loads have ballooned. In my own department, student enrolment numbers at first- and second-year levels have nearly doubled in the past five or so years, yet our full-time lecturing capacity has decreased as university budget priorities have shifted towards an ever-growing administrative bureaucracy and a set of ceaselessly reinvented corporate transformation agendas – exacted, in turn, via an interminable stream of administrative tasks and "quality control" exercises offloaded onto academic faculty. As Wamuwi Mbao phrases it in his assessment of the state of higher education in contemporary South Africa,

> The assumption that the modern university needs highly managerial scaffolding has resulted in the absurd situation where management posts have swelled even as faculties have been locked in the dulling clasp of diminishing subsidies and social expectations ... Universities are companies now, with shareholders, capital and assets, and the employees who staff them must be encouraged to see themselves as stakeholders in the enterprise, even as management directly disregards the views of those who teach.

Even though the "temporal regimes of the neoliberal university and their embodied effects" (Mountz et al.) have been well documented in the Global North, these studies have not filtered into the governing priorities of local university management teams, who have outsourced concerns about the well-being of staff to the now-ubiquitous "Centres for Health and Wellness" on university campuses, thereby individualizing responsibility for larger structural dysfunction.[3] Anecdotal evidence from academic faculty across the country suggests that inhabiting what Sarah Nuttall calls the tension between the "redistributed university" ("Afterword" 282) and the "toxic university" (Smyth 3) is experienced as increasingly unsustainable, and is incrementally shutting down the space and the time required for forms of cultural theorizing accountable to the complexities and growing planetary vulnerabilities of the present.

A brief look at the workings of the redistributed university may help here to map alternatives to these frequently debilitating institutional dynamics, and to reassess what it might mean to feel wayward in the post-rainbow university and beyond. In brief, Nuttall locates the redistributed university, on the one hand, in the decolonial "call for a radical politics of reparation and change" (282) made audible by the hashtag generation, and, on the other, in the pressures placed by cognitive and algorithmic capitalism (Moulier Boutang; Peters) on the forms of knowledge conventionally generated from within the university and its disciplinary scaffolding. Meeting the challenges of the redistributed university for the humanities, Nuttall suggests, requires more than harnessing the politics of negation and shutdown deployed so powerfully by student activists. Following Rosi Braidotti's reading of an emergent "critical posthumanities" (88), Nuttall also calls for accompanying forms of affirmative knowledge production as a means towards reimagining the African university as a site of social justice-driven epistemic and social renewal and regeneration. She explains:

> Both forms of critique, as Braidotti has pointed out, are ways of honouring alternative sources of knowledge, and both draw on feminist epistemologies and anti-racist thought. Both seek to draw in [those] rendered invisible by history and theory. And both base their analyses around structural differences people face and the inequalities that inhabit our present. ("Afterword" 284)

These supplementary forms of critique – the one propagated through a politics of negation, the other invested in affirmation – in fact harmonize with the kinds of theorizing privileged in this book, theorizing likewise indebted to non-Cartesian feminist, queer, and decolonial knowledge ecologies attuned to the complex entanglement of the ideational and non-ideational as socially embedded domains of embodied experience. Even as the toxic university closes in on the ground available for such work, *Wayward Feeling* has sought in both method and substance to amplify alternatives to epistemic and emotional injustice regulating "public time" and "intimate time" in the university and beyond (Highmore, *Ordinary* 88).[4]

Breathe

Post-rainbow publics have continued to contest varieties of affective containment and exclusion, particularly those that mitigate against the "everyday struggle to live free … when there is little room to breathe" (Hartman 227, 228). As I indicate at the start of this book, we have, for some time now, been living through a planet-wide respiratory crisis brought on by extractive and racial capitalism's history of ever-increasing CO_2 and other greenhouse gas emissions, in turn exacerbating human vulnerability to the effects of the respiratory coronavirus that started to shut down conventional forms of social and economic life across the globe in early 2020. The breath, as my discussion of Gabrielle Goliath's multisensory installations emphasizes, not only acts as an animating force central to the body's capacity to regulate its own regeneration. The breath also signals a larger context of material interdependence, as the future of human life is inseparable from the life-enabling futures of non-human ecologies and atmospheres.

In its insistence upon the intimacy of matter and mind, *Wayward Feeling* has deliberately blurred the boundary between breathing as an autonomic respiratory function of the body, and the breath – or lack thereof – as a metaphor for varieties of experience in both post-rainbow South Africa and further afield. I have offered waywardness as a term for the creative, life-affirming ways in which variously entangled forms of suffocation – emotional, epistemic, economic, environmental, institutional – are being affectively mitigated by the post-rainbow body and its aesthetically mediated forms. These include the labours of undoing the harmful effects of the toxic university outlined above, frequently found in forms of refusal that make it possible for academics and students alike to take back time, to pause, breathe, listen, engage, read, and critique with care (Berg and Seeber 33–70). This work finds expression also in ongoing struggles to survive the asphyxiating emotional cultures against which protesting students rose up – including against what Shose Kessi referred to as the stifling ways in which white feeling excludes and silences "under the guise of 'logical reasoned argument.'" Beyond the university, examples of these oxygenating forms of affective agency can be identified in this book also, for instance, in the mood work whereby the subjects of Chu and Maruping's films straddle the tension between expectation and experience in their everyday lives, as well as in the daily psychic labours of those navigating the afterlives of extractive capitalism's state-sponsored violence, of colonial and apartheid-era infrastructure planning and commemoration, and of the unremitting scourge of gender-based violence that accompanies all of these, discussed respectively in the preface and chapters 3 to 5.

I have further conceived of waywardness as a framework for thinking about the capacity of audio-visual culture and aesthetic activism to enliven South African publics to forms of bodily suffering and psychic alienation obscured by the spectacle of the promise and its distorted temporalities. The word "enliven" is significant here as a referent for the meaning of aesthetics I have privileged throughout, namely "a form of cognition, achieved through taste, touch, hearing, seeing, smell – the whole corporeal sensorium" (Buck-Morrs 6). The filmmakers and artists whose work I have considered in this book all to a certain extent suspend "the normal coordinates of sensory experience" (Rancière, *Aesthetics* 25); each engages in a reapportioning of "spaces and times, of the visible and the invisible, and of noise and speech" (24). Yet these interventions are far from redemptive, predictable, or straightforward in their mediation of the often combustive and capricious energies coursing through post-rainbow, and more recently also post-Zuma, times. They offer no guarantees, certitudes or easy resolutions. Instead, archives of wayward feeling might be understood as giving affective form to what Joanna Ruth Evans suggestively theorizes as "the multiple, cusping potentialities of the dense and dangerous nonhomogeneous and noncontemporaneous present, in which each moment and matter holds the potential for the emergence of a new politic, an upheaval, an insurrection, or a redistribution of the sensible" (136).

More than simply providing a descriptive map, however, the audiovisual activisms that made it into this book *intervene*; they harness the powers of attention – of being present and alive, of listening, breathing, seeing, sensing – to engage, to varying degrees, in forms of sensorial and emotional pedagogy driven by an ethics and epistemics of regeneration and feminist care. Propelled as such by a "recursive but ultimately future-oriented critical melancholia" (Wenzel 235), they reveal that if, as Leigh-Ann Naidoo explains,

> we are to be custodians of a future that will have dismantled the violence of the past and its stubborn hold on the present, then we cannot get stuck in a politics of shut down. Shutting down is indeed necessary for the arresting of the present. But if we do not use the space that the shut down grants to work, seriously, on our vision of the future, if we do not allow ourselves, too, to be challenged and pushed, to read, and talk to each other, to work out our strategies, to doubt, and to find a vision of a future world [beyond] the many oppressions that beset this one ... then the door we have opened will have closed again. (5)

I opened this conclusion with reference to Mississauga Nishnaabeg writer and musician Leanne Betasamosake Simpson's declaration that the systems of the Michi Saagiig Nishnaabeg people – including their "knowledge system, the education system, the economic system, and the political system" (3) – were designed to promote more life. She goes on to say that this way of living was designed to generate not only "human life but the life of all living things" (3). Simpson's words are taken up by journalist and social activist Naomi Klein to advocate for the right of all life to "renew, regenerate, and heal itself" (443). A regenerative mindset, she explains, is "the very antithesis of extractivism, which is based on the premise that life can be drained indefinitely, and which, far from promoting future life, specializes in turning living systems into garbage, whether it's ... the armies of discarded people roving the world looking for temporary work, or the particulates and gases that choke the atmosphere that were once healthy parts of the ecosystem" (442).

I reach here, by way of conclusion, across the Atlantic to situate the wayward post-rainbow South African sensorium within a larger planetary struggle for breath at this time of the ongoing global pandemic. Even as the virus has exposed the fragility of the boundaries of nation-states, the risks of late capitalism continuing to retreat into xenophobic, racist, and authoritarian nationalisms remain. In the suffocating global present, the exemplary violence of South Africa's history of extraction will continue to generate new forms of unevenly distributed suffering, as the murder of anti-mining and environmental activist Fikile Ntshangase, mentioned at the start of this book, so painfully demonstrates. As the long-term effects of the pandemic make themselves known, a wayward planetary ethics of regeneration anchored in a "resurgent present" of reciprocal "movements with other humans and nonhumans radically imagining their ways out of domination" (Simpson, *As We Have* 10) will yet again require that we harness our attentions, with renewed creativity, towards hallucinating "a new time" by "forcing an awareness of a time when things are not this way" (Naidoo 2). Such regenerative hallucinations will have to power the difficult projects of reckoning and reworlding that our contemporary moment of planetary crisis so urgently demands.

Notes

Introduction

1 For an overview of some of the forms that protest has taken in South Africa in recent years, see for instance Brown, *Insurgent*, and Duncan, *Protest Nation*.

2 The Rhodes Must Fall collective uses the lower-case term "black" to refer to "all racially oppressed people of colour" (6). Throughout this book I likewise use the term to designate a resistant political identity, though in line with the preferences of the South African Students' Organisation (SASO), founded in 1968 and in turn spearheading the Black Consciousness Movement (BCM), I privilege the upper-case usage of the term. As such, the term "Black" includes those historically categorized as Indian, Coloured, and African. The terms "Indian" and "Coloured" are used when referring specifically to either a self-identified member of, or one previously legislated as belonging to, either of these groups. This is not an attempt at hardening these classifications, but serves as an acknowledgment of the extent to which these inherited categories still mark social interaction, access, and daily living in a society that continues to be profoundly divided and defined by race. When referring only to the group historically designated as "African," I use the lower-case term "black." Each of these categories is used, ultimately, with awareness of the contested histories within which they came into signification, of heterogeneities of identification that operate both within and beyond their confines, and of the creative and resistant ways in which imposed labels have been and continue to be renegotiated. Formulated in response to apartheid racial labelling and discrimination, the BCM was sensitive to the fact that racism historically preceded the invention of "race."

3 For a discussion of the aesthetics of "wayward feeling" in South African "New Wave" cinemas, see Strauss, "Waywardness." This article, first

presented as part of a panel with Y-Dang Troeung and Christopher Patterson on "Wayward Politics" at the 2016 "Crossroads in Cultural Studies" conference in Sydney, Australia, conveys some of my early thinking on "wayward feeling" that I develop in this book.

4 I use the terms visual and audio-visual somewhat interchangeably throughout this book. Though my primary focus in chapters 1 to 4 is the visual, elements of the aural are analysed throughout these pages as well. It is only, however, in chapter 5 that sound becomes the dominant focus.

5 Founded in 2013 by expelled former president of the African National Congress Youth League Julius Malema, the EFF quickly rose to power to become the country's third-largest political party.

6 See van der Vlies, *Present Imperfect* (12–14), for a compelling reading of post-apartheid temporality by way of Ernst Bloch's understanding of the circulation of past utopian surplus in the present, and, by extension, of what van der Vlies calls "educated hope" (14) as a method of literary analysis. I consider Naidoo's reference to hallucinated time to be a variant of this educated hope.

7 See for instance Veblen, *Leisure Class*, and Bourdieu, *Distinction*.

8 The disciplinary and moral gate-keeping that saw aesthetics develop "a bad reputation" (Rancière, *Aesthetics* 1) – in 1868 Walter Pater, for instance, used the term to refer to the nineteenth-century movement that advocated the study and creation of "art for art's sake" – in truth failed to fully appreciate its own entanglement with politics, history, and ordinary, corporeal life. In fact, aesthetics carried a political valence even in the narrower senses in which it came to signify in the German Romantic tradition. Friedrich von Schiller's *On the Aesthetic Education of Man in a Series of Letters* (1794), for instance, identifies in an aesthetic education the route towards achieving the French Revolution's never fully realized ideals. The elevation of a person's moral character, he suggests, "is brought about by means of aesthetic education, which subjects to laws of beauty all those spheres of human behavior in which neither natural laws, nor yet rational laws, are binding upon human caprice, and which, in the form it gives to outer life, already opens up the inner" (169). As Gayatri Spivak phrases it, "the aesthetic, for Schiller, is a powerful thing, fit for princes, which can save the world from itself" (*An Aesthetic Education* 32).

9 The Online Etymology Dictionary defines the English term "aesthetics" as deriving from the German *Ästhetisch* or French *esthétique*, which both, in turn, derive from the Greek "*aisthetikos* 'sensitive, perceptive,' [and] from *aisthanesthai* 'to perceive (by the senses or by the mind), to feel.'"

10 See also Strauss, "Affective Return," for more on this point.

11 Theorists including Gayatri Spivak (*An Aesthetic*), Jacques Rancière (*Aesthetics and Its Discontents*), Russ Castronovo (*Beautiful*), and Ben

Highmore (*Ordinary*) have explored ways of narrowing the gap between aesthetics and politics. For Spivak, an "aesthetic education" – conceptualized in part as the pursuit of "deep language learning, qualitative social sciences, philosophizing into unconditional ethics" (*An Aesthetic Education* 27) – might be our best defence against the depersonalizing and homogenizing effects of globalization. See also Buck-Morrs, "Aesthetics and Anaesthetics," for an account of the journey the term aesthetics undertook from its classical to contemporary usage.

12 See for instance Stevens, Duncan, and Hook, eds., *Race, Memory and the Apartheid Archive: Towards a Transformative Psychosocial Praxis* (2013); Ratele and Duncan, eds., *Social Psychology and Inter-group Relations in South Africa* (2003); Ratele, ed., *Inter-group Relations: South African Perspectives* (2006); Gobodo-Madikizela, *A Human Being Died That Night* (2003); Gobodo-Madikizela and Van Der Merwe, eds., *Memory, Narrative and Forgiveness: Perspectives on the Unfinished Journeys of the Past*; and Gobodo-Madikizela, "Trauma" (2008); and Hook, *(Post)apartheid Conditions* (2013). See also Zimitri Erasmus's *Race Otherwise: Forging a New Humanism for South Africa* (2017) – which grew from the Apartheid Archive Project that I briefly discuss in chapter 5 – for some of the affective dimensions of apartheid-era racialization and subsequent political practice (through an exploration of the concepts of *eros* and *aimance* in particular).

13 See also the important work done by Keguro Macharia to theorize the wayward experiential dimensions that conventional approaches to (imperial) archives of queer life in African contexts fail to reveal. Drawing inspiration from the work of Ugandan feminist Stella Nyanzi, Macharia finds waywardness accumulated in "odd stories, little moments, folksy wisdom, and seemingly disconnected anecdotes" (188).

14 Some of the early inspiration for this book can be traced to a reading group on "Postcolonial Intimacies" in which I participated with Phanuel Antwi, Sarah Brophy, and Y-Dang Troeung at McMaster University in Canada roughly ten years ago. Much of our attention was focused on the work of Ahmed. For more on this topic, see for instance an interview that we conducted with Ahmed for a 2013 special issue of the journal *Interventions*.

15 Readers interested in the affective dimensions of political behaviour, and the shortcomings of critical models that explain these behaviours with a focus primarily on rationality, may also consult Clarke, Hoggett, and Thompson, *Emotion*; Demertzis, *Emotions*; and Ross, *Mixed*.

16 See for instance, Harari, *21 Lessons*, for an account of the contemporary "post-truth" moment as in fact anything but new to the human species. See also Siva Vaidhyanathan's *Antisocial Media* for an exploration of the ways in which Facebook in particular has contributed to the amplification of sophistry, lies, bigotry, and extremism through an erosion of our

capacity for slow, sustained forms of rational deliberation. Even though Facebook "amplifies content that hits strong emotional registers, whether joy or indignation" (5), the problem lies not in the tension between reason and emotion, but in the fact that their interdependence has been largely overlooked.

17 A cursory list of theorists here includes Sara Ahmed, Lauren Berlant, Kimberlé Crenshaw, Ann Cvetkovich, Moira Gatens, Pumla Dineo Gqola, bell hooks, Desiree Lewis, Audre Lorde, Zethu Matebeni, Patricia McFadden, Danai Mupotsa, Clare Hemmings, Arlie Hochschild, Stella Nyanzi, Carolyn Pedwell, Eve Kosofsky Sedgwick, Elizabeth Spelman, Sylvia Tamale, Anne Whitehead, and Iris Marion Young.

18 For an overview of some of these inheritances, see, for instance, Pedwell and Whitehead, "Affecting"; Cvetkovich, *Depression*; and Ahmed, "Afterword."

19 Studies of affect were declared to represent a "turn" most prominently in the 2007 and 2010 anthologies *The Affective Turn* (ed. Patricia Ticineto Clough and Jean Halley) and *The Affect Theory Reader* (ed. Melissa Gregg and Gregory Seigworth), yet a rapidly growing, interdisciplinary focus on affect has more recently produced volumes such as *Affective Societies: Key Concepts* (2019, ed. Jan Slaby and Christian von Scheve), *Public Spheres of Resonance: Constellations of Affect and Language* (2020, ed. Anne Fleig and Christian von Scheve), and *Analyzing Affective Societies: Methods and Methodologies* (2019, ed. Antje Kahl). As a number of feminist theorists have pointed out, there has been a tendency in some of the more recent declarations of a "turn" to affect to elide a longer legacy of feminist, queer, antiracist, and other work on related concerns and concepts. As Cvetkovich phrases it, "I have to confess I am somewhat reluctant to use the term *affective turn* because it implies that there is something new about the study of affect when in fact ... this work has been going on for quite some time" (*Depression* 3–4; emphasis in original). Sara Ahmed likewise points out that "when the affective turn becomes a turn to affect, feminist and queer work are no longer positioned as part of that turn" (*Cultural Politics* 206).

20 For an overview of some of the meanings historically assigned to terms such as affect, feeling, emotion, sensation, sentiment, mood, and so forth, see, for instance, Ahmed, *Cultural Politics*; Anderson, *Encountering Affect*; Flatley, *Affective Mapping*; Slaby and Von Scheve, *Affective Societies*; and Staiger, Cvetkovich and Reynolds, eds., *Political Emotions*.

21 For examples of feminist work on "feelings," see for instance Sedgwick, *Touching Feeling*; Ngai, *Ugly Feelings*; Love, *Feeling Backward*; and Cvetkovich, *Archives* and *Depression*. In her work on depression as a public feeling in the context of the contemporary United States, Ann Cvetkovich,

for instance, explains the preference she gives to the term feelings in much of her work as follows: "Because it is intentionally imprecise, retaining the ambiguity between feelings as embodied sensations and feelings as psychic or cognitive experiences. It also has a vernacular quality that lends itself to exploring feelings as something we come to know through experience and popular usage and that indicates, perhaps only intuitively but nonetheless significantly, a conception of mind and body as integrated" (*Depression* 4). *Wayward Feeling* is in fact indebted throughout to Cvetkovich's trailblazing work in this field.

1. Troubling the Rainbow Promise

1 An earlier, shorter version of this chapter was published in volume 16, no. 2, of the journal *Safundi: The Journal of South African and American Studies* (2014). Disappointment has subsequently been taken up by a number of cultural and literary critics to diagnose the post-apartheid present. See for instance Van der Vlies *Present Imperfect* (2017), and Wright "Ruined Time" (2019).

2 Muholi explains that "the title is taken from a collection/series of photographs in [their] publication *Only Half the Picture*" (Muholi).

3 My usage of the phrase emotional cultures builds on work in the field of affect theory on the relationship between emotion and politics. See for instance John Spurlock and Cynthia Magistro's *New and Improved: The Transformation of American Women's EmotionalCulture* for a definition of the phrase. My understanding of an "emotional culture" is heavily indebted to Raymond Williams's concept of "structures of feeling" (134), but also grows out of work done by theorists referenced in the introduction on the sociality of emotions, and on the relationship between intimate affects and the public sphere. I further draw here on work done on "affective publics," particularly in the context of digitally mediated and amplified protest movements. Margreth Lünenborg explains, for instance, that in these contexts, publics are understood to be affective "due to the highly dynamic character of news distributed instantaneously, usually through social media, during an ongoing event. In this context, publics take part affectively in waves of solidarity within online and offline communities" (320). See also, for instance, Ahmed, *Cultural Politics*; Berlant, *Cruel Optimism*; Cvetkovich, *Depression*; and Papacharissi, *Affective Publics*.

4 For further discussion of some of these aspects of their work, see for instance Baderoon, "African Oceans"; Farber, "Beyond"; Gqola, "Through Zanele Muholi's Eyes" and "Memory"; Imma, "(Re)visualizing"; Lewis, "Conceptual"; Sides, "Framing"; Thomas, "Intimate Archive"; and Van der Vlies, "Queer Knowledge."

5 Timothy Wright, for instance, identifies in South Africa after the 2012 Marikana massacre a "new temporal moment" marked by "a thematics of disappointment and ruin" (202).

6 Cvetkovich goes on to situate her analysis of negative feeling within larger debates in queer theory about the antisocial thesis, but notes that her approach "ultimately resists reductive binarisms between the social and the antisocial and between positive and negative affect, as well as paranoid critical tendencies that are on the lookout for premature forms of utopia or futurity or that presume the superiority of negative affect" (*Depression* 6).

7 See for instance Robins, "Slow Activism in Fast Times," for a reading of the politics of the instant media spectacle post-apartheid, and the creative ways in which a number of social justice movements have combined the latter with the longer-term activism of litigation, grassroots mobilization, as well as other slower forms of civic pedagogy.

8 This is taken from the Oxford English Dictionary's instructive definition of the term spectacle: "A person or thing exhibited to, or set before, the public gaze as an object either *(a)* of curiosity or contempt, or *(b)* of marvel or admiration."

9 Readers interested in the role played by Nelson Mandela in particular in manufacturing the euphoric optimism of the early transitional years may consult the generative set of essays included in *The Cambridge Companion to Nelson Mandela* (2014), edited by Rita Barnard. As Deborah Posel phrases it, "far more than anyone else, it was Mandela who performed the breach with the past and the 'national reconciliation' that went with it ... And in the dramatic spectacles of 'the rainbow nation' – in 1994 and 1995 – the old South African sclerosis of race and class had likewise seemed to 'melt away just like that' in the euphoric moment, as if self-evidently possible and, in fact, already emergent" ("Madiba Magic," 71; 88).

10 Writing, for instance, about the commodity as spectacle, Debord explains that, "with the coming of the industrial revolution, the division of labor specific to that revolution's manufacturing system, and mass production for a world market, the commodity emerged in its full-fledged form as a force aspiring to the complete colonisation of social life ... The spectacle corresponds to the historical moment at which the commodity completes its colonisation of social life" (29).

11 Numerous public intellectuals, politicians, and political commentators have been vocal in their criticism of those who have openly flaunted their wealth in public exhibitions of consumer excess (see for instance Tabane, "An Embarrassment," and Ndebele "Part 1"). Economic Freedom Front (EFF) leader Julius Malema in particular attracted criticism during his time as the president of the ANC Youth League (2008–12) for excessive consumer display, though he was quick to refashion the iconography of

consumer spectacle central to his public persona during these years into the highly emotive visuals of working-class solidarity as he assumed the role of EFF leader in 2013 (the EFF has from the outset been highly skilled at using sartorial and other forms of political theatre to convert media attention into political currency, as their political brand has come to be associated with the red overalls, hard hats, housecoats, and headscarves typically worn by miners, manual labourers, cleaners, and domestic workers). For more on this, see for instance Posel, "Malema." Criticism of Malema and others notwithstanding, it is worth taking note of the general absence, until fairly recently, of similar expressions of outrage in relation to longer-term forms of conspicuous consumer display on the part of a significant portion of South Africa's white citizenry, many of whom own lavish vacation homes in addition to their primary residences.

12 The 52nd National Conference of the ANC that took place in Polokwane, Limpopo, from 16 to 20 December in 2007 is often seen as a turning point in South African post-apartheid history. At this conference, Jacob Zuma was elected as ANC president, which in turn set in motion the events that led to the resignation of then president Thabo Mbeki on 20 September 2008, and Zuma's own ascent to the national presidency following the 2009 general election.

13 For more on these periodizations, see for instance Barnard and van der Vlies, *Writing*; Frenkel and MacKenzie, "Conceptualizing"; Chapman, "Conjectures"; Samuelson, "Scripting"; and Akpome "Towards."

14 See for instance Alexander, "Protests"; Bianco, "Protest Capital"; Ornellas et al., "Neoliberalism"; Bond and Mottiar, "The Politics of Discontent"; and work published by the Institute for Security Studies (https://www.issafrica.org). The mid-2000s features in these sources as roughly the time when protests started to drastically increase across the country. As dissenting publics continue the search for political platforms from which to be heard, protests have frequently turned violent, though it must be noted that the definition of violence privileged in dominant public discourse tends to be "profoundly anti-black and anti-poor" (Godsell, "#WitsFeesMustFall"). In his overview of eight studies on insurgent citizenship and collective violence in contemporary South Africa, Karl von Holdt indicates that, in recent years, "protests have become increasingly violent, marked by the destruction of public and private property, and confrontations between armed police and stone-throwing crowds" (5). Yet his findings must be qualified by acknowledging the many faces of violence, and of the ways in which the structural violence inherent South Africa's legacy of racial capitalism has come to be normalized.

15 See for instance Hoeane, "Race," and Habib, "Myth."

16 For more on the many forms of corruption that plagued the Zuma presidency, see for instance *No Longer Whispering to Power* (2017), Thandeka Gqubule's biography of then public protector Thuli Madonsela, and Ivor Chipkin and Mark Swilling, eds., *Shadow State: The Politics of State Capture* (2018).

17 It bears stating here that the boundary between those considered members of the South African national community and those believed to be foreign is blurry at best, as is evidenced by the fact that xenophobic attacks frequently involve the assault of significant numbers of South African citizens as well. See for instance Strauss, "Cinema."

18 The argument regarding the relationship between the apartheid and colonial production of alterity and contemporary xenophobic hatred is made most explicitly, perhaps, in Landau ("Loving"), but variations thereof can also be found, for instance, in Comaroff and Comaraff ("Nature"); Neocosmos (*From*); Nyamnjoh (*Insiders*); Monson ("Citizenship"); and Steinberg ("Xenophobia"). For additional details regarding the 2008 xenophobic attacks, as well as incidents predating and following these, see for instance Hassim et al. (*Go Home*) and Landau (*Exorcising*). See also the research and reports on migration and xenophobic violence published, for instance, by the African Centre for Migration and Society (http://www.migration.org.za/publications/); the Consortium for Refugees and Migrants in South Africa (https://www.cormsa.org.za/); the South African Migration Programme (https://samponline.org/samp-special-reports/); as well as the essays included, for instance, in the 2016 special issue of the journal *Agenda: Empowering Women for Gender Equity* on "Xenophobia, Nationalism and Techniques of Difference." In their collective study of insurgent citizenship across South Africa since 2008, Adèle Kirsten and Karl van Holdt point out that community protests and xenophobic violence require comparative analysis not least because community protests more often than not involved episodes of xenophobic violence (2). See Bond and Bond, "The Politics of Discontent," and Kirsten and Von Holdt, eds., *The Smoke That Calls*, for analyses of a selection of community protests in South Africa since 2008.

19 See Mbembe, "Necropolitics," passim. Police brutality has assumed staggering proportions in recent years, as evidenced by the fact that between April 2012 and March 2019, more than 42,000 criminal complaints were lodged against police, including allegations of rape, torture, murder, and assault (Knoetze). There is no question that the South African police forces are under considerable strain. Yet a point made by Jacob Dlamini in an analysis of social protests in the town of Voortrekker in June 2008 bears repeating here: "It is significant that in Voortrekker, as in many other sites of collective violence, police intervention is justified in the name of

maintaining law and order. But in the use of rubber bullets and teargas the state is acting as a patron of violence. Clearly the protests cannot be treated only as a law and order problem and should involve inquiries into their causes and exploring solutions through negotiations" (38).

20 Williams coined the now widely used phrase a "structure of feeling" to refer to "social experiences *in solution*, as distinct from other social semantic formations which have been *precipitated* and are more evidently and more immediately available" (133–4).

21 Debord, *Spectacle*, 144–6. Here the spectacle is conceptualized specifically as a form of false consciousness generated by the mass circulation of images under consumer capitalism.

22 As Andrew Loman phrases it, "Rubber has an extravagantly bloody history … The rubber death toll that midwifed the petroleum age is a shattering vindication of Walter Benjamin's melancholy apothegm that a document of civilization is always a document of barbarism" (297). For an overview of some of the death and human suffering resulting from the extraction of wild rubber in the Congo under King Leopold II of Belgium, see for instance Adam Hochschild's *King Leopold's Ghost* (1998).

23 Sense memories of the spectacle of necklacing serve as a particularly potent affective force here. For an analysis of the affective politics of representation that pertain specifically to the phenomenon of necklacing in both apartheid and post-apartheid contexts, see Thomas, "Wounding."

24 The N2 Gateway Housing Project was arguably the most ambitious housing project to emerge post-apartheid, with the ultimate aim to provide low-cost housing to people living in informal settlements along the N2 corridor in Cape Town – the highway that stretches from Cape Town to the airport and beyond. The project has been mired in controversy from scratch for reasons that include poor planning, failure to consult with local residents, forced relocations, and substandard building practices and construction materials. In 2009, the Centre on Housing Rights and Evictions (COHRE), Geneva, Switzerland, published a report criticizing various aspects of this project, including failures to respect the "right of affected persons to participate in developments that will directly affect their lives and livelihoods" (*N2*, 38) as well as the manner in which the project has thus far been managed.

25 Thanks are due to Jesse Arseneault for helping me think through this point. For important overviews of recent debates regarding the relationship between the human and the nonhuman, particularly from queer, feminist, and decolonial theoretical vantage points, see the special issues of the journals *GLQ: A Journal of Lesbian and Gay Studies* and the *Cambridge Journal of Postcolonial Literary*, co-edited respectively by Dana Luciano and Mel Chen, and Rosemary Jolly and Alexander Fyfe.

26 See Highmore, *Ordinary*, x, 52. The work of playful re-signification that marks the video installations of Searle and Muholi has long been a hallmark of carnivalesque forms of resistance in, for instance, contexts of anti-colonial or anti-homophobic struggle (pride marches constituting just one example). In post-rainbow South Africa, playfulness has been central also to some of the public spectacles contesting the authority of patriarchal power. Feminist resistance marches, as Desiree Lewis puts it, are often "marked by the spirited and noisy display of bodies and dress" ("Gendered Spectacle" 135), thus revealing spectacles of disappointment as possible arenas for the performance of subversive agency.

27 See Butler's "Is Kinship Always Already Heterosexual?" for a detailed discussion of this tension.

28 See also Van der Vlies, "Queer Knowledge," 152.

29 Muholi changed their pronouns from "she" to "they" while working on their series "Somnyama Ngonyama." This change reflects not only Muholi's resistance to binary gender pronouns; it also conveys their rejection to forms of individualism that would sever them from their historical community of African ancestors: "I'm not coming alone … I walk in with my ancestors" (qtd. in Gqola, "Muholi Walks").

30 In 2009, the South African Minister of Arts and Culture at the time, Lulu Xingwana, walked out of an art exhibition featuring some of Muholi's work. She took offence at what she considered to be the "immoral, offensive" nature of Muholi's images featuring Black lesbian intimacy (though in response to charges of homophobia she later claimed that she was "not even aware as to whether the 'bodies in the images were of men or women or both for that matter'" [Xingwana]). She further suggested that these artworks worked against "nation-building" (qtd. in Van Wyk). In some way Minister Xingwana's statements reflect precisely the kinds of "not" seeing that Muholi addresses in the title of the video installation at issue here. For a fuller analysis of the problems raised by the minister's comments, see for instance Thomas, "Intimate Archive," and Van der Vlies, "Queer Knowledge."

2. Moody, Expectant Teens

1 This chapter is dedicated to the memory of Sarah Chu.

2 *Coconut*, 1.

3 The films were the result of a rigorous selection and mentorship process. First, 28 semi-finalists were selected from 120 applications following a nationwide call in May 2010. These semifinalists attended a 10-day workshop at the Big Fish School of Digital Filmmaking in Johannesburg.

These aspirant filmmakers were then asked to pitch their ideas to a panel of judges, who chose seven of these pitches for development into film.

4 Sarah Nuttall and Cheryl-Ann Michael, who map out a number of these shifts in autobiographical representation, also point to gendered anxieties about individual self-assertion that percolated through women's autobiographical writing at the time. These concerns about the relationship between self and community were less prominent in the autobiographies published, for instance, by male authors such as Bloke Modisane and Ezekiel Mphahlele in the 1950s, in which individuality is more confidently asserted (3036).

5 Posel draws here on the work done by Martin Conboy on the meaning and ethics of contemporary tabloid journalism.

6 See, for instance, the work of Anna McCarthy ("Reality"), Beverley Skeggs and Helen Wood (*Reacting*), and Rita Barnard ("Oprah") on some of these contemporary forms of governmentality.

7 Even though Chu and Maruping were not independently responsible for directing these films (Chu was in fact the producer of *Made in China* whereas Maruping served as a co-director and editor alongside a director mentor [Gersch Kgamedi] and another director [Dipolelo Ditshego]), I give them primary credit here because they were the main subjects of these films and were both centrally involved in how their life stories took documentary shape.

8 Herbert Zettl explains that, in addition to the ways in which cinematographic factors help viewers to orient themselves in relation to so-called "outer" elements such as screen space and time, a number of elements such as sound, music, lighting, and so forth contribute to the manipulation of the "inner orientation" of viewers, namely the emotions and feelings that films aim to arouse. An example of this can be found, for instance, in the difference between the above-eye-level and the below-eye-level lighting of a face. Whereas the former ensures that shadows on a face are as expected, the latter casts shadows in unexpected positions, leading to affective disorientation on the part of the viewer: "We affix to this outer disorientation an inner disorientation: the face appears unusual, ghostly, and frightening" (31).

9 For some reflections on this global shift, see for instance Mik Thobo-Carlsen and Victor Chateaubriand's "How Tattoos Went from Subculture to Pop Culture."

10 There are many historical precursors to this individualization of responsibility for hardship via the injunction to think positively, not least of which Norman Vincent Peale's influential 1952 book *The Power of Positive Thinking*.

11 The word documentary, significantly, comes from the Latin *docere*: to teach and, according to the OED, as late as 1800 "documentary" meant "a lesson; a warning." The genre chosen for telling Sarah Chu's life narrative is thus entangled with the work of education.
12 This publication was published under Halberstam's former name, "Judith."
13 Like Lisa Baraitser, I use the terms motherhood and maternity interchangeably. For while the former is conventionally taken to signal the heteropatriarchal institution within which the experience of maternity and the relationship women have with their offspring have come to be regulated, the distinction between the two terms does risk making the latter seem disconnected from the institutionality assumed to be central to the former. As Baraitser puts it, "I use the terms interchangeably throughout this work, in a bid to trouble the notion that 'experience' may lie outside of the cultural, political and social institutions that both shape and are shaped by it" (160).
14 My translation. The subtitles here were not entirely accurate.
15 See for instance Baraitser, *Maternal*, and Nnaemeka, *Politics*, for details on some of the emotional complexities and contradictions that motherhood presents.
16 On some of the challenges delivered to the maternal subject by the alterity of the child, see, for instance, Buchanan, *Mother*; Baraitser, *Maternal*; Nnaemeka, *Politics*; and Oliver, *Subjects*.
17 I distinguish here between schooling and education in an effort to differentiate between colonial forms of schooling, to which I refer here, and the much longer legacy of African forms of education to which Maxeke and her peers did have access.

3. Managing Public Feeling

1 Zuma later declared the week of 20–26 August 2012 a period of national mourning to commemorate the lives of everyone who died violently at Marikana.
2 A much shorter version of this chapter was published in vol. 30, no. 4, of the journal *Critical Arts: South-North Cultural and Media Studies* (2016).
3 These include paintings made by the widows of the miners killed at Marikana (collected in a volume titled *Speaking Wounds: Voices of Marikana Widows through Art and Narrative*); urban graffiti by the activist collective Tokolos Stencils; paintings by artists such as Lehlohonolo Dhlamini, Jeannette Unite, Ayanda Mabulu, and Mary Wafer; sculptures by Haroon Gunn-Salie; as well as the documentaries *Night Is Coming: A Threnody for the Victims of Marikana* (2014), *Precious Metal* (2016), and *Strike a Rock* (2017),

directed respectively by Aryan Kaganof, Isis Thompson, and Aliki Saragas. A 2019 special issue of the journal *Social Dynamics: A Journal of African Studies*, edited by Ronit Frenkel and Pamila Gupta, is dedicated explicitly to thinking South Africa post-Marikana.

4 As Neville Hoad phrases it in his assessment of the extent to which US-centric public feelings projects might be transposable to other national contexts: "many of the major questions that the rubric of public feelings wish to address are evident in an event like the South African Truth and Reconciliation Commission (TRC), where narrative testimony was imagined as having emotionally reparative force in a wider project of nation-building" ("Three Poems" 135).

5 See for instance, Fogel, "The Selling of a Massacre," and Duncan, "South African Journalism and the Marikana Massacre." Duncan reveals, for instance, that the voices of miners accounted for only 3 per cent of the early sources of information used by journalists to report on the events (she surveyed 153 articles published between the 13 and 22 August 2012). Remarkably, "of all 153 articles, only one showed any attempt by a journalist to obtain an account from a worker about their version of events" (70).

6 Traditional medicine.

7 Duncan explains that the framing of the strikes in terms, for instance, of the damage it might do to investor confidence "was clearly and unashamedly biased towards the business case, further deligitimising the legitimate (albeit legally unprotected) attempt of the miners to secure a living wage (given that the formal bargaining structures had failed them)" ("South African" 74).

8 Tyler is concerned in her study with the dual meanings of the term "revolt": "the processes through which minoritized populations are imagined and configured as revolting and become subject to control, stigma and censure, and the practices through which individuals and groups resist, reconfigure and revolt against their subjectification" (3–4).

9 See for instance "Lonmin Admits Exerting Political Pressure."

10 The emails between Ramaphosa and Lonmin management were the subject of considerable controversy at the Farlam Commission, where conflicting testimony about their implications were given respectively by Ramaphosa and Shabangu. For more on this, see Kgosana, "Susan."

11 See for instance Zembylas, "Affective Modes."

12 See for instance the details provided in Alexander et al., *Marikana*; Marinovich, *Murder*; and Sinwell and Mbatha, *The Spirit*. Evidence presented at the Farlam Commission revealed that, contrary to claims that the miners who were fatally shot at "Scene One" (where 17 of the 34 miners were killed) were rushing in suicidal, muti-fuelled charge

towards the SAPS's Tactical Response Team (TRT), these miners were in fact being corralled in the direction of the TRT. Not only was their path of exit being blocked by armoured vehicles and barbed wire, seconds before police opened fire, the miners were being sprayed from behind by jets of water from a water cannon while stun grenades were being set off behind them, creating the appearance that they were running towards the TNT in attack. Video footage commissioned by the South African Human Rights Commission that shows all events in chronological order reveals the police version of events to have been largely misleading. This footage also indicates that police had by no means exhausted non-lethal means of dispersing the miners prior to the massacre. See Marinovich and Nicholson, "Marikana Commission" and "Marikana Video."

13 Though all workers have the right to strike, only workers engaged in a protected strike are safeguarded from dismissal. See De Vos, "Sharp." Details surrounding the fear-mongering strategies listed here are documented, for instance, in Alexander et al., *Marikana*; Desai, *Miners*; Duncan, "South African"; and Fogel, "The Selling."

14 Butler elaborates on this in the chapter titled "Melancholy Gender/ Refused Identification" in *The Psychic Life of Power*.

15 Aside from the studies that I discuss below, examples of work on melancholia in the fields of queer theorizing, critical race, and postcolonial studies include Paul Gilroy's *Postcolonial Melancholia*, Douglas Crimp's *Melancholia and Moralism*, and Sarah Ahmed's work on the "melancholic migrant" in *The Promise of Happiness*.

16 See for instance Mark Sanders's analysis of the testimony of Joyce N. Mtimkhulu in 1996 for a discussion of some of the ways in which the process of mourning was enabled through the invitation of acts of public condolence (Sanders 40–9). As he puts it, "mourning would make good for the violations of the apartheid era. As a system of social separation, apartheid would be undone through condolence" (49).

17 For a discussion of the use of the "common-purpose doctrine" at Marikana, see De Waal, "Apartheid." For more on the afterlife of the murder charges, see Meeson-Frizelle, "Murder." The murder charges were provisionally dropped on 3 September 2012. The arrested miners were also charged with public violence, illegal gathering, possession of dangerous weapons, and intimidation until August 2014, when these charges were finally dropped. At the time, Andries Nkome, a member of the defence team stated, "The charges were dropped due to the fact that the State would not be able to prove their cases if the matter went to trial" ("State Drops").

18 Thanks are due to Nthombizodwa Japhta for the translation.

19 Evidence presented at the Farlam Commission revealed that Lonmin had been engaging in questionable tax evasion practices for years. This

evidence has, in turn, called into doubt Lonmin's claims at the time of the strikes that it could not afford the wage increases demanded by the miners. See for instance McKune, "16"; McKune and Makinana, "Cyril"; as well as evidence presented in the documentary *Strike a Rock* (dir. Saragas) regarding Lonmin's unfulfilled Social Labour Plan obligations at a time when they had shown significant growth in revenue.

20 One of the primary concerns of the families of miners presenting their case at the Farlam Commission has been the fact that medical treatment for miners was delayed. One of these miners, Bongani Mdze, bled to death at the scene of the first shootings. He could have been saved if he had received timely medical attention. See "What Have We Learned?"

21 Phiyega was suspended from her post as police commissioner by Zuma following an investigation into her fitness for the post recommended by the Farlam Commission, though her suspension did not relate directly to her conduct at the time of the Marikana massacre.

22 For an early account of the workings of emotional labour see for instance Arlie Hochschild's *The Managed Heart: Commercialization of Human Feeling*, also discussed in the previous chapter. Of subsequent engagements with the notion of "affective labour," the work of Michael Hardt and Antonio Negri in *Empire* and *Multitude* is arguably the most widely discussed.

23 The Facebook group Justice Now for Marikana Strikers, for instance, to which Desai and others involved with the film are regular contributors, has over ten thousand members. The filmmakers also maintain a website; the film's own Facebook group, called Miners Shot Down; as well as a Twitter and Youtube presence. See https://minersshotdown.co.za/.

24 It is worth noting here that eight police officers are, at the time of this writing, charged with crimes related to the massacre, though these charges only materialized in 2017 and the National Prosecuting Authority has yet to convict anyone for the shooting of the miners on 16 August 2012. See Evans, "Seven."

25 As my reading of South Africa's long history of gender-based violence in chapter 5 indicates, not all cases of misogynist violence and femicide earn the kind of attention the Oscar Pistoruis trial did. The latter could be ascribed in no small part to the celebrity status and race of the man involved in the killing, and has little to do with widespread public concern regarding the routine killing and sexual assault/rape of women and gender-nonconforming people in the country.

4. Feeling the Fall

1 A study conducted already in 1998 by the Centre for the Study of Violence and Reconciliation (CSVR) and the Khulumani Support Group (a group

that has, over the years, been at the forefront of the struggle for reparations for apartheid survivors who testified at the TRC) found that most of the survivors of apartheid-era violence interviewed about their views on the TRC "felt that even if perpetrators were held accountable through the amnesty process for their deeds, justice still had to be done" and "that reconciliation and reparation were integrally linked" (Hamber et al.).

2 The assumption that students were driven to a greater extent by emotion than reason featured particularly prominently on social media platforms and in conversations that I had with numerous colleagues at the University of the Free State. Interestingly, not all of these colleagues were necessarily politically right-leaning or unsupportive of student protestors.

3 The repetition of the words serious in this intervention is notable. In a university context, seriousness might be read as signalling forms of intellectual engagement "untainted" by emotion, play, or silliness. I read this investment in seriousness as tied, at least in part, to the historical instrumentalization of the emotion-reason binary to exclusionary effect (a history I address shortly). It is further worth noting that one of the intellectual and activist legacies of 2015–16 student organizing has been a sustained insistence, on the part of particularly Black queer, trans, non-binary, and feminist activists, that intersectionality as a mode of critique be central to addressing forms of internal violence and complicity. The claim by Nattrass and Seekings, then, that the so-called racialization of pain would lead to a foreclosing of "serious consideration of other forms of injustice and indignity," did not bear out in the long term, and particularly not in the more reflexive, intersectional versions of student activism.

4 The question of particularly student violence has been a flashpoint issue in a number of commentaries on the 2015–17 protests, usually taken up differently by those in management and students respectively. See for instance Wits activist and former student Sarah Godsell's "On Violent Protest and Solidarity" for an overview of some of the ways in which the definitions of violence informing responses to student activisms in South Africa have historically tended to be "profoundly anti-black and anti-poor." For an analysis of the difficulties faced by university vice-chancellors during this time, see Jonathan Jansen's *As by Fire: The End of the South African University* and Adam Habib's *Rebels and Rage: Reflecting on #FeesMustFall*. See also the response to the latter from those derided by Habib as the "the far-left" (*Rebels* 71) or the "Pol Pot Brigade" (24) in "Open Letter," as well as Wamuwi Mbao's widely circulated review of the text in the Johannesburg Review of Books ("Dry"). My own position as part of a network of faculty members at South African universities supportive of student concerns regarding access, outsourcing, and decolonization is that the question of violence on the part of some students

cannot be separated from the manner in which university campuses came to be securitized both pre-emptively and in response to student protest. The case of former Wits SRC president Shaeera Khalla getting shot in the back 13 times at close range with rubber bullets by public order police at the time of a peaceful student protest (Pather and Whittles) is one of many examples of police or private security brutality in response to student activism at the time. For Khalla's perspective on the securitization of campuses, see McNulty. For more on student protests and the question of violence, see Malabela, "We Are Not," as well as Brooks, "In the Aftermath." The latter specifically explores the slow violence of legal foot dragging that many student protesters faced post #FMF.

5 In an essay titled "Malcolm X and Black Rage," Cornel West describes Malcolm X as a "prophet of black rage primarily because of his great love for black people. His love was neither abstract nor ephemeral. Rather, it was a concrete connection with a degraded and devalued people in need of psychic conversion. This is why Malcolm X's articulation of black rage was not directed first and foremost at white America. Rather, Malcolm believed that if black people felt the love that motivated that rage, the love would produce a psychic conversion in black people; they would affirm themselves as human beings, no longer viewing their bodies, minds and souls through white lenses, and believing themselves capable of taking control of their own destinies" (95–6).

6 As Smith phrases it, for instance, in his commentary on the Obama presidency, "Black rage was being channeled into black hope. On its face, that isn't entirely bad, but the particular brand of black hope that Obama represented was one that muted black rage, and its possibilities, altogether." See also Cooper, *Eloquent Rage*, and Thompson "An Exoneration of Black Rage."

7 This is not to say that there were not problems with how activism came to unfold in some student quarters, as I state earlier in this chapter. The point here is simply to acknowledge some of the ways in which questions of experiential embodiment were in fact central to much student theorizing from the outset.

8 Duncan explains that "when property is damaged but no one is injured or killed in such protests, journalists often automatically apply the label 'violent service delivery protests'" (*Protest* 143). She further points out that there are many reasons why protests could become violent, including in response to police violence, and that journalists have a responsibility to not simply focus on the moments of spectacular violence, but on the circumstances leading up to the violence, and so to avoid reinforcing "stereotypes that protesting is a form of expression of first, not last, resort" (142–3). Duncan's important assessment of protest reporting is part of a

larger study of protest as a key form of democratic expression, and of the extent to which this right is being variously upheld or placed under threat in contemporary South Africa.

9 See for instance Taibbi, *I Can't Breathe: The Killing That Started a Movement*, on the origins of the Black Lives Matter Movement in the United States, which, as I point out at the start of this book, took on renewed significance in 2020 with the death of George Floyd. The widely circulated meme "We revolt simply because for many reasons, we can no longer breathe," attributed to Franz Fanon, is actually a slightly altered version of the original in *Black Skin, White Masks*: "It is not because the Indo-Chinese has discovered a culture of his own that he is in revolt. It is because 'quite simply' it was, in more than one way, becoming impossible for him to breathe" (226).

10 "I have no use for human feelings," Modisane writes. "I stripped myself of them that day I looked upon the battered remains of the man who was my father; I pushed down the pain, forced it down, refused to cry and never cried since … I have long ceased to experience the sensation of feeling a hurt. I am a corpse" (qtd. in Nyamnjoh 83).

11 Translated from the original "antiblanke woede" and "antiwit haat" (Roodt, "Rhodes-standbeeld"). For an entertaining jeremiad on some of the anxieties awakened by the #RMF protests on the part of some liberal white male commentators, see Gillian Schutte's "Rhodes Arouses White Male Fears."

12 Incidentally, Rhodes's statue was meant, according to the booklet accompanying the statue's unveiling, to portray Rhodes's "immense and brooding spirit" (qtd. in Schmahmann 94).

13 In their captivating analysis of the history and politics of sanitation in Cape Town, Jackson and Robins point out, for instance, that urban segregation in South Africa has its deep roots in the nineteenth-century imperial governance of sanitation: "It was in the thick of struggle over sanitation expenditure and reform that Africans living in Cape Town were classified as an objectively distinct population, and then pushed outside the city … The colonial government in Cape Town … insisted on minimal investment in the city, with the idea that resources and wealth should flow *from* the African periphery to the European centre, not the other way around" (78; emphasis in original). Owing to the inadequacy of these investments, by the late nineteenth century the city of Cape Town had earned the label the "city of stinks." As a remedy, the "Cape Colonial response was to reduce the weight of its responsibility and access to modern infrastructure … The passing of the Native Reserve Locations Act of 1902 resulted in forcibly moving Africans to a sewage farm just outside Cape Town called Uitvlugt. This created safe distance, a more formidable

boundary separating the city's centre from its periphery, and stabilised interpretations of an ethnic or racial location for contamination. Africans, as a result, were spatially, bodily conflated with waste and pushed once-and-for-all outside the city" (80).

14 As co-translator Rodolphe el-Khoury explains in his introduction to the 2000 translation of *The History of Shit*, first published in 1978, the book constitutes an elaborate parody of conventional academic discourse: "with his convoluted prose, which this translation attempts to preserve; for it stands as a backhanded attempt to reverse the deodorization of language by means of a reeking syntax" (ix). Laporte further explicitly engages the intersections between colonial forms of racial othering and the historical management of odour and waste. As he phrases it, "since the sixteenth century, capitalism has persistently trapped the city in the Möbius strip of a discourse whose very unity is predicated on a division that can only be dialectically related. On one side lies the rich man's discourse, which associates the poor with the vile, the vulgar, the corrupt – in other words, with shit. On the other side lies the poor man's law, which suspects corruption within luxury and wealth at the source of stench. Needless to say, both the discourse of the master and that of the slave can smell the Jew a mile away, and their olfactory sense is all the keener when it comes to the black man. If rich and poor cling to similar racist views, it is because a capitalist dynamic locks each into place as the other's filth" (40).

15 *iQhiya* is an isiXhosa term for a headwrap or headscarf worn by women. For an overview of some of the ways in which the headscarf has recently been reclaimed by Black South African women as a sign of cultural celebration, see Fihlani. Massa Lemu offers a generative reading of iQhiya, alongside the group Gugulective, as engaged in forms of "biopolitical collectivism," namely "socially engaged practices, operating within a neoliberal capitalist environment, which focus on the production of critical subjectivities" (334). As Lemu points out, iQhiya is deeply sensitive to the harmful effects of labelling, and "has categorically rejected the 'performance collective' label," asserting "that the scope of their work is much broader than the title 'performance collective' suggests" (334). The group includes the following female artists: Asemahle Ntlonti, Bronwyn Katz, Buhlebezwe Siwani, Bonolo Kavula, Charity Matlhogonolo Kelapila, Lungiswa Gqunta, Sethembile Msezane, Sisipho Ngodwana, Thandiwe Msebenzi, Thule Gamedze, and the late Pinky Mayeng (Lemu 333).

16 Photographs of these and other similar performances can be viewed on Msezane's webpage under the heading "Public Holiday Series": http://www.sethembile-msezane.com/public-holiday-series/ol5m6r2x4m1tkhvm8iq1a0mvy8ha7s.

17 This is the title of Msezane's MFA exhibition from the Michaelis School of Fine Art, which was presented at the Cape Town Gallery MOMO from 15 February until 18 March 2017. The exhibition included sculptural installations that reimagine Black women into public space and official memory, and that rethink the binary between the public and private specifically in relation to the ways in which women's histories have been archived. See also the installations "Gog' Mashange," "Ovezi," and "Signal Her Return 1" on exhibition at the Zeitz Museum of Contemporary Art Africa in Cape Town: https://zeitzmocaa.museum/artists/sethembile-msezane/.

18 In the apartheid context, the infamous "pencil test" was used, for instance, to determine racial identity whenever officials were in doubt. If a pencil slid into a person's hair remained stuck, he/she could not be classified as "white." As sociologist Zimitri Erasmus phrases it, "scientific racism of the late nineteenth century made the body the sign of race. The naming of biological markers that came to validate European/ white superiority and African/ black inferiority was central to this science. Next to skin colour, hair texture was regarded as one of the most reliable markers of racial heritage" (380). See also Dabiri, *Twisted*, for a recent discussion of Black hairstyling cultures and histories.

19 Increased awareness surrounding the cultural politics of hair have arguably informed some of the resistance to the regulation of Black girls' hair at South African schools that started at Pretoria High School for Girls in August 2016, went viral, and subsequently compelled many schools to rethink their rules about hair. See, for instance, Ngoepe, "Black Girls." I noticed for instance that at the school my daughter attends, the rules regarding hair – and about what the school previously referred to as "ethnic hair" in particular – were changed the year following these protests.

20 The play in question was published under Ndlovu's former name, Lueen Conning.

5. Feminist Resonance

1 The most recent statistics available from the South African Police Service report that a woman is murdered every three hours in South Africa, and that 137 sexual offences are committed per day in the country (Head, "Femicide"; Francke, "Thousands"). This places the country fourth out of 183 countries ranked by the World Health Organization for the frequency of femicide committed. August 2019 was declared the most deadly month yet for violent crimes against women in the country (Francke).

2 Though I use the terms woman/women throughout this chapter and book, I take these terms to include all who identify with the category, if not the terms, but who may nonetheless reject cis/gender normativity, including trans women and gender- or sex-nonconforming and non-binary persons. I do so in the interest of gender/sex inclusivity even as I acknowledge that this terminology may be inadequate and that, at various points through the chapter, terms including womxn, womyn, wommon/wimmin, womyn-born-womyn, wombyn, and non-binary folx may well be more appropriate. I only use alternative terminology in cases where its use was explicitly stated as preferred, thereby accounting for the fact that the traditional spelling of "woman/women" may in fact at times be privileged also by those who nonetheless reject its historically binary underpinnings.

3 See also Strauss, "Affective Return."

4 Of the few studies of the role of sound in South African popular culture, Liz Gunner's work on radio drama is particularly worth noting. See for instance, *Radio Soundings: South Africa and the Black Modern* (2019).

5 The distrust of the personal, the sensory, and the emotional that has long been an object of critique on the part of feminist theorists has increasingly become the target of more mainstream cultural theory in Europe, the United States and elsewhere. This shift (which is not much of a shift if one's point of departure is feminist, queer, and decolonial) has been accompanied by a transition from ocularcentric approaches to (visual) culture towards forms of inquiry awake to the complex ways in which aesthetic texts and audio-visual technologies call upon the full human sensorium, encompassing both the distance (vision and hearing) and proximal (touch, smell, and taste) senses. My own thinking on the embodied sensorium has been shaped in many ways by work deriving from the global field of film, cultural, and sound studies, particularly that of theorists such as Vivian Sobchack, Steven Shaviro, Anna Rutherford, Laura Marks, Brandon LaBelle, Jonathan Sterne, and Frances Dyson.

6 Though some of the scholars involved in the Apartheid Archives project (including Tamara Shefer, Kopano Ratele, LaKeasha Sullivan, and Garth Stevens) take an explicitly intersectional approach to the afterlives of apartheid-era racisms, highlighting the intersections of gender, race, and sexuality in the apartheid archive, no study or social project of South Africa's long history of violent misogyny on the scale of the TRC has been attempted thus far.

7 Gqola explores the concept of the "female fear factory," first introduced in her Alan Paton Award–winning book *Rape: A South African Nightmare* (2015), in compelling detail in *Female Fear Factory* (2021).

8 See also literary critic Barbara Boswell's interview with Tlali in 2006 on some of the challenges the latter faced as a novelist under apartheid (Tlali,

"Interview"), as well as Boswell's analysis of *Muriel at Metropolitan* in *And Wrote My Story Anyway: Black South African Women's Novels as Feminism* (2020).

9 In spite of South African law stating that a rape complainant may not be named, the Afrikaans newspaper *Beeld* did so, in part to affirm the veracity of the charge against Zuma in the face of multiple initial denials, thus making Kuzwayo vulnerable to considerable victimization and stigmatization. For closer discussion of the question of Kwuzayo's anonymity, see Thlabi's *Khwezi: The Remarkable Story of Fezekile Ntsukela Kuzwayo*, and the fifth chapter, titled "Making Sense of Responses to the Jacob Zuma Rape Trial," of Gqola's *Rape: A South African Nightmare.*

10 See https://www.youtube.com/watch?v=kPnxkR2hFw8 for Dlamini's full response.

11 The 1956 Women's March had a significant, lesser-known, precursor in 1913, when a group of women, led by Charlotte Maxeke, staged a protest against colonial pass laws by tearing apart and burning their passes in front of municipal offices, leading to the arrest of over 80 women in Bloemfontein, Jagersfontein, Winburg, and Fauresmith.

12 "Gabrielle."

13 For more on the introduction of film sound, and of aurality as a central component of spectatorial reception, see, for instance, the chapter titled "Cinema as Ear" in *Film Theory: An Introduction through the Senses*, Thomas Elsaesser and Malte Hagener's reframing of the history of film theory through the lens of the embodied sensorium.

14 For a discussion of Nancy's meditations on listening as part of a larger "anti-ocular turn" in critical theory, see Adrienne Janus's article "Listening: Jean-Luc Nancy and the 'Anti-Ocular' Turn in Continental Philosophy and Critical Theory."

15 Bennett's reference to "finding ears" derives from a poem by Constance Mkombwe titled "Shopping for an Ear" (1993).

Conclusion: Shutting Down

1 "Speaking."

2 Former vice-chancellor Jonathan Jansen for instance implemented the "No Student Hungry Programme" to address the reality that close to 60 per cent of UFS's students face considerable food insecurity, with many going hungry for days on end. See: https://www.ufs.ac.za/docs/librariesprovider37/no-student-hungry-programme-(nsh)-documents/the-nsh-story-2015-18-eng.pdf?sfvrsn=0. Though the Free State is one of the country's poorest provinces, the problem is countrywide. See for instance Wegerif and Adeniyi, "Student Hunger."

3 Some of the studies my colleagues and I have returned to in recent years to make sense of the corporatization of higher education and its embodied effects include Berg and Seeber, *Slow*; Mountz et al., "Slow"; Readings, *University*; Smyth, *Toxic*; and Whelan, Walker, and Moore, *Zombie*.

4 Highmore defines public time as the "time of clocks, of eight-hour shifts, of hourly news bulletins, of national holidays." Intimate time, in contrast, is "the time of the body, of hunger, of stream of consciousness." It is in the relationship between work and life, he explains, "where the conflict between public and intimate forms of time is often experienced most starkly" (*Ordinary* 88).

Works Cited

Abrahams, Peter. *Mine Boy*. Oxford: Heineman, 1946.

Ahmed, Sara. "Afterword." *The Cultural Politics of Emotion*, 2nd ed. New York: Routledge, 2014, pp. 204–33.

– "Broken Bones." *feministkilljoys*, 15 Aug. 2014, https://feministkilljoys.com/2014/08/15/broken-bones/. Accessed 17 Aug. 2014.

– *The Cultural Politics of Emotion*. New York: Routledge, 2004.

– "Multiculturalism and the Promise of Happiness." *New Formations*, vol. 63, winter 2007–8, pp. 121–37.

– "Not in the Mood." *New Formations*, vol. 82, 2014, pp. 13–28.

– *The Promise of Happiness*. Durham: Duke UP, 2010.

– *Willful Subjects*. Durham: Duke UP, 2014.

Akoob, Rumana. "We Need to Talk about the Long-Term Effects of FMF on Students' Mental Health." *The Daily Vox*, 1 Nov. 2017, https://www.thedailyvox.co.za/we-need-to-talk-about-the-long-term-effects-of-fmf-on-students-mental-health-rumana-akoob/. Accessed 25 Mar. 2020.

Akpome, Aghogho. "Towards a Reconceptualisation of '(Post)Transitional' South African Cultural Expression." *English in Africa*, vol. 43, no. 2, 2016, pp. 39–62.

Alexander, Peter. "Protests and Police Satatistics: Some Commentary." Unpublished note. Johannesburg: Research Chair in Social Change, University of Johannesburg.

Alexander, Peter, Thapelo Lekgowa, Botsang Mmope, Luke Sinwell, and Bongani Xezwi. *Marikana: A View from the Mountain and a Case to Answer*. Johannesburg: Jacana Media, 2012.

Anderson, Ben. *Encountering Affect: Capacities, Apparatuses, Conditions*. Farnham: Ashgate, 2014.

Antwi, Phanuel, Sarah Brophy, Helene Strauss, and Y-Dang Troeung. "'Not without Ambivalence': An Interview with Sara Ahmed on Postcolonial

Intimacies." *Interventions: International Journal of Postcolonial Studies*, vol. 15, no. 1, 2013, pp. 110–26.

– "Postcolonial Intimacies: Gatherings, Disruptions, Departures." *Interventions: International Journal of Postcolonial Studies*, vol. 15, no. 1, 2013, pp. 1–9.

Apata, Gabriel O. "I Can't Breathe': The Suffocating Nature of Racism." *Theory, Culture & Society* , vol. 37, no. 7–8, pp. 241–54. *Sage Journals*, https://doi.org/10.1177/0263276420957718.

Aradau, Claudia, and Rens van Munster. "Taming the Future: The *Dispositive* of Risk in the War on Terror." *Risk and the War on Terror*, edited by Marieke de Goede and Louise Amoore. London: Routledge, 2008, pp. 23–40.

Areff, Ahmed, and Derrick Spies. "Zuma Announces Free Higher Education for Poor and Working Class Students." *News24*, 16 Dec. 2017, https://www.news24.com/SouthAfrica/News/zuma-announces-free-higher-education-for-poor-and-working-class-students-20171216. Accessed 25 Mar. 2020.

Arendt, Hannah. *Crises of the Republic: Lying in Politics, Civil Disobedience, On Violence, Thoughts on Politics and Revolution*. New York: Harcourt Brace, 1972.

Athanasiou, Athena, and Judith Butler. *Dispossession: The Performative in the Political*. Cambridge, MA: Polity Press, 2013.

Baderoon, Gabeba. "The African Oceans – Tracing the Sea as Memory of Slavery in South African Literature and Culture." *Research in African Literatures*, vol. 40, no. 4, 2009, pp. 89–107.

Badiou, Alain. *The Meaning of Sarkozy*. Translated by David Fernbach. London and New York: Verso, 2008.

Baraitser, Lisa. *Maternal Encounters: The Ethics of Interruption*. London and New York: Routledge, 2009.

Barber, Karin. "Introduction: Hidden Innovators in Africa." *Africa's Hidden Histories: Everyday Literacy and Making the Self*, edited by Karin Barber. Bloomington, Indiana UP, 2006, pp. 1–24.

Barchiesi, Franco. *Precarious Liberation: Workers, the State and Contested Social Citizenship in Postapartheid South Africa*. Albany: State U of New York P, 2011.

– "That Melancholic Object of Desire: Work and Official Discourse before and after Polokwane." *The Johannesburg Salon*, vol. 1, 2009, pp. 51–5.

Barnard, Rita. "Introduction." *South African Writing in Transition*, edited by Rita Barnard and Andrew van der Vlies. London: Bloomsbury Academic, 2019, pp. 1–32.

– "Oprah's Paton, or South Africa and the Globalization of Suffering." *Safundi: The Journal of South African and American Studies*, vol. 7, no. 3, 2006, pp. 1–21.

Bauman, Zygmunt. *Wasted Lives: Modernity and Its Outcasts*. Cambridge, UK: Polity Press, 2004.

– *Does Ethics Have a Chance in a World of Consumers?* Cambridge, MA: Harvard UP, 2008.

Bennett, Jane. "'Enough Lip Service!' Hearing Post-colonial Experience of Gender-Based Violence." *Agenda: Empowering Women for Gender Equity*, vol. 50, 2001, pp. 88–96.

Berg, Maggie, and Barbara Seeber. *The Slow Professor: Challenging the Culture of Speed in the Academy.* Toronto: U of Toronto P, 2016.

Berlant, Lauren. "Cruel Optimism." *The Affect Theory Reader*, edited by Melissa Gregg and Gregory Seigworth, Durham, NC: Duke UP, 2010, pp. 93–117.

– *Cruel Optimism.* Durham, NC: Duke UP, 2011.

– *The Female Complaint: The Unfinished Business of Sentimentality in America.* Durham, NC: Duke UP, 2008.

– "Life Writing and Intimate Publics: A Conversation with Lauren Berlant." By Jay Prosser. *Biography*, vol. 34, no. 1, winter 2011, pp. 180–7.

Berlant, Lauren, and Lee Edelman. *Sex or the Unbearable.* Durham, NC: Duke UP, 2014.

Bestall, Lucienne. "The Lives of Others: Gabrielle Goliath's 'This song is for …'" *Arttrob*, 20 Dec. 2019, https://artthrob.co.za/2019/12/20/the-lives-of-others-gabrielle-goliaths-this-song-is-for/. Accessed 22 Dec. 2019.

Bhabha, Homi. *The Location of Culture.* London and New York: Routledge, 1994.

Bianco, Silvia. "South Africa: The 'Protest Capital of the World.'" *The South African*, 20 June 2013, http://www.thesouthafrican.com/south-africa-the-protest-capital-of-theworld. Accessed 12 Dec. 2019.

Bloch, Ernst. *Das Prinzip Hoffnung: Erster Band.* Frankfurt am Main: Suhrkamp Verlag, 1959.

– *The Principle of Hope*, translated by Neville Plaice, Stephen Plaice, and Paul Knight. Oxford: Basil Blackwell, 1986.

Bond, Patrick, and Shauna Mottiar. "Movements, Protest and a Massacre in South Africa." *Journal of Contemporary African Studies*, vol. 31, no. 2, 2013, pp. 283–302.

– "The Politics of Discontent and Social Protest in Durban." *Politikon*, vol. 39, no. 3, Dec. 2012, pp. 309–30.

Bordwell, David, and Kristin Thompson. *Film Art: An Introduction.* 7th ed. New York: McGraw-Hill, 2004.

Borralho, Carina. "Mitigating the Environmental Effects of Opencast Mining." *Creamer Media's Mining Weekly*, 9 May 2014, https://www.miningweekly.com/article/mitigating-the-environmental-effects-of-opencast-mining-2014-05-09#:~:text=%E2%80%9COpencast%20mining%20also%20impacts%20negatively,life%20cycle%2C%E2%80%9D%20he%20says. Accessed 25 Oct. 2020.

Boswell, Barbara. *And Wrote My Story Anyway: Black South African Women's Novels as Feminism*. Johannesburg: Wits UP, 2020.

Bourdieu, Pierre. *Distinction*. Translated by Richard Nice. Cambridge, MA: Harvard UP, 1987.

Braidotti, Rosi. "Critical Posthuman Knowledges." *South Atlantic Quarterly*, vol. 116, no. 1, 2017, pp. 83–96.

Brooks, Shirley. "In the Aftermath of #FeesMustFall: Scapegoats, Race, and the Question of Individual Responsibility." *The Journalist*, 29 Mar. 2018, http://www.thejournalist.org.za/spotlight/in-the-aftermath-of-feesmustfall-scapegoats-race-and-the-question-of-individual-responsibility. Accessed 29 Mar. 2018.

Brophy, Sarah, and Janice Hladki. "Visual Autobiography in the Frame: Critical Embodiment and Cultural Pedagogy." *Embodied Politics in Visual Autobiography*, edited by Sarah Brophy and Janice Hladki, Toronto: U of Toronto P, 2014, pp. 3–28.

Brown, Elspeth, and Thy Phu. *Feeling Photography*. Durham, NC: Duke UP, 2014.

Brown, Julian. *South Africa's Insurgent Citizens: On Dissent and the Possibility of Politics*. London: Zed Books, 2015.

Buchanan, Andrea. *Mother Shock: Loving Every (Other) Minute of It*. Emeryville, CA: Seal Press, 2003.

Buck-Morrs, Susan. "Aesthetics and Anaesthetics: Walter Benjamin's Artwork Essay Reconsidered." *October*, vol. 62, autumn 1992, pp. 3–41.

Butler, Judith. *Gender Trouble: Feminism and the Subversion of Identity*. New York and London: Routledge, 1990.

– "Is Kinship Always Already Heterosexual?" *Differences: A Journal of Feminist Cultural Studies*, vol. 13, no. 1, 2002, pp. 14–44.

– *The Psychic Life of Power: Theories in Subjection*. Stanford: Stanford UP, 1997.

Bystrom, Kerry. *Democracy at Home in South Africa: Family Fictions and Transitional Culture*. New York: Palgrave Macmillan, 2016.

Bystrom, Kerry, and Sarah Nuttall. "Private Lives and Public Cultures in South Africa." *Cultural Studies*, vol. 27, no. 3, 2013, pp. 307–32.

Carlson, Jennifer, and Kathleen Stewart. "The Legibilities of Mood Work." *New Formations*, vol. 82, 2014, pp. 114–33.

Castronovo, Russ. *Beautiful Democracy: Aesthetics and Anarchy in a Global Era*. Chicago: U of Chicago P, 2007.

Chapman, Michael. "Conjectures on South African Literature." *Current Writing*, vol. 21, no. 1–2, 2009, pp. 1–23.

Cheng, Anne Anlin. *The Melancholia of Race: Psychoanalysis, Assimilation and Hidden Grief*. Oxford: Oxford UP, 2001.

Chidgey, Red. *Feminist Afterlives: Assemblage Memory in Activist Times*. London: Palgrave Macmillan, 2018.

Chion, Michel. *Audio-Vision: Sound on Screen*. New York. Columbia UP, 1994.

Chipkin, Ivor, and Mark Swilling, editors. *Shadow State: The Politics of State Capture*. Johannesburg: Wits UP, 2018.

Cho, Lily. "Affecting Citizenship: The Materiality of Melancholia." *Narratives of Citizenship: Indigenous and Diasporic Peoples Unsettle the Nation-State*, edited by Aloys Fleischman, Nancy van Styvendale, and Cody McCarroll. Edmonton: U of Alberta P, 2011, pp. 107–27.

Clarke, Simon, Paul Hoggett, and Simon Thompson, editors. *Emotion, Politics, and Society*. New York: Palgrave Macmillan, 2006.

Clough, Patricia Ticineto, and Jean Halley, editors. *The Affective Turn*. Durham, NC: Duke UP, 2007.

Cock, Jacklyn, and Alison Bernstein. *Melting Pots and Rainbow Nations: Conversations about Difference in the United States and South Africa*. Urbana: U of Illinois P, 2002.

Coleman, Daniel. "Epistemological Crosstalk: Between Melancholia and Spiritual Cosmology in David Chariandy's *Soucouyant* and Lee Maracle's *Daughters Are Forever*." *Crosstalk: Canadian and Global Imaginaries in Dialogue*, edited by Diana Brydon and Marta Dvorak. Waterloo, ON: Wilfrid Laurier UP, 2012, pp. 53–72.

– *White Civility: The Literary Project of Early Canada*. Toronto: U of Toronto P, 2006.

– "Why Does Reading Matter?" Comment on "Why Does It Matter: Perspectives on Humanities Education in Canada." Blog, 29 June 2013, http://whydoesitmattercanada.wordpress.com/2013/06/29/why-does-reading-matter/. Accessed 13 July 2013.

Comaroff, Jean, and John Comaroff. "Naturing the Nation: Aliens, Apocalypse and the Postcolonial State." *Journal of Southern African Studies*, vol. 27, no. 3, 2001, pp. 627–51.

– "Theory from the South: A Rejoinder." *Cultural Anthropology Online*, 25 Feb. 2012, http://www.culanth.org/fieldsights/273theoryfromthesoutharejoinder. Accessed 18 Apr. 2016.

Conboy, Martin. "The Popular Press: Surviving Postmodernity." *The Tabloid Culture Reader*, edited by Anita Biressi and Heather Nunn. Maidenhead, Berkshire: Open UP, 2008, pp. 45–52.

Cooper, Brittney. "In Defense of Black rage: Michale Brown, Police and the American Dream." *The Salon*, 12 Aug. 2014, https://www.salon.com/2014/08/12/in_defense_of_black_rage_michael_brown_police_and_the_american_dream/. Accessed 12 December 2017.

– *Eloquent Rage: A Black Feminist Discovers Her Superpower*. New York: St. Martin's Press, 2018.

Coulthard, Lisa. "Haptic Aurality: Listening to the Films of Michael Haneke." *Film-Philosophy*, vol. 16, no. 1, 2012, pp. 16–29.

Crimp, Douglas. *Melancholia and Moralism: Essays on AIDS and Queer Politics.* Cambridge, MA: MIT Press, 2002.

Cvetkovich, Ann. "Affect." *Keywords for American Cultural Studies.* Edited by Bruce Burgett and Glenn Hendler. New York: New York UP, 2014, pp. 13–16.

– *An Archive of Feelings: Trauma, Sexuality and Lesbian Public Cultures.* Durham, NC: Duke UP, 2003.

– *Depression: A Public Feeling.* Durham, NC: Duke UP, 2012.

– "Public Feelings." *South Atlantic Quarterly*, vol. 106, no. 3, 2007, pp. 459–68.

Dabiri, Emma. *Twisted: The Tangled History of Black Hair Culture.* Glasgow: HarperCollins, 2020.

Da Costa, Dia. "Cruel Pessimism and Waiting for Belonging: Towards a Global Political Ecomomy of Affect." *Cultural Studies*, vol. 30, no. 1, 2016, pp. 1–23.

Davenport, Thomas. "elearning and the Attention Economy: Here, There and Everywhere?" *LiNE Zine*, 2001, pp. 1–4.

Debord, Guy. *The Society of the Spectacle.* Translated by Donald Nicholson-Smith. New York: Zone Books, 1995. Originally published as *La société du spectacle* (Paris: Buchet-Chastel, 1967).

Demertzis, Nicolas, editor. *Emotions in Politics: The Affect Dimension in Political Tension.* New York: Palgrave Macmillan, 2013.

Derrida, Jacques, and Eric Prenowitz. *Archive Fever: A Freudian Impression.* Chicago: U of Chicago P, 1996.

Desai, Rehad, director. *Miners Shot Down.* Produced by Anita Khanna and Rehad Desai. Uhuru Productions, DVD, 2014.

De Vos, Pierre. "Sharp Divisions on the Constitutional Court about the Right to Strike." *Constitutionally Speaking*, 25 Sept. 2012, https://constitutionallyspeaking.co.za/sharp-divisions-on-the-constitutional-court-about-the-right-to-strike/. Accessed 3 Mar. 2020.

De Waal, Mandy. "Apartheid and the Marikana Murder Charges: A Common Purpose Indeed." *Daily Maverick*, 31 Aug. 2012, https://www.dailymaverick.co.za/article/2012-08-31-apartheid-and-the-marikana-murder-charges-a-common-purpose-indeed/#.VEy72fmSxqU. Accessed 3 Mar. 2020.

De Wet, Phillip. "Zuma Announces Inquiry into Marikana Shooting." *Mail and Guardian Online*, 17 Aug. 2012, http://mg.co.za/article/2012-08-17-police-go-with-bravado-on-marikana. Accessed 3 Mar. 2020.

Diangelo, Robin. *White Fragility: Why It's So Hard for White People to Talk about Racism.* Boston: Beacon Press, 2018.

Ditshego, Dipolelo, director, and Evelyn Maruping, co-director. *Where Is the Love.* Produced by Mokete Leroibaki. Born Free Media, DVD, 2010.

Dlakavu, Simamkele. "Is There Space for White Allies in Black Student Uprisings?" *Vanguard Magazine*, 12 May 2015, http://vanguardmagazine.

co.za/is-there-space-for-white-allies-in-black-student-uprisings/. Accessed 31 May 2015.

– "Khwezi Protest: We Came as 4, but Stood as 10 000." *City Press*, 14 Aug. 2016, https://city-press.news24.com/Voices/khwezi-protest-we-came-as-4-but-stood-as-10-000-20160814. Accessed 12 Nov. 2019.

Dlamini, Jacob. "Voortrekker: The Smoke That Calls." *The Smoke That Calls: Insurgent Citizenship, Collective Violence and the Struggle for a Place in the New South Africa*, edited by Adèle Kirsten and Karl von Holdt. Johannesburg: Centre for the Study of Violence and Reconciliation and the Society, Work and Development Institute, 2011, pp. 33–44.

Duncan, Jane. *Protest Nation: The Right to Protest in South Africa*. Pietermaritzburg: U of KwaZulu-Natal P, 2016.

– "South African Journalism and the Marikana Massacre: A Case Study of an Editorial Failure." *The Political Economy of Communication*, vol. 1, no. 2, 2013, pp. 65–88.

Dussel, Enrique. *1492: El encubrimiento del Otro: Hacia el origen del "mito de la modernidad."* La Paz: Plural Editores, 1994.

Elsaesser, Thomas, and Malte Hagener. *Film Theory: An Introduction through the Senses*. New York: Routledge, 2015.

Eng, David, and David Kazanjian. "Introduction: Mourning Remains." *Loss*, edited by David Eng and David Kazanjian. Berkeley: U of California P, 2003, pp. 1–25.

Erasmus, Zimitri. "Hair Politics." *Senses of Culture*, edited by Sarah Nuttall and Cheryl-Ann Michael. Oxford: Oxford UP, 2000, pp. 380–92.

– *Race Otherwise: Forging a New Humanism for South Africa*. Johannesburg: Wits UP, 2017.

Erlmann, Veit. *Reason and Resonance: A History of Modern Aurality*. New York: Zone Books, 2010.

Esty, Joshua. "Excremental Postcolonialism." *Contemporary Literature*, vol. 40, no. 1, spring 1999, pp. 22–59.

Evans, Jenni. "Seven Years since Marikana Massacre and Still No Justice, Says Rights Institute." *News24*, 16 Aug. 2019, https://www.news24.com/SouthAfrica/News/seven-years-since-marikana-massacre-and-still-no-justice-says-rights-institute-20190815. Accessed 3 Mar. 2020.

Evans, Joanna Ruth. "Unsettled Matters, Falling Flight: Decolonial Protest and the Becoming-Material of an Impertial Statue." *TDR: The Drama Review*, vol. 62, no. 3, 2018, pp. 130–44.

Falkof, Nicky, and Cobus van Staden, editors. *Anxious Joburg: The Inner Lives of a Global South City*. Johannesburg: Wits UP, 2020.

Fanon, Frantz. *Black Skin, White Masks*. 1952. London: Pluto Press, 1986.

Farber, Leora. "Beyond the Ethnographic Turn: Refiguring the Archive in Selected Works by Zanele Muholi." *Critical Arts*, vol. 31, no. 2, 2017, pp. 12–27.

Fekisi, Linda, and Sylvia Vollenhoven. "We Love UCT: Says Student Who Covered Rhodes in Shit." *The Journalist*, 25 Mar. 2015, http://www.thejournalist.org.za/spotlight/we-love-uct-says-student-who-covered-rhodes-in-shit. Accessed 25 June 2017.

Felski, Rita, and Susan Fraiman. "Introduction: In the Mood." *New Literary History*, vol. 43, 2012, pp. v–xii.

Ferguson, James. *Global Shadows: Africa in the Neoliberal World Order.* Durham, NC: Duke UP, 2006.

– "Theory from the Comaroffs, or How to Know the World Up, Down, Backwards and Forwards." *The Salon*, vol. 5, 2013, pp. 1–4.

Fick, Angelo. "Decolonising Institutions, Organisations, and Minds." *eNCA*, 26 Mar. 2015, https://www.enca.com/opinion/decolonising-institutions-organisations-and-minds. Accessed 15 Apr. 2015.

Fihlani, Pumza. "How South African Women Are Reclaiming the Headscarf." *BBC News*, 11 June 2016, https://www.bbc.com/news/world-africa-36461213. Accessed 29 May 2017.

Fikeni, Lwandile. "Protest, Art and the Aesthetics of Rage: Social Solidarity and the Shaping a Post-Rainbow South Africa." *Ruth First Lecture*, 17 Aug. 2016, University of the Witwatersrand, http://witsvuvuzela.com/wp-content/uploads/2016/08/Final-1-Lwandile-2016.pdf. Accessed 30 Sept. 2017.

Flatley, Jonathan. *Affective Mapping: Melancholia and the Politics of Modernism*, Cambridge, MA: Harvard UP, 2008.

Fleig, Anne, and Christian von Scheve, editors. *Public Spheres of Resonance: Constellations of Affect and Language.* London and New York: Routledge, 2020.

Fogel, Benjamin. "The Selling of a Massacre: Media Complicity in Marikana Repression." *Ceasefire*, 5 Nov. 2012, https://ceasefiremagazine.co.uk/south-africa-marikana/. Accessed 3 Mar. 2020.

Foucault, Michel, and Colin Gordon. *Power/Knowledge: Selected Interviews and Other Writings, 1972–1977.* New York: Pantheon Books, 1980.

Francke, Robin-Lee. "Thousands Protest in South Africa over Rising Violence against Women." *The Guardian*, 5 Sept. 2019, https://www.theguardian.com/world/2019/sep/05/thousands-protest-in-south-africa-over-rising-violence-against-women. Accessed 3 Oct. 2019.

Frenkel, Ronit, and Pamila Gupta. "Yo-yo Culture: Thinking South Africa after Marikana." *Social Dynamics: A Journal of African Studies*, vol. 45, no. 2, 2019, pp. 1–8.

Freud, Sigmund. "The Ego and the Id." 1923. *The Standard Edition of the Complete Psychological Works of Sigmund Freud, Volume 19*, edited by James Strachey, London: Hogarth, 1961, pp. 13–66.

– "Mourning and Melancholia." 1917. *The Freud Reader*, edited by Peter Gay. New York: W.W. Norton, 1989, pp. 584–89.

Friend. "Tribute to Koketso 'Queen'." *Elegy* by Gabrielle Goliath, Sept. 2016, https://www.gabriellegoliath.com/tributekoketso-queen. Accessed 15 Nov. 2019.

Gill, Rosalind, and Imogen Tyler. "Postcolonial Girl: Migrant Audibility and Mediated Intimacy." *Interventions: International Journal of Postcolonial Studies*, vol. 15, no. 1, 2013, pp. 78–94.

Gilroy, Paul. *Postcolonial Melancholia*. New York: Columbia UP, 2005.

Gobodo-Madikizela, Pumla. *A Human Being Died That Night*. Boston, MA: Houghton Mifflin, 2003.

– "Trauma, Forgiveness and the Witnessing Dance: Making Public Spaces Intimate." *Journal of Analytical Psychology*, vol. 53, no. 2, 2008, pp. 169–88.

Gobodo-Madikizela, Pumla, and Chris Van Der Merwe, editors. *Memory, Narrative and Forgiveness: Perspectives on the Unfinished Journeys of the Past*. Newcastle upon Tyne: Cambridge Scholars Publishing, 2009.

Godsell, Sarah. "#WitsFeesMustFall" Op-Ed: On Violent Protest and Solidarity." *Daily Maverick*, 19 Oct. 2015, https://www.dailymaverick.co.za/article/2015-10-19-witsfeesmustfall-op-ed-on-violent-protest-and-solidarity/#.V96sShGNLlI. Accessed 20 Oct. 2015.

– "On Violent Protest and Solidarity." *Daily Maverick*, 19 Oct. 2015, https://www.dailymaverick.co.za/article/2015-10-19-witsfeesmustfall-op-ed-on-violent-protest-and-solidarity/#.Wmr_VxG9hlI. Accessed 20 Oct. 2015.

Goliath, Gabrielle. *Elegy*. 2015, https://www.gabriellegoliath.com/elegy. Accessed 17 Nov. 2019.

– "Gabrielle Goliath: Embracing the Capacious." Goliath interviewed by *National Arts Festival*, 21 May 2019, https://www.nationalartsfestival.co.za/news/sbya2019-visual-art-gabrielle-goliath/. Accessed 13 Nov. 2019.

– *Personal Accounts*. 2014, https://www.gabriellegoliath.com/personal-accounts. Accessed 17 Nov. 2019.

– "Re: Query." Email received by Helene Strauss, 29 Jan. 2020.

– *This song is for …* 2019, https://www.gabriellegoliath.com/this-song-is-for. Accessed 17 Nov. 2019.

Gould, Deborah. "On Affect and Protest." *Political Emotions: New Agendas in Communication*, edited by Janet Staiger, Ann Cvetkovich, and Ann Reynolds. New York: Routledge, 2010, pp. 18–44.

Gouws, Amanda. "#EndRapeCulture Campaign in South Africa: Resisting Sexual Violence through Protest and the Politics of Experience." *Politikon*, vol. 45, no. 1, 2018, pp. 3–15.

Gqola, Pumla Dineo. "'The Difficult Task of Normalizing Freedom': Spectacular Masculinities, Ndebele's Literary/Cultural Commentary and Post-Apartheid Life." *English in Africa*, vol. 36, no. 1, May 2009, pp. 61–76.

– *Female Fear Factory*. Cape Town: Melinda Ferguson Books, 2021.

– "Gabrielle Goliath Creates Songs for Survivors in Scratched Melodies." *New Frame*, 12 July 2019, https://www.newframe.com/gabrielle-goliath-creates-songs-for-survivors-in-scratched-melodies/. Accessed 29 Oct. 2019.

– "Memory, Diaspora, and Spiced Bodies in Motion: Berni Searle's Art." *African Identities*, vol. 3, no. 2, 2005, pp. 123–38.

– *Rape: A South African Nightmare*. Johannesburg: MFBooks, Jacana Media, 2015.

– *Reflecting Rogue: Inside the Mind of a Feminist*. Johannesburg: MFBooks, Jacana Media, 2017.

– "Through Zanele Muholi's Eyes: Re/Imagining Ways of Seeing Black Lesbians." *African Sexualities: A Reader*, edited by Sylvia Tamale. Cape Town: Pambazuka Press, 2011, pp. 622–9.

– "Zanele Muholi Walks in with the Ancestors." *New York Times*, 2 Dec. 2020, https://www.nytimes.com/2020/12/02/arts/zanele-muholi-tate-modern.html. Accessed 5 Dec. 2020.

Gqubule, Thandeka. *No Longer Whispering to Power: The Story of Thuli Madonsela*. Cape Town: Jonathan Ball Publishers, 2017.

Grandey, Alicia, James Diefendorff, and Deborah Rupp, editors. *Emotional Labor in the 21st Century: Diverse Perspectives on the Psychology of Emotional Regulation at Work*. New York and London: Routledge, 2013.

Greenfield, Patrick. "South African Environmental Activist Shot Dead in Her Home." *The Guardian*, 23 Oct. 2020, https://www.theguardian.com/world/2020/oct/23/south- african-environmental-activist-shot-dead-in-her-home. Accessed 24 Oct. 2020.

Gregg, Melissa, and Gregory Seigworth, editors. *The Affect Theory Reader*. Durham, NC: Duke UP, 2010.

Grosfoguel, Ramón. "The Structure of Knowledge in Westernized Universities: Epistemic Racism/Sexism and the Four Genocides/Epistemicides of the Long 16th Century." *Human Architecture: Journal of the Sociology of Self-Knowledge*, vol. 11, no. 1, 2013, pp. 73–90.

Guignon, Charles. "Moods in Heidegger's *Being and Time*." *What Is an Emotion? Classic and Contemporary Readings*, edited by Robert C. Solomon. Oxford, Oxford UP, 2003, pp. 81–190.

Gumede, William. "Unfinished Revolutions: The North African Uprisings and Notes on South Africa." *Fees Must Fall: Student Revolt, Decolonisation and Governance in South Africa*, edited by Susan Booysen, Johannesburg: Wits UP, 2016, pp. 169–90.

Gunner, Liz. *Radio Soundings: South Africa and the Black Modern*. Johannesburg: Wits UP, 2019.

Habib, Adam. "Myth of the Rainbow Nation: Prospects for the Consolidation of Democracy in South Africa." *African Security Review*, vol. 5, no. 6, 1996, pp. 15–37.

– "Politics of Rage Puts Our Gains in Danger." *Sunday Times*, 15 May 2016, p. 13.

– *Rebels and Rage: Reflecting on #FeesMustFall*. Johannesburg and Cape Town: Jonathan Ball, 2019.

Hage, Ghassan. "The Politics of White Restoration Has to 'Go Back Where It Came From.'" *The Guardian*, 19 July 2019, https://www.theguardian.com/commentisfree/2019/jul/20/the-politics-of-white-restoration-has-to-go-back-where-it-came-from. Accessed 19 July 2019.

Hamber, Brandon, Traggy Maepa, Tlhoki Mofokeng, and Hugo van der Merwe. "Survivors' Perception of the Truth and Reconciliation Commission and Suggestions for the Final Report." Centre for the Study of Violence and Reconciliation, 1998, https://web.archive.org/web/20060925181412/http://www.csvr.org.za/papers/papkhul.htm#note1. Accessed 24 Jan. 2017.

Hamilton, Carolyn, Verne Harris, and Graeme Reid. "Introduction." *Refiguring the Archive*, edited by Carolyn Hamilton et al. Cape Town: Springer, 2002, pp. 1–17.

Halberstam, Judith. *In a Queer Time and Place: Transgender Bodies, Subcultural Lives*. New York: New York UP, 2005.

Harari, Yuval Noah. *21 Lessons for the 21st Century*. Toronto: Signal, Penguin Random House Canada, 2018.

Haraway, Donna. *Staying with the Trouble: Making Kin in the Chthulucene*. Durham, NC: Duke UP, 2016.

Hardt, Michael, and Antonio Negri. *Empire*. London: Harvard UP, 2000.

– *ultitude: War and Democracy in the Age of Empire*. New York: Penguin, 2004.

Harper, Stephen. "Text of Prime Minister Harper's Apology." 11 June 2008, http://www.fns.bc.ca/pdf/TextofApology.pdf. Accessed 3 Mar. 2014.

Hartman, Saidiya. *Wayward Lives, Beautiful Experiments: Intimate Histories of Social Upheaval*. New York: W.W. Norton, 2019.

Harrisberg, Kim. "Murders of South African Women Surge as 9-Week Lockdown Eases." *Global Citizen*, 23 June 2020, https://www.globalcitizen.org/en/content/gender-violence-covid-19-lockdown-south-africa/. Accessed 29 Oct 2020.

Hassim, Shireen. "Why, a Decade On, a New Book on Zuma's Rape Trial Has Finally Hit Home." *The Conversation*, 5 Oct. 2017, https://theconversation.com/why-a-decade-on-a-new-book-on-zumas-rape-trial-has-finally-hit-home-85262. Accessed 18 Feb. 2018.

Hassim, Shireen, Tawana Kupe, and Eric Worby, editors. *Go Home or Die Here: Violence, Xenophobia and the Reinvention of Difference in South Africa.* Johannesburg: Wits UP, 2008.

Head, Tom. "Femicide Rates: South Africa vs the Rest of the World." *The South African,* 4 Sept. 2019, https://www.thesouthafrican.com/news/how-many-women-killed-south-africa-femicide/. Accessed 3 Oct. 2019.

Hebdige, Dick. *Subculture: The Meaning of Style.* New York: Routledge, 1981.

Hedges, Chris. *Empire of Illusion: The End of Literacy and the Triumph of Spectacle.* New York: Nation Books, 2009.

Heidegger, Martin. *Being and Time.* Translated by John Macquarrie and Edward Robinson. Oxford: Basil Blackwell, 1967.

Hemmings, Clare. "In the Mood for Revolution: Emma Goldman's Passion." *New Literary History,* vol. 43, no. 3, summer 2012, pp. 527–45.

– "Invoking Affect: Cultural Theory and the Ontological Turn." *Cultural Studies.* vol. 19, no. 5, 2005, pp. 548–67.

Highmore, Ben. *Ordinary Lives: Studies in the Everyday.* London and New York: Routledge, 2011.

– "Finding Our Way: Mood and Cultural Studies." *Communication and Critical/Cultural Studies,* vol. 10, no. 4, 2013, pp. 427–38.

Highmore, Ben, and Jane Bourne Taylor. "Introducing Mood Work." *New Formations,* vol. 82, 2014, pp. 5–12.

Hirsch, Marianne. *Family Frames: Photography, Narrative, and Postmemory.* Cambridge, MA: Harvard UP, 1997.

Hoad, Neville. *African Intimacies: Race, Homosexuality, and Globalization.* Minneapolis: U of Minnesota P, 2007.

– "Three Poems and a Pandemic." *Political Emotions: New Agendas in Communication,* edited by Janet Staiger, Ann Cvetkovich, and Ann Reynolds. New York: Routledge, 2010, pp. 134–50.

Hochschild, Adam. *King Leopold's Ghost: A Story of Greed, Terror and Heroism in Colonial Africa.* Boston: Houghton Mifflin, 1998.

Hochschild, Arlie Russell. "Emotion Work, Feeling Rules, and Social Structure." *American Journal of Sociology,* vol. 85, no. 3, 1979, pp. 551–75.

– *The Managed Heart: Commercialization of Human Feeling.* Berkeley: U of California P, 1983.

Hoeane, Thabisi. "Race Relations: Is There Hope?" *SA Reconciliation Barometer: Tracking Socio-political trends,* vol. 2, no. 3, 2004, pp. 5–6.

Hook, Derek. *(Post)apartheid Conditions: Psychoanalysis and Social Formation,* New York: Palgrave Macmillan, 2013.

– "A Threatening Personification of Freedom or: Sobukwe and Repression." *Safundi: Journal of South African and American Studies,* vol. 17, no. 2, pp. 189–212.

hooks, bell. *Talking Back: Thinking Feminist, Thinking Black.* London: Sheba Feminist Publishers, 1989.

Hunt, Nancy Rose. "An Acoustic Register: Rape and Repetition in Congo." *Imperial Debris: On Ruins and Ruination*, edited by Ann Laura Stoler. Durham, NC, Duke UP, 2013, pp. 47–66.

Imma, Z'étoile. "(Re)visualizing Black lesbian Lives, (Trans)masculinity, and Township Space in the Documentary Work of Zanele Muholi." *Journal of Lesbian Studies*, vol. 21, no. 2, 2017, pp. 219–41.

Isaacs, Lisa. "Maxwele under fire from #FeesMustFall feminists." *IOL News*, 6 Apr. 2016, https://www.iol.co.za/news/maxwele-under-fire-from-feesmustfall-feminists-2005721. Accessed 22 May 2016.

Jackson, Shannon, and Steven Robins. "Making Sense of the Politics of Sanitation in Cape Town." *Social Dynamics: A Journal of African Studies*, vol. 44, no. 1, 2018, pp. 69–87.

Jacobs, Sean, and Herman Wasserman. "It Is Time to Be Offended." *The Daily Maverick*, 5 May 2011, https://www.dailymaverick.co.za/opinionista/2011-05-05-it-is-time-to-be-offended/. Accessed 18 Oct. 2019.

Jaffer, Zubeida. *Beauty of the Heart: The Life and Times of Charlotte Mannya Maxeke*. Bloemfontein: Sun Press, 2016.

Jaggar, Allison. "Love and Knowledge: Emotion in Feminist Epistemology." *Women, Knowledge, and Reality: Explorations in Feminist Philosophy*, edited by Ann Garry and Marilyn Pearsall. Boston: Unwin Hyman, 1989, pp. 129–56.

James, Deborah. *Money from Nothing: Indebtedness and Aspiration in South Africa*. Stanford: Stanford UP, 2015.

Jansen, Jonathan. *As by Fire: The End of the South African University*. Cape Town: Tafeberg, 2017.

Janus, Adrienne. "Listening: Jean-Luc Nancy and the 'Anti-Ocular' Turn in Continental Philosophy and Critical Theory." *Comparative Literature*, vol. 63, no. 2, spring 2011, pp. 182–202.

Jappie, Saarah. "Tribute to Louisa van de Caab." *Elegy*, by Gabrielle Goliath, 2019, https://www.gabriellegoliath.com/full-videolouisa-van-de-caab Accessed 15 Nov. 2019.

Jappie, Zayaan. "Meet South African Artist Gabrielle Goliath, the 2019 Recipient of the Prestigious Standard Bank Young Artist Award." *okayafrica*, 18 Feb. 2019, https://www.okayafrica.com/south-african-artist-gabrielle-goliath-the-2019-recipient-of-the-prestigious-standard-bank-young-artist-award/. Accessed 12 Oct. 2019.

Jasper, James. "Emotions and Social Movements: Twenty Years of Theory and Research." *Annual Review of Sociology*, vol. 37, Aug. 2011, pp. 285–303.

Jayawardane, M. Neelika. "Bad Education." *Even Magazine*, fall 2016, http://evenmagazine.com/bad-education-south-africa/. Accessed 20 May 2018.

– "Gabrielle Goliath's 'Elegy' Is a Powerful Lamentation for the Victims of Sexual Violence." *Frieze*, 31 May 2019, https://frieze.com/article/gabrielle-goliaths-elegy-powerful-lamentation-victims-sexual-violence. Accessed 24 Sept. 2019.

Jinnah, Zaheera. "South Africa Is Burning: Femicide, Xenophobia and Protests." *Mail and Guardian*, 4 Sept. 2019, https://mg.co.za/article/2019-09-04-sa-is-burning-femicide-xenophobia-and-protests/. Accessed 16 Oct. 2019.

Jolly, Rosemary, and Alexander Fyfe. "Introduction: Reflections on Postcolonial Animations of the Material." *Cambridge Journal of Postcolonial Literary Inquiry*, vol. 5, no. 3, 2018, pp. 296–303.

Jones, Megan. "Conspicuous Destruction, Aspiration and Motion in the South African Township." *Safundi: The Journal of South African and American Studies*, vol. 14, no. 2, 2013, pp. 209–24.

Jordheim, Helge, Anne Kveim Lie, Erik Ljungberg, and Einar Wigen. "Epidemic Times." *Somatosphere: Science, Medicine, and Anthropology*, 2 Apr. 2020, http://somatosphere.net/2020/epidemic-times.html/. Accessed 30 Oct. 2020.

Kahl, Antje, editor. *Analyzing Affective Societies: Methods and Methodologies*. London and New York: Routledge, 2019.

Kelly, Christy. "Reflections on Oscar Pistorius, Marikana and the Media." *Felix Online*, 6 Nov. 2014, https://old.felixonline.co.uk/articles/2014-11-6-reflections-on-oscar-pistorius-marikana-and-the-media/. Accessed 3 Mar. 2020.

Kennedy, Michael. "Moonlight Sonata." *Oxford Dictionary of Music*. Oxford: Oxford UP, 2006.

Kessi, Shose. "Of Black Pain, Animal Rights and the Politics of the Belly." *Mail and Guardian Thought Leader*, 25 Sept. 2015, https://thoughtleader.co.za/blackacademiccaucus/2015/09/25/of-black-pain-animal-rights-and-the-politics-of-the-belly/. Accessed 29 Apr. 2017.

Kesting, Marietta. *Affective Images: Post-apartheid Documentary Perspectives*. Albany: State U of New York P, 2017.

Kgamedi, Gersh, director. *Driving Force*. Produced by Amos Mathebula Nanziwe Mzuzu and co-produced by Mawande Stemela. Born Free Media, 2011.

Kgosana, Caiphus. "Susan Shabangu Says Cyril Ramaphosa Is Lying about Marikana." *City Press*, 26 Aug. 2014, http://www.citypress.co.za/politics/susan-shabangu-says-cyril-ramaphosa-lying-marikana-call/. Accessed 17 Sept. 2014.

Khanna, Ranjana. "Post-Palliative: Coloniality's Affective Dissonance." *Postcolonial Text*, vol. 2, no. 1, 2006. https://www.postcolonial.org/pct/article/viewArticle/385/815.

Kimani, Hazel. "Gabrielle Goliath's *Elegy* // A Deadly Sonic Experience." *Bubblegumclub*, Dec. 2017, https://bubblegumclub.co.za/art-and-culture/gabrielle-goliaths-elegy-deadly-sonic-experience/. Accessed 26 Sept. 2019.

Kirsten, Adèle, and Karl von Holdt. "Introduction." *The Smoke That Calls: Insurgent Citizenship, Collective Violence and the Struggle for a Place in the New South Africa*, edited by Adèle Kirsten and Karl von Holdt. Johannesburg: Centre for the Study of Violence and Reconciliation and the Society, Work and Development Institute, 2011, pp. 2–4.

Klein, Naomi. *This Changes Everything: Capitalism vs. the Climate.* New York: Simon and Schuster, 2014.

Knoetze, Daneel. "Nine Key Takeaways: IPID's Cover-up of Police Brutality in SA." *Daily Maverick*, 7 Oct. 2019, https://www.dailymaverick.co.za/article/2019-10-07-key-takeaways-ipids-cover-up-of-police-brutality-in-sa/. Accessed 19 Dec. 2019.

Kockott, Fred, and Matthew Hattingh. "Fikile Ntshangase Opposed a Mine Extension: Last Night She Was Murdered." *Fin24*, 23 Oct. 2020, https://www.news24.com/fin24/companies/mining/fikile-ntshangase-opposed-a-mine-extension-last-night-she-was-murdered-20201023. Accessed 24 Oct. 2020.

Kuklick, Henrika. "Contested Monuments: The Politics of Archeology in Southern Africa." *Colonial Situations: Essays on the Contextualization of Ethnographic Knowledge*, edited by George Stocking. Madison: U of Wisconsin P, 1991, pp. 135–69.

Kuzwayo, Ellen. *Call Me Woman.* Johannesburg: Ravan Press, 1985.

LaBelle, Brandon. "Auditory Relations." *The Sound Studies Reader*, edited by Jonathan Sterne, London and New York, Routledge, 2012, pp. 468–74.

– *Sonic Agency: Sound and Emergent Forms of Resistance.* London: Goldsmith's Press, 2018.

Landau, Loren, editor. *Exorcising the Demons Within: Xenophobia, Violence and Statecraft in Contemporary South Africa.* Johannesburg: Wits UP, 2011.

– "Loving the Alien? Citizenship, Law, and the Future in South Africa's Demonic Society." *African Affairs*, vol. 109, 2010, pp. 213–30.

Laporte, Dominique. *A History of Shit.* Translated by Nadia Benabid and Rodolphe el-Khoury. Cambridge, MA: MIT Press, 2000.

Lekabe, Thapelo. "Ramaphosa Bombshell: Yes I Would Believe Khwezi Was Raped." *The Citizen*, 8 Dec. 2017, https://citizen.co.za/news/54th-anc-national-conference/1752892/ramaphosa-bombshell-yes-i-would-believe-khwezi-was-raped/. Accessed 12 Jan. 2018.

Lemu, Massa. "Performance in Biopolitical Collectivism: A Study of Gugulective and iQhiya." *Acts of Transgression: Contemporary Live Art in South Africa*, edited by Jay Pather and Catherine Boulle. Johannesburg: Wits UP, 2019.

Lewis, Desiree. "The Conceptual Art of Berni Searle." *Agenda*, vol. 16, no. 50, 2001, pp. 108–17.

– "Gendered Spectacle: New Terrains of Struggle in South Africa." *Sida Studies*, vol. 24, 2009, pp. 127–37.

Lewis, Desiree, and Cheryl Hendricks. "Epistemic Ruptures in South African Standpoint Knowledge-Making: Academic Feminism and the #FeesMustFall Movement." *Gender Questions*, vol. 4, no. 1, 2016, pp. 64–81.

Lincoln, Sarah. "Precarious Time and the Aesthetics of Community." *South African Writing in Transition*, edited by Rita Barnard and Andrew van der Vlies. London: Bloomsbury Academic, 2019, pp. 99–121.

"Lonmin Admits Exerting Political Pressure." *Times Live*, 10 Sept. 2014, http://www.timeslive.co.za/local/2014/09/10/lonmin-admits-exerting-political-pressure. Accessed 17 Sept. 2014.

Lorde, Audre. "The Uses of Anger: Women Responding to Racism." *Sister Outsider: Essays and Speeches*. Berkeley: Crossing Press, 1984, pp. 124–33.

Love, Heather. *Feeling Backwards: Loss and the Politics of Queer History*. Cambridge, MA: Harvard UP, 2007.

Lowman, Andrew. "Rubber." *Fueling Culture: 101 Words for Energy and Environment*, edited by Imre Szeman, Jennifer Wenzel, and Patricia Yaeger. New York: Fordham UP, pp. 296–9.

Luciano, Dana, and Mel Chen. "Introduction: Has the Queer Ever Been Human?" *GLQ: A Journal of Lesbian and Gay Studies*, vol. 21, no. 2–3, 2015, pp. 182–207.

Lujabe, Ndileka. "The Struggle within the struggle." *City Press*, 16 June 2016, https://city-press.news24.com/News/the-struggle-within-the-struggle-20160611. Accessed 12 Apr. 2017.

Lünenborg, Margreth. "Affective Publics." *Affective Societies: Key Concepts*, edited by Jan Slaby and Christian von Scheve. London and New York: Routledge, 2019, pp. 319–29.

Lyster, Rosa. "The Death of Uyinene Mrwetyana and the Rise of South Africa's #AmINext Movement." *The New Yorker*, 12 Sept. 2019, https://www.newyorker.com/news/news-desk/the-death-of-uyinene-mrwetyana-and-the-rise-of-south-africas-aminext-movement. Accessed 13 Sept. 2019.

Macharia, Keguro. "On Being Area-Studied: A Litany of Complaint." *Journal of Lesbian and Gay Studies*, vol. 22, no. 2, 2014, pp. 183–9.

Macleod, Catriona. *"Adolescence," Pregnancy and Abortion: Constructing a Threat of Degeneration*. London and New York: Routledge, 2011.

Maingard, Jacqueline. "Trends in South African Documentary Film and Video: Questions of Identity and Subjectivity." *Journal of Southern African Studies*, vol. 21, no. 4, December 1995, pp. 567–667.

Makhulu, Anna-Maria. "Reckoning with Apartheid: The Conundrum of Working through the Past." *Comparative Studies of South Asia, Africa and the Middle East*, vol. 36, no. 2, 2016, pp. 256–62.

– "Trump, Zuma, Brexit: Anti-Black Racism and the Truth of the World." *Safundi*, vol. 21, no. 4, pp. 493–503. *Taylor & Francis Online*, https://doi.org/10.1080/17533171.2020.1835300.

Malabela, Musawenkosi. "We Are Not Violent but Just Demanding Free Decolonized Education: University of the Witwatersrand." *#Hashtag: An Analysis of the #FeesMustFall Movement at South African Universities*, edited by Malose Langa. Johannesburg: Centre for the Study of Violence and Reconciliation, 2017, pp. 132–47.

Mandela, Nelson. *Long Walk to Freedom*. Boston: Little Brown, 1994.

Marinovich, Greg. *Murder at Small Koppie: The Real Story of the Marikana Massacre*. Johannesburg: Zebra Press, 2016.

Marinovich, Greg, and Greg Nicolson. "Marikana Commission: Police's Defence Collapsing." *Daily Maverick*, 9 Sept. 2014, https://www.dailymaverick.co.za/article/2014-09-09-marikana-commission-polices-defence-collapsing/#.VB_q0fmSxqX. Accessed 3 Mar. 2020.

"Marikana Inquiry Updates." *Times Live*, 23 Oct. 2012, https://en.wikipedia.org/wiki/Marikana_miners'_strike. Accessed 3 Mar. 2020.

"Marikana Video Casts Doubt on Police Version." *Mail and Guardian*, 5 Sept. 2014, https://mg.co.za/article/2014-09-05-marikana-video-casts-doubt-on-police-version. Accessed 3 Mar. 2020.

Maroga, Kopano. "The Poetics of Remembrance as Resistance: The Work of Sethembile Msezane." *Artthrob*, 27 Feb. 2017, https://artthrob.co.za/2017/02/27/the-poetics-of-remembrance-as-resistance-the-work-of-sethembile-msezane/. Accessed 23 May 2017.

Mashinini, Emma. *Strikes Have Followed Me All My Life: A South African Autobiography*. London: The Woman's Press, 1989.

Massumi, Brian. "The Future Birth of Affective Fact: The Political Ontology of Threat." *The Affect Theory Reader*, edited by Melissa Gregg and Gregory Seigworth. Durham, NC: Duke UP, 2010, pp. 52–70.

Mathews, James, and Gladys Thomas. *Cry Rage*. Johannesburg: Spro-cas Publications, 1972.

Matlwa, Kopano. *Coconut*. Johannesburg: Jacana, 2007.

Maxwele, Chumani. "Black Pain Led Me to Throw Rhodes Poo." *Business Live*, 16 Mar. 2016, https://www.businesslive.co.za/bd/opinion/2016-03-16-black-pain-led-me-to-throw-rhodes-poo/. Accessed 10 Apr. 2017.

Maylam, Paul. *The Cult of Rhodes: Remembering an Imperialist in Africa*. Claremont: New Africa Books, 2005.

Mbandazayo, Kwezilomso. "Kanga and Khwezi: Kwezilomso Mbandazayo Challenges the Memorialisation of Fezekile Ntsukela Kuzwayo." *Johannesburg Review of Books*, 15 Jan. 2018, https://johannesburgreviewofbooks.com/2018/01/15/conversation-issue-kanga-and-khwezi-kwezilomso-mbandazayo-challenges-the-memorialisation-of-fezekile-ntsukela-kuzwayo/. Accessed 31 Jan. 2018.

Mbao, Wamuwi. "Dry Like Steel: A Wrecking Ball of a Book." *Johannesburg Review of Books*, 6 May 2019, https://johannesburgreviewofbooks

.com/2019/05/06/dry-like-steel-a-wrecking-ball-of-a-book-from-the-hashtag-seasons-wamuwi-mbao-reviews-adam-habibs-rebels-and-rage-reflecting-on-feesmustfall/. Accessed 8 May 2019.

Mbembe, Achille. "Class, Race and the New Native." *Mail and Guardian*, 26 Sept. 2014, https://mg.co.za/article/2014-09-25-class-race-and-the-new-native/. Accessed 3 Mar. 2020.

– "Necropolitics." *Public Culture*, vol. 15, no. 1, 2003, pp. 11–40.

– "Ruth First Lecture." *New Frame*, 4 Oct. 2019, https://www.newframe.com/ruth-first-memorial-lecture-2019-achille-mbembe/. Accessed 10 Oct. 2019.

– "SA's Death Penalty Is Not Yet Dead." *City Press*, 16 Aug. 2015, https://www.news24.com/citypress/Voices/SAs-death-penalty-is-not-yet-dead-20150814. Accessed 3 Mar. 2020.

McCarthy, Anna. "Reality Television: A Neoliberal Theater of Suffering." *Social Text*, vol. 25, no. 4, 2007, pp. 17–41.

McKune, Craig. "16 Questions Lonmin Must Answer." *Mail and Guardian*, 16 Oct. 2014, https://mg.co.za/article/2014-10-16-questions-lonmin-must-answer. Accessed 3 Mar. 2020.

McKune, Craig, and Andisiwe Makinana. "Cyril Ramaphosa's Lonmin Tax-Dodge Headache." *Mail and Guardian*, 19 Sept. 2014, https://mg.co.za/article/2014-09-18-cyril-ramaphosas-lonmin-tax-dodge-headache. Accessed 3 Mar. 2020.

McNulty, Kyla. "Interview with Shaeera Khalla, former SRC President at Wits University." *South African History Online*, n.d., https://www.sahistory.org.za/archive/interview-shaeera-kalla-former-src-president-wits-university-interviewed-kyla-mc-nulty. Accessed 4 Jan. 2018.

Meeson-Frizelle, "Murder Charges Dropped against Marikana Miners." *The South African*, 3 Sept. 2012, http://www.thesouthafrican.com/murder-charges-dropped-against-marikana-miners. Accessed 3 Mar. 2020.

Mercier, Hugo, and Dan Sperber. "Why Do Humans Reason? Arguments for an Argumentative Theory." *Behavioral and Brain Sciences*, vol. 34, no. 2, 2011, pp. 57–74.

Mgqolozana, Thando. "Rhodes Falling Is an Acknowledgement of Black Pain." Interview by Nick Pawson. *News24 Video*, 13 Apr. 2015, https://www.news24.com/news24/video/southafrica/news/rhodes-falling-is-acknowledgement-of-black-pain-20150410. Accessed 15 May 2016.

Mitchell, W.J.T. *Picture Theory: Essays on Verbal and Visual Representation.* Chicago: U of Chicago P, 1994.

Modisane, Bloke. *Blame Me on History*. New York: Dutton, 1963.

Mohsen, Lamiaa. *UN Chronicle*, 26 Oct. 2020, https://www.un.org/en/un-chronicle/covid-19-and-need-action-mental-health. Accessed 27 Oct. 2020.

Molope, Kagiso Lesego. *This Book Betrays My Brother.* Oxford: Oxford UP, 2012.

Monson, Tamlyn. *Citizenship, "Xenophobia" and Collective Mobilisation in a South African Settlement: The Politics of Exclusion at the Threshold of the State.* PhD dissertation, London School of Economics, 2015.

Morrison, Toni. 1993. "Nobel Lecture." *Nobel Media,* 19 Dec. 2019, https://www.nobelprize.org/prizes/literature/1993/morrison/lecture/. Accessed 20 Dec. 2019.

Motsei, Mmatshilo. *The Kanga and the Kangaroo Court: Reflections on the Rape Trial of Jacob Zuma.* Johannesburg: Jacana, 2007.

Motsemme, Nthabiseng. "'Loving in a Time of Hopelessness': On Township Women's Subjectivities in a Time of HIV/AIDS." *African Identities,* vol. 5, no. 1, 2007, pp. 61–87.

– "The Mute Always Speaks: On Women's Silences at the Truth and Reconciliation Commission." *Current Sociology,* vol. 52, no. 5, Sept. 2004, pp. 909–32.

Moulier Boutang, Yann. *Cognitive Capitalism.* Cambridge: Polity, 2012.

Mountz, Alison, et al. "For Slow Scholarship: A Feminist Politics of Resistance through Collective Action in the Neoliberal University." *ACME: An International Journal for Critical Geographies,* vol. 14, no. 4, 2015, pp. 1235–59.

Msezane, Sethembile. "Gallery MOMO: Sethembile Msezane." *Creative Feel,* 20 Feb. 2017, https://creativefeel.co.za/2017/02/gallery-momo-sethembile-msezane/. Accessed 20 May 2017.

– "Living Sculptures That Stand for History's Truths." *TedEx Talk,* 2017, https://www.ted.com/talks/sethembile_msezane_living_sculptures_that_stand_for_history_s_truths/transcript. Accessed 2 Feb. 2020.

– "Sethembile Msezane: Kwasuka Sukela: Re-Imagined Bodies of a (South African) 90s Born Woman." *IAM: Intense Art Magazine,* 18 Apr. 2017, http://www.iam-africa.com/sethembile-msezane-kwasuka-sukela/. Accessed 3 May 2017.

– "Sethembile Msezane Performs at the Fall of the Cecil Rhodes Statue, 9 April 2015." *The Guardian,* 15 May 2015, https://www.theguardian.com/artanddesign/2015/may/15/sethembile-msezane-cecil-rhodes-statue-cape-town-south-africa. Accessed 17 Oct. 2016.

Msimang, Sisonke. "Belonging – Why South Africans Refuse to Let Africa In." *Africa Is a Country,* 15 Apr. 2014, https://africasacountry.com/2014/04/belonging-why-south-africans-refuse-to-let-africa. Accessed 12 Aug. 2019.

– "Making South Africa Great Again." *New York Times,* 8 Dec. 2016, https://www.nytimes.com/2016/12/08/opinion/making-south-africa-great-again.html?_r=0. Accessed 8 Dec. 2016.

– "Zuma's South Africa: When Shame Means Nothing at All." *Daily Maverick*, 25 Apr. 2016, https://www.dailymaverick.co.za/opinionista/2016-04-25-zumas-south-africa-when-shame-means-nothing-at-all/#. Accessed 3 Dec. 2019.

Mthonti, Fezokuhle. "A Rapist State's Children: Jacob Zuma & Chumani Maxwele." *The Con*, 8 Apr. 2016, http://www.theconmag.co.za/2016/04/08/a-rapist-states-children-jacob-zuma-chumani-maxwele/. Accessed 23 May 2017.

Muholi, Zanele. "what don't you see when you look at Me?" Artist's statement and video installation. *ZaneleMuholi.com*, 2008, http://www.zanelemuholi.com/videos.htm.

Mühlhoff, Rainer. "Affective Resonance." *Affective Societies: Key Concepts*, edited by Jan Slaby and Christian von Scheve. London and New York: Routledge, 2019, pp. 189–99.

Mukhuba, Theophilus. "Miriam Tlali's Muriel at Metropolitan: Black Conciousness and the Search for Self-Affirmation." *Mediterranean Journal of Social Sciences*, vol. 5, no. 23, 2014, pp. 2469–74.

Munro, Brenna. *South Africa and the Dream of Love to Come: Queer Sexuality and the Struggle for Freedom*. Minneapolis: U of Minnesota P, 2012.

Munusamy, Ranjeni. "Marikana One Week On: SA's War with Itself, for All to See." *Daily Maverick*, 24 Aug. 2012, https://www.dailymaverick.co.za/article/2012-08-24-marikana-one-week-on-sas-war-with-itself-for-all-to-see/. Accessed 18 Apr. 2018.

Mupotsa, Danai. "The Promise of Happiness: Desire, Attachment and Freedom in Post/Apartheid South Africa." *Critical Arts*, vol. 29, no. 2, 2015, pp. 183–98.

– "Sophie's Special Secret: Public Feeling, Consumption and Celebrity Activism in Post-apartheid South Africa." *Celebrity Humanitarianism and North-South Relations*, edited by Lisa Ann Richey. London: Routledge, 2016, pp. 88–105.

Murphy, Kate. *You're Not Listening*. New York: Celadon Books, 2019.

Murray, Jessica. "'Pain Is Beauty': The Politics of Appearance in Kopano Matlwa's *Coconut*." *English in Africa*, vol. 39, no. 1, May 2012, pp. 91–107.

Murray, Paul. *Zimbabwe*. 3rd ed. Chalfont St Peter: Bradt Travel Guides, 2016.

N2 Gateway Project: Housing Rights Violations as "Development" in South Africa. Geneva: Centre on Housing Rights and Evictions, 2009.

Naidoo, Leigh-Ann. "Hallucinations." *Ruth First Memorial Lecture*, 2016, http://witsvuvuzela.com/wp-content/uploads/2016/08/Hallucinations_RUTHFIRST_August2016_FINAL.pdf. Accessed 16 Sept. 2016.

Nancy, Jean-Luc. *Listening*. Translated by Charlotte Mandell. New York: Fordham UP, 2007.

Ndebele, Njabulo. "'Iph' Indlela? Finding Our Way into the Future – the First Steve Biko Memorial Lecture." *Social Dynamics: A Journal of African Studies*, vol. 26, no. 1, 2000, pp. 43–55.

– "Liberation Betrayed by Bloodshed." *Social Dynamics: A Journal of African Studies*, vol. 39, no. 1, 2013, pp. 111–14.

– "Part 1: Our Dream Is Turning Sour." *Times Live*, 25 Sept. 2011, http://www.timeslive.co.za/opinion/commentary/2011/09/25/part-1-our-dream-is-turning-sour. Accessed 18 May 2013.

– *Rediscovery of the Ordinary: Essays on South African Literature and Culture*. Scottsville: U of Kwazulu Natal P, 2006.

Neocosmos, Michael. *From "Foreign Natives" to "Native Foreigners": Explaining Xenophobia in Post-apartheid South Africa*. Dakar: CODESRIA, 2010.

Ngai, Sianne. *Ugly Feelings*. Cambridge, MA: Harvard UP, 2005.

Ngcobo, Lauretta. *And They Didn't Die*. Braamfontein: Skotaville, 1990.

Ngoepe, Karabo. "Black Girls in Tears at Pretoria School Hair Protest." *News 24*, 29 Aug. 2016, https://www.news24.com/SouthAfrica/News/black-girls-in-tears-at-pretoria-school-hair-protest-20160829. Accessed 3 Sept. 2017.

Nichols, Bill. *Introduction to Documentary*. 2nd ed. Bloomington: Indiana UP, 2010.

Nixon, Rob. *Slow Violence and the Environmentalism of the Poor*. Cambridge, MA: Harvard UP, 2011.

Nnaemeka, Obioma, editor. *The Politics of (M)othering: Womanhood, Identity and Resistance in African Literature*. London and New York: Routledge, 1997.

Nuttall, Sarah. "Afterword: The Shock of the New Old." *Social Dynamics: A Journal of African Studies*, vol. 45, no. 2, 2019, pp. 280–5.

– "Literature and the Archive: The Biography of Texts." *Refiguring the Archive*, edited by Carolyn Hamilton et al. Cape Town: Springer, 2002, pp. 283–300.

– "Upsurge." *Acts of Transgression: Contemporary Live Art in South Africa*, edited by Jay Pather and Catherine Boulle. Johannesburg: Wits UP, 2019, pp. 41–59.

Nuttall, Sarah, and Cheryl-Ann Michael. "Autobiographical Acts." *Senses of Culture*, edited by Sarah Nuttall and Cheryl-Ann Michael. Oxford: Oxford UP, 2000, pp. 298–317.

Nyamnjoh, Francis. *Insiders and Outsiders: Citizenship and Xenophobia in Contemporary South Africa*. Dakar: CODESRIA, 2006.

– *#RhodesMustFall: Nibbling at Resilient Colonialism in South Africa*. Mankon, Bamenda: Langaa Research and Publishing CIG, 2016.

Oliver, Kelly. *Subjects without Subjectivity: From Abject Fathers to Desiring Mothers*. Lanham, MD: Rowan and Littlefield, 1998.

– *Witnessing beyond Recognition*. Minneapolis: U of Minnesota P, 2001.

"An Open Letter to the Readers of Adam Habib's 'Rebels in Rage.'" *Mail and Guardian*, 1 Apr. 2019, https://mg.co.za/article/2019-04-01-an-open-letter-to-the-readers-of-adam-habibs-rebels-and-rage/. Accessed 2 Apr. 2019.

Ornellas, Abigail, et al. "Neoliberalism and Austerity in Spain, Portugal and South Africa: The Revolution of Older Persons." *Journal of Gerontological Social Work*, vol. 60, no. 6–7, 2017, pp. 535–52.

Papacharissi, Zizi. *Affective Publics: Sentiment, Technology, and Politics*. New York: Oxford UP, 2015.

Papadopoulos, Dimitris, Stephenson Niamh, and Vassilis Tsianos. *Escape Routes: Control and Subversion in the 21st Century*. London: Pluto Press, 2008.

Pather, Jay. "Negotiating the Postcolonial Black Body as a Site of Paradox." *Theatre Journal*, vol. 47, no. 2, 2017, pp. 143–52.

Pather, Jay, and Catherine Boulle. "Introduction." *Acts of Transgression: Contemporary Live Art in South Africa*, edited by Jay Pather and Catherine Boulle. Johannesburg: Wits UP, 2019, pp. 1–16.

Pather, Ra-eesa. "A Liberation Reimagined Takes Root." *Mail and Guardian*, 22 Dec. 2016, https://mg.co.za/article/2016-12-22-00-a-liberation-reimagined-takes-root. Accessed 22 Dec. 2016.

Pather, Ra-eesa, and Govan Whittles. "Cops Who Shot Shaeera Kalla to Be Subject of Investigation." *Mail and Guardian*, 20 Oct. 2016, https://mg.co.za/article/2016-10-20-cops-who-shot-shaeera-kalla-to-be-subject-of-investigation. Accessed 20 Oct. 2016.

Peale, Norman Vincent. *The Power of Positive Thinking*. New York: Prentice-Hall, 1952.

Pedwell, Carolyn, and Anne Whitehead. "Affecting Feminism: Questions of Feeling in Feminist Theory." *Feminist Theory*, vol. 13, no. 2, 2012, pp. 115–29.

Peerbhay, Mumtaaz Mahomed, director. *Made in China*. Produced by Sarah Chu. Born Free Media, DVD, 2010.

Peters, Michaels. "Algorithmic Capitalism in the Epoch of Digital Reason." *Fast Capitalism*, vol. 14, no. 1, 2017, pp. 65–74.

Phillimore, Roger. "Lonmin Statement on Marikana." 16 Aug. 2012, https://www.lonmin.com/downloads/media_centre/news/press/2012/Lonmin_Statement_on_Marikana_-_16_08_12_-_FINAL.pdf. Accessed 19 Sept. 2014.

Phillips, Dana. "Excremental Ecocriticism and the Global Sanitation Crisis." *Material Ecocriticism*, edited by Serenella Iovina and Serpil Opperman. Bloomington: UP, 2014, pp. 172–85.

"Police Acted to Defend Themselves: Phiyega." *South African Government News Agency*, 17 Aug. 2012, https://www.sanews.gov.za/south-africa/police-acted-defend-themselves-phiyega. Accessed 3 Mar. 2020.

Posel, Deborah. "The ANC Youth League and the Politicization of Race" *Thesis 11*, vol. 115, no. 1, 2013, pp. 58–76.

– "Julius Malema and the Post-apartheid Public Sphere." *Acta Academica: Critical Views on Society, Culture and Politics*, vol. 46, no. 1, 2014, pp. 32–54.

– "'Madiba Magic': Politics as Enchantment." *The Cambridge Companion to Nelson Mandela*, edited by Rita Barnard. New York: Cambridge UP, 2014, pp. 70–91.

– "Races to Consume: Revisiting South Africa's History of Race, Consumption and the Struggle for Freedom." *Ethnic and Racial Studies*, vol. 33, no. 2, 2010, pp. 157–75.

"Proclamation by the President of the Republic of South Africa." *Saatskoerant*, 12 Sept. 2012, https://www.politicsweb.co.za/politics/marikana-terms-of-reference-for-the-farlam-inquiry. Accessed 4 Sept. 2014.

Putuma, Koleka. *Collective Amnesia*. Cape Town: uHlanga, 2017.

Rabkin, Franny. "Law Matters: Scant Coverage of Marikana Commission." *Business Day*, 6 Nov. 2014, https://www.businesslive.co.za/archive/2014-11-06-law-matters-scant-coverage-of-marikana-commission/. Accessed 6 Nov. 2016.

Rancière, Jacques. *Aesthetics and Its Discontents*. Cambridge: Polity Press, 2009.

– *Dissensus: On Politics and Aesthetics*. Translated by Steven Corcoran. London: Continuum International Publishing, 2010.

– *The Philosopher and His Poor*. Edited by Andrew Parker. Translated by John Drury, Corrine Oster, and Andrew Parker. Durham, NC: Duke UP, 2004.

Rao, Rahul. "What Do We Mean When We Talk about Statues?" Africa Day Memorial Lecture, University of the Free State, Equitas Auditorium, Bloemfontein, 23 May 2018.

Ratele, Kopano, editor. *Inter-group Relations. South African Perspectives*. Cape Town: Juta, 2006.

Ratele, Kopano, and Norman Duncan, editors. *Social Psychology: Identities and Relationships*. Lansdowne: U of Cape Town P, 2003.

Readings, Bill. *The University in Ruins*. Cambridge: Harvard UP, 1997.

Rhodes Must Fall Movement. "UCT Rhodes Must Fall Mission Statement." *The Salon*, vol. 9, 2015, pp. 6–8.

Robins, Steven. "Back to the Poo That Started It All." *IOL News*, 9 Apr. 2015, https://www.iol.co.za/news/opinion/back-to-the-poo-that-started-it-all-1842443. Accessed 15 May 2016.

– "How Poo Became a Political Issue." *Daily News*, 3 July 2013, https://www.iol.co.za/dailynews/opinion/how-poo-became-a-political-issue-1541126. Accessed 29 May 2017.

– "How Toilets Became 'Political' in South Africa in 2011: Between the Exceptional and the Everyday after Apartheid." *Development and Change*, vol. 45, no. 3, 2014, pp. 479–501.

– "Poo Wars and Matter Out of Place: 'Toilets for Africa' and Sanitation Activism in Cape Town." *Anthropology Today*, vol. 30, no. 1, 2013, pp. 1–3.

– "Slow Activism in Fast Times: Reflections on the Politics of Media Spectacles after Apartheid." *Journal of Southern African Studies*, vol. 40, no. 1, 2014, pp. 91–110.

Roodt, Dan. "Rhodes-standbeeld en Afrikaner se Engelse problem." *Praag*, 22 Mar. 2015, http://praag.co.za/?p=30792. Accessed 15 June 2017.

Rosfort, René, and Giovanni Stanghellini. "The Person in between Moods and Affects." *Philosophy, Psychiatry, and Psychology*, vol. 16, no. 3, 2009, pp. 251–66.

Ross, Andrew. *Mixed Emotions: Beyond Fear and Hatred in International Conflict*. Chicago: U of Chicago P, 2014.

Samuelson, Meg. "Scripting Connections: Reflections on the Post-Transitional." *English Studies in Africa*, vol. 53, no. 1, 2010, pp. 113–17.

Sanders, Mark. *Ambiguities of Witnessing: Law and Literature in the Time of a Truth Commission*. Stanford: Stanford UP, 2007.

Saragas, Aliki, director. *Strike a Rock*. Produced by Aliki Saragas, Liani Maasdorp, and Anita Khanna. Uhuru Productions, DVD, 2017.

Sartre, Jean-Paul. "Preface." *The Wretched of the Earth*, by Frantz Fanon, 1961, translated by Richard Philcox. New York: Grove Press, 2004, pp. xliiii–lxii.

Scarry, Elaine. *The Body in Pain: The Making and Unmaking of the World*. New York: Oxford UP, 1985.

Schaeffer, Pierre. *Treatise on Musical Objects: An Essay Across Disciplines*. 1996. Translated by Christine North and John Dack. Berkeley: U of California P, 2017.

Schmahmann, Brenda. "The Fall of Rhodes: The Removal of a Sculpture from the University of Cape Town." *Public Art Dialogue*, vol. 6, no. 1, 2016, pp. 90–115.

Schutte, Gillian. "Rhodes Arouses White Make Fears." *Sunday Independent*, 12 Apr. 2015, http://www.iol.co.za/sundayindependent/rhodes-arouses-white-male-fears-1843789. Accessed 25 June 2017.

Scott, David. *Omens of Adversity: Tragedy, Time, Memory, Justice*. Durham, NC: Duke UP, 2014.

Searle, Berni. "*Black Smoke Rising*: Archived Artist Statement and Still Frames." *The Pandorian*, 2009, http://thepandorian.com/2009/12/berni-searle-black-smoke-rising/. Accessed 14 May 2013.

– "*Gateway* from the *Black Smoke Rising* Series: 26 May–23 July: Archived Still Frames from Video Installation." Cape Town: Michael Stevenson, 2011, https://archive.stevenson.info/exhibitions/searle/black_smoke_rising/gateway.html. Accessed 14 May 2013.

– "*Lull* from the *Black Smoke Rising* Series: 26 May–23 July: Archived Still Frames from Video Installation." Cape Town: Michael Stevenson, 2011, https://archive.stevenson.info/exhibitions/searle/black_smoke_rising/lull.html. Accessed 14 May 2013.

– "*Moonlight* from the *Black Smoke Rising* Series: 26 May–23 July: Archived Still Frames from Video Installation." Cape Town: Michael Stevenson, 2011, https://archive.stevenson.info/exhibitions/searle/black_smoke_rising/moonlight.html. Accessed 14 May 2013.

Sedgwick, Eve Kosofsky. *Touching Feeling: Affect, Pedagogy, Performativity.* Durham, NC: Duke UP, 2003.

Seekings, Jeremy, and Nicoli Nattrass. "Rhodes and the Politics of Pain." *Daily Maverick,* 31 Mar. 2015, https://www.dailymaverick.co.za/opinionista/2015-03-31-rhodes-and-the-politics-of-pain/#.WOsmDRG9gII. Accessed 2 Apr. 2015.

Sides, Kirk. "Framing the Debate on Race: Global Historiography and Local Flavor in Berni Searle's 'Colour Me' Series." *Image and Text,* vol. 17, 2011, pp. 120–36.

Simpson, Leanne Betasamosake. *As We Have Always Done: Indigenous Freedom through Radical Resistance.* Minneapolis: U of Minnesota P, 2017.

– "Leanne Simpson Speaking at Beit Zatoun Jan 23rd 2012." *Youtube,* uploaded by Dreadedstar, 25 Jan. 2012, https://www.youtube.com/watch?v=EkrkCTZWWJU.

Sinwell, Luka, and Siphiwe Mbatha. *The Spirit of Marikana: The Rise of Insurgent Trade Unionism in South Africa.* Johannesburg: Wits UP, 2016.

Skeggs, Beverley, and Helen Wood. *Reacting to Reality Television: Performance, Audience and Value.* London: Routledge, 2012.

Slaby, Jan, and Christian von Scheve, editors. *Affective Societies: Key Concepts.* London and New York: Routledge, 2019.

– "Introduction." *Affective Societies: Key Concepts,* edited by Jan Slaby and Christian von Scheve. London and New York, Routledge, 2019, pp. 1–24.

Slaughter, Joseph. *Human Rights Inc: The World Novel, Narrative Form and International Law.* New York: Fordham UP, 2007.

Smith, Mychal Denzel. "The Rebirth of Black Rage: From Kanye to Obama, and Back Again." *The Nation,* 13 Aug. 2015, https://www.thenation.com/article/the-rebirth-of-black-rage/. Accessed 13 Sept. 2015.

Smyth, John. *The Toxic University: Zombie Leadership, Academic Rock Stars and Neoliberal Ideology.* London: Palgrave Macmillan, 2017.

Spearey, Susan. Email received by Helene Strauss, 23 Jan. 2020.

Spelman, Elizabeth. "Anger and Insubordination." *Women, Knowledge, and Reality: Explorations in Feminist Philosophy,* edited by Ann Garry and Marilyn Pearsall. Boston: Unwin Hyman, 1989, pp. 263–74.

Spivak, Gayatri Chakravorty. *An Aesthetic Education in the Era of Globalization.* Cambridge, MA: Harvard UP, 2012.

– *Death of a Discipline.* New York: Columbia UP, 2003.

Spurlock, John, and Cynthia Magistro. *New and Improved: The Transformation of American Women's Emotional Culture.* New York: New York UP, 1998.

Staiger, Janet, Ann Cvetkovich, and Ann Reynolds, editors. *Political Emotions: New Agendas in Communication.* New York: Routledge, 2010.

"State Drops Charges against Marikana Miners." *City Press*, 20 Aug. 2014, http://www.citypress.co.za/politics/state-drops-charges-marikana-miners/. Accessed 20 Aug. 2014.

Steinberg, Jonny. "Xenophobia and Collective Violence in South Africa: A Note of Skepticism about the Scapegoat." *African Studies Review*, vol. 61, no. 3, 2018, pp. 119–34.

Stern, Daniel. *The Interpersonal World of the Infant.* 1985. London: Karnac Books, 1998.

Stern, Eddie. *One Simple Thing: A New Look at the Science of Yoga and How It Can Transform Your Life.* New York: North Point Press, 2019.

Stevens, Garth, Norman Duncan, and Derek Hook, editors. "Introduction." *Race, Memory and the Apartheid Archive: Towards a Transformative Psychosocial Praxis*, edited by Garth Stevens, Norman Duncan, and Derek Hook. New York and London: Palgrave Macmillan, 2013, pp. 1–17.

– *Race, Memory and the Apartheid Archive: Towards a Transformative Psychosocial Praxis.* New York and London: Palgrave Macmillan, 2013.

Stevens, Garth, Norman Duncan, and Christopher C. Sonn. "Memory, Narrative and Voice as Liberatory Praxis in the Apartheid Archive." *Race, Memory and the Apartheid Archive: Towards a Transformative Psychosocial* Praxis, edited by Garth Stevens, Norman Duncan, and Derek Hook. New York and London: Palgrave Macmillan, 2013, pp. 25–44.

Stockdale, Liam. "The Governance of Time and the Politics of (In)Security." *McMaster Institute on Globalization and the Human Condition Working Paper Series*, vol. 12, no. 3, Sept. 2012, pp. 20–4.

Strauss, Helene. "Affective Return: Anachronistic Feeling and Contemporary South African Documentary Form." *Social Dynamics: A Journal of African Studies*, vol. 45, no. 2, 2019, pp. 218–33.

– "Cinema of Social Recuperation: Xenophobic Violence and Migrant Subjectivity in Contemporary South Africa." *Subjectivity*, vol. 4, no. 2, 2011, pp. 103–20.

– "Energy Archives: of Rocks, Rubbish, and Feminist Feeling in Aliki Saragas's *Strike a Rock.*" *Subjectivity*, vol. 13, no. 4, 2020, pp. 254–80. *SpringerLink*, https://doi.org/10.1057/s41286-020-00107-8.

– "Interrupting the International Narrative of South Africa's Neoliberal Rainbow Family: Winnie Madikizela-Mandela in the Canadian Print Media since the Late 1980s." *Regarding Winnie: Feminism, Race and Nation in*

Global Representations of Winnie Madikizela-Mandela, edited by Pumla Dineo Gqola, Casava Republic Press. Forthcoming.

– "Managing Public Feeling: Temporality, Mourning and the Marikana Massacre in Rehad Desai's *Miners Shot Down*." *Critical Arts: South-North Cultural and Media Studies*, vol. 30, no. 4, Aug. 2016, pp. 58–73.

– "Memory, Masculinity and Responsibility: Searching for 'Good Men' in Mtutuzeli Nyoka's *I Speak to the Silent*." *English in Africa*, vol. 36, no. 1, May 2009, pp. 77–89.

– "Waywardness of Mood and Mode in *Love the One You Love* and *Necktie Youth*." *Journal of African Cinemas*, vol. 9, nos. 2–3, 2017, pp. 273–86.

Stuurman, Ziyanda. "Police Brutality in South Africa Exposed Once Again." *Mail and Guardian*, 28 Aug. 2020, https://mg.co.za/opinion/2020-08-28-police-brutality-in-south-africa-exposed-once-again/. Accessed 28 Oct. 2020.

Suttner, Raymond. "Reinvigorating Our vocabulary for freedom and emancipation." *Daily Maverick*, 9 Oct. 2019, https://www.dailymaverick.co.za/article/2019-10-08-reinvigorating-our-vocabulary-for-freedom-and-emancipation/. Accessed 3 Jan. 2020.

Swan, Elaine. "What Are White People to Do? Listening, Challenging Ignorance, Generous Encounters and the 'Not Yet' as Diversity Research Praxis." *Gender, Work and Organization*, vol. 24, no. 5, 2017, pp. 547–63.

Szalavitz, Maia, and Bruce Perry. *Born for Love: Why Empathy Is Essential – And Endangered*. New York: Harper Collins, 2010.

Szeman, Imre. "Crude Aesthetics: The Politics of Oil Documentaries." *A Companion to Contemporary Documentary Film*, edited by Alexandra Juhasz and Alisa Lebow. Minneapolis: John Wiley & Sons, 2015, pp. 28–42.

Tabane, Rapule. "An Embarrassment of Riches." *Mail and Guardian Online*, 22 Dec. 2010, https://mg.co.za/article/2010-12-22-an-embarrassment-of-riches/. Accessed 3 May 2013.

Tafeni, Viwe. "This song is for … An Audio-Visual Installation by Gabrielle Goliath." *Artsvark*, 12 Nov. 2019, https://artsvark.co.za/this-song-is-for-an-audio-visual-installation-by-gabrielle-goliath/. Accessed 3 Dec. 2019.

Taibbi, Matt. *I Can't Breathe: The Killing That Started a Movement*. New York: Spiegel & Grau, 2017.

Taylor, Diana. "Trauma in the Archive." *Feeling Photography*, edited by Elspeth Brown and Thy Phu. Durham, NC: Duke UP, 2014, pp. 239–51.

Terreblanche, Sampie. *A History of Inequality in South Africa 1652–2002*. Pietermaritzburg: U of Natal P, 2002.

Thamm, Marianne. "Afrikaner Singer Chains Herself to Vandalised South African Statue." *The Guardian*, 10 Apr. 2015, https://www.theguardian.com/world/2015/apr/10/afrikaner-singer-chains-herself-to-vandalised-south-african-statue. Accessed 12 May 2017.

Thobo-Carlsen, Mik, and Victor Chateaubriand. "How Tattoos Went from Subculture to Pop Culture." *Huffpost Arts and Culture*, 27 Oct. 2014, https://www.huffpost.com/entry/how-tattoos-went-from-sub_b_6053588. Accessed 5 Apr. 2016.

Thomas, Kylie. "Wounding Apertures: Violence, Affect and Photography during and after Apartheid." *Kronos*, vol. 38, no. 1, 2012, pp. 204–18.

– "Zanele Muholi's Intimate Archive: Photography and Post-Apartheid Lesbian Lives." *Safundi: The Journal of South African and American Studies*, vol. 11, no. 4, 2010, pp. 421–36.

Thompson, Debra. "An Exoneration of Black Rage." *South Atlantic Quarterly*, vol. 116, no. 3, 2017, pp. 457–81.

Tlali, Miriam. *Between Two Worlds*. Peterborough: Broadview Press, 2004.

– "Interview by Barbara Boswell." Tape Recording. Johannesburg, 4 July, 2006.

– *Muriel at Metropolitan*. Johannesburg: Ravan Press, 1975.

Tlhabi, Redi. *Khwezi: The Remarkable Story of Fezekile Ntsukela Kuzwayo*. Johannesburg and Cape Town: Jonathan Ball Publishers, 2017.

Tokolos-Stencils. https://tokolosstencils.tumblr.com. Accessed 16 Mar. 2015.

Trippe, Katie. "Pandemic Policing: South Africa's Most Vulnerable Face a Sharp Increase in Police-Related Brutality." *Atlantic Council*, 24 June 2020, https://www.atlanticcouncil.org/blogs/africasource/pandemic-policing-south-africas-most-vulnerable-face-a-sharp-increase-in-police-related-brutality/. Accessed 28 Oct. 2020.

Tsing, Anna Lowenhaupt. *The Mushroom at the End of the World: On the Possibility of Life in Capitalist Ruins*. Princeton, NJ: Princeton UP, 2015.

Tyler, Imogen. *Revolting Subjects: Social Abjection and Resistance in Neoliberal Britain*. London and New York: Zed Books, 2013.

Vaidhyanathan, Siva. *Antisocial Media: How Facebook Disconnects Us and Undermines Democracy*. Oxford: Oxford UP, 2018.

Valji, Nahla. "Race and Reconciliation in a Post-TRC South Africa." Paper presented at the "Ten Years of Democracy in Southern Africa" conference, 2–5 May 2004, Queen's University, Kingston, Canada. https://www.csvr.org.za/race-and-reconciliation-in-a-post-trc-south-africa/. Accessed 27 Feb. 2007.

Van der Kolk, Bessel, and Rita Fisler. "Dissociation and the Fragmentary Nature of Traumatic Memories: Overview and Exploratory Study." *Journal of Traumatic Stress*, vol. 8, no. 4, 1995, pp. 505–25.

Van der Vlies, Andrew. *Present Imperfect: Contemporary South African Writing*. Oxford: Oxford UP, 2017.

– "Queer Knowledge and the Politics of the Gaze in Contemporary South African Photography: Zanele Muholi and Others." *Journal of African Cultural Studies*, vol. 24, no. 2, 2012, pp. 140–56.

Van Wyk, Lisa. "Xingwana: Homophobic Claims 'Baseless, Insulting.'" *Mail and Guardian Online*, 5 Mar. 2012, https://www.mg.co.za/article/2010-03-05-xingwana-homophobic-claims-baseless-insulting. Accessed 14 July 2014.

Veblen, Thorstein. *The Theory of the Leisure Class*. New York: New American Library, 1953.

Venn, Couze. "Identity, Diasporas and Subjective Change: The Role of Affect, the Relation to the Other, and the Aesthetic." *Subjectivity*, vol. 26, no. 1, 2009, pp. 3–28.

Vidal, John. "Destroyed Habitat Creates the Perfect Conditions for Coronavirus to Emerge." *Scientific American*, 18 Mar. 2020, https://www.scientificamerican.com/article/destroyed-habitat-creates-the-perfect-conditions-for-coronavirus-to-emerge/. Accessed 27 Oct. 2020.

Volz, Ulrich. "Investing in a Green Recovery." *International Monetary Fund: Finance and Development*, Sept. 2020, https://www.imf.org/external/pubs/ft/fandd/2020/09/pdf/investing-in-a-green-recovery-volz.pdf. Accessed 27 Oct. 2020.

Von Holdt, Karl. "Overview: Insurgent Citizenship and Collective Violence: An Analysis of Case Studies." *The Smoke That Calls: Insurgent Citizenship, Collective Violence and the Struggle for a Place in the New South Africa*, edited by Adèle Kirsten and Karl von Holdt. Johannesburg: Centre for the Study of Violence and Reconciliation and the Society, Work and Development Institute, 2011, pp. 5–32.

Von Schiller, Friedrich. *On the Aesthetic Education of Man in a Series of Letters*. 1965. Translated by Reginald Snell. New York: Friedrich Unger, 1974.

Wazar, Mishka. "So You Want to #RememberKhwezi? Here's What You Need to Know." *The Daily Vox*, 16 Aug. 2016, https://www.thedailyvox.co.za/want-rememberkhwezi-need-know/. Accessed 17 Apr. 2017.

Wegerif, Marc, and Oluwafunmiola Adeniyi. "Student Hunger at South African Universities Needs More Attention." *The Conversation*, 18 Sept. 2019, https://theconversation.com/student-hunger-at-south-african-universities-needs-more-attention-123378. Accessed 25 Mar. 2020.

Wenzel, Jennifer. *Bulletproof: Afterlives of Anticolonial Prophecy in South Africa and Beyond*. Chicago: U of Chicago P, 2009.

West, Cornel. "Malcolm X and Black Rage." *Race Matters*, by Cornel West. Boston: Beacon Press Books, 1993, pp. 93–105.

"What Have We Learned from the Farlam Commission?" *Amandla!*, vol. 35, Aug./Sept. 2014, pp. 30–1.

Whelan, Andrew, Ruth Walker, and Christopher Moore, editors. *Zombies in the Academy: Living Death in Higher Education*. Chicago: U of Chicago P, 2013.

Williams, Raymond. *Marxism and Literature*. Oxford: Oxford UP, 1977.

Wright, Timothy. "Ruined Time and Post-revolutionary Allegory in Nthikeng Mohlele's *Small Things*." *Social Dynamics: A Journal of African Studies*, vol. 45, no. 2, 2019, pp. 198–212.

Xingwana, Lulu. "Statement by Minister of Arts and Culture Ms Lulu Xingwana on Media Reports around the Innovative Women Exhibition." *South African Government*, 2010, https://www.gov.za/statement-minister-arts-and-culture-ms-lulu-xingwana-media-reports-around-innovative-art-exhibition. Accessed 15 May 2012.

Yusoff, Kathryn. *A Billion Black Anthropocenes or None*. Minneapolis: U of Minnesota P, 2018.

Zembylas, Michalinos. "The Affective Modes of Right-Wing Populism: Trump Pedagogy and Lessons for Democratic Education." *Studies in Philosophy and Education*, vol. 39, no. 1, 2020, pp. 151–66.

Zettl, Herbert. *Sight Sound Motion: Applied Media Aesthetics*. 7th ed. Boston, MA: Wadsworth, 2014.

Zhang, Lei, and Carlton Clark. *Affect, Emotion, and Rhetorical Persuasion in Mass Communication*. New York: Routledge, 2018.

Žižek, Slavoj. *Violence*. New York: Picador, 2008.

Zuma, Jacob. "Statement from President Jacob Zuma on the Marikana Lonmin Mine Workers Tragedy, Rustenburg." 17 Aug. 2012, https://www.thepresidency.gov.za/speeches/statement-president-jacob-zuma-marikana-lonmin-mine-workers-tragedy%2C-rustenburg. Accessed 16 Aug. 2015.

Index

African and Diasporic Cultural Studies

www.ingramcontent.com/pod-product-compliance
Lightning Source LLC
LaVergne TN
LVHW090155080826
844660LV00013B/817/J

* 9 7 8 1 4 8 7 5 4 0 5 8 6 *